GLOBALIZATIONS AND THE ANCIENT WORLD

In this book, Justin Jennings argues that globalization is not just a phenomenon limited to modern times. Instead he contends that the globalization of today is just the latest in a series of globalizing eras in human history. Using the Uruk, Mississippian, and Wari civilizations as case studies, Jennings examines how the growth of the world's first great cities radically transformed their respective areas. The cities required unprecedented exchange networks, creating long-distance flows of ideas, people, and goods. These flows caused cascades of interregional interaction that eroded local behavioral norms and social structures. New, hybrid cultures emerged within these globalized regions. Although these networks did not span the whole globe, people in these areas developed globalized cultures as they interacted with one another. Jennings explores how understanding globalization as a recurring event can help in the understanding of both the past and the present.

Justin Jennings is Associate Curator of New World Archaeology at the Royal Ontario Museum and Assistant Professor of Anthropology at the University of Toronto. He writes widely on archaeology for both scholarly and general audiences and recently edited *Drink, Power, and Society in the Andes* and *Beyond Wari Walls*.

For Adrienne, my best friend and true love

Globalizations and the Ancient World

Justin Jennings

Royal Ontario Museum, Toronto

CAMBRIDGE
UNIVERSITY PRESS

CAMBRIDGE UNIVERSITY PRESS
Cambridge, New York, Melbourne, Madrid, Cape Town, Singapore,
São Paulo, Delhi, Dubai, Tokyo, Mexico City

Cambridge University Press
32 Avenue of the Americas, New York, NY 10013-2473, USA

www.cambridge.org
Information on this title: www.cambridge.org/9780521760775

First published 2011

Printed in the United States of America

A catalog record for this publication is available from the British Library.

Library of Congress Cataloging in Publication data
Jennings, Justin.
   Globalizations and the ancient world / Justin Jennings.
      p.   cm.
   Includes bibliographical references and index.
   ISBN 978-0-521-76077-5
   1. Cities and towns – History.   2. Globalization – History.   I. Title.
   HT111.J46 2011
   303.48'2091732–dc22   2010035560

ISBN 978-0-521-76077-5 Hardback

Contents

Figures and Tables

FIGURES

TABLES

Acknowledgments

More than anything else, this book is the product of a late-night challenge. My fiancée wasn't particularly fond of the book ideas I was giving her, and she said that I should write a book that she might want to read. This is not exactly the book she had in mind, but it does attempt to address a larger audience to explain why the past mattered. My fiancée (now wife), Adrienne Rand, is a social marketer, and she was one of two people who read the complete early draft of this book. The second person was my mother, Kay Jennings (a retired psychologist turned hockey player). Both offered valuable advice on the content of my argument as well as on how to write in plain English. My wife and mom are perhaps a biased sample of the general public, but first and foremost I wanted to make a book that made sense to them. I also benefited from wide-ranging conversations on the book's topics with friends from various walks of life: Fernando Aloise, David Haverkamp, Daniel Heimpel, Dick Jennings, Alon Levitan, and Michael Samulon are just a few of the people who helped along the way to make my arguments more clear and the book more palatable.

Many academic colleagues were also quite generous with their time. They looked over portions of the text and also discussed the idea of ancient globalizations with me at length. These colleagues include Robin Beck, Christopher Chase-Dunn, Rowan Flad, Tom Hall, Randy McGuire, Clemens Reichel, Jason Ur, Willy Yépez Álvarez, and two anonymous reviewers. They helped by sharing references, correcting my errors, and challenging me to think more clearly. I did not take all of their advice, but I know that the book has benefited enormously from their efforts.

Finally, this book was made possible by the support of three institutions. I wrote this book in my office at the Royal Ontario Museum, and this venerable institution deserves thanks for creating an atmosphere that is conducive to doing research. The book is also made possible by the institution where I teach – the University of Toronto. The conversations that I have had with students in my graduate courses on urbanization and interregional interaction have been especially valuable. Finally, this book would not have been possible without Cambridge University Press. My acquisition editor, Beatrice Rehl, provided good advice and steady guidance, and my book editors, Camilla Knapp and Sara Black, have fixed many of the grammatical errors and muddled thinking that plagued earlier drafts.

1

Modernity's Greatest Theft

Globalization seems quintessentially modern. Up until very recently, the images that sprang to my mind when I heard the word were a jumble of post–World War II vignettes – someone sharing files over the Internet with a friend across the ocean, a woman hunkered down at her sewing machine in a vast third-world sweatshop, the flags flapping outside of the United Nations. These mental snapshots evoked a feeling that I lived in a rapidly shrinking, ever-changing, and perhaps out-of-control world. I no longer see just these images. These recent pictures are now joined by images from antiquity when I think of globalization. A thousand-year-old megalith in Mexico is as vivid as an MTV broadcast in India; a luxury hotel in Dubai is juxtaposed to a colony of the Indus Valley civilization (Figure 1.1).

For most readers, these new pairings may seem silly. You might understandably argue that globalization is a modern phenomenon that is categorically different from anything in the past. After all, ancient civilizations did not have a truly "global" impact, and enormous leaps in technology, transformed socioeconomic systems, and new ways of thinking all separate us from the deep past. In short, you could argue that globalization is a new process, and you could find dozens of well-regarded books in the library to bolster your argument. Nonetheless, I will try to show that globalization has occurred many times in history and that these earlier globalizations can help us better understand the future of the world that we live in today.

Despite the use of the word "global" in "globalization," many definitions of modern globalization stress *only* that interactions are occurring increasingly over long distances, and even those who stress worldwide connections in their definitions of globalization acknowledge that vast regions of the world today lack many of these connections (el-Ojeili and Hayden 2006: 12–13; Scholte 2000: 41–61). Definitions of modern globalization tend to describe it as a process of widespread social change that is related to the establishment of extensive, dense networks (e.g., el-Ojeili and Hayden 2006: 13; Eriksen 2007: 14; Held and McGrew 2000: 3; Inda and Rosaldo 2008: 4; Ritzer 2007: 1; Tilly 1995: 1–2). For these authors, the emphasis is placed on the transformative nature of expanding networks today rather than their geographic extent.

One of the more influential definitions of globalization is by John Tomlinson. In his book *Globalization and Culture*, Tomlinson defines globalization succinctly as "complex connectivity" (1999: 2): a dense network of intense interaction and interdependencies between people in different parts of the world that is created by a significant increase in the flow of information, goods, and people across cultural and geographic boundaries. For Tomlinson, a network reaches the stage of complex connectivity when it triggers the array of social changes that are associated with the formation of global culture (don't think McWorld when you read the term "global culture," but

Figure 1.1 Although we think of a Maya stela and the billboards at Times Square as fundamentally different, both can be seen as advertising (stela lithograph by Frederick Catherwood [1844] and photo by Kay Jennings).

rather imagine a fractured, hybrid, and often contentious amalgamation of people who know that they are stuck together whether they like it or not).

Although Tomlinson and many other scholars argue that globalization is unique to the modern era, their definition of globalization paradoxically provides us with a straightforward criterion that we can use to identify earlier periods of globalization. I suggest that if the same social changes identified with the creation of our modern global culture can also be found during an earlier period of intense interregional interaction, then we should consider the definitional demands of globalization met and accept the earlier period as an era of globalization. If these changes fail to occur as a result of earlier interactions, then we should recognize that the period fails to measure up to the definition of globalization even though some social changes and systematic connections likely occurred.

This book uses their widely held definitional criteria to determine if globalization occurred after the sudden growth of early cities like Cahokia, Teotihuacan, Tiwanaku, and Harappa. We know that the exchange networks created by these cities led to the long-distance flows of ideas, people, and goods. People outside of these cities reacted to these flows by creating their own networks, and a chain reaction of interactions ensued that transformed broad regions. Although these networks did not span the globe, they radically changed the known "world" of these people. In this book, I present a general model of the changes associated with early urbanization and demonstrate how the social changes associated with the spread of the Uruk, Mississippian, and Wari civilizations relate to those that are occurring in today's global culture.

THE GREAT WALL

Although looking for past globalizations may sound easy in theory, the reality is that putting an "s" at the end of globalization won't feel right to most readers. Our knee-jerk reaction to the juxtaposition of images in Figure 1.1 might be to exclaim that there was nothing comparable to the Internet in ancient Egypt or there was nothing like McDonald's two thousand years ago. At the most basic level, we all find it difficult to compare a megalith to a McNugget because we think of them as categorically different. Why do we think this way? There are a variety of reasons (you can't eat a megalith), but one is that we consider them as belonging to two categorically different eras. One of the largest problems that we face in thinking about globalizations in the plural is our preconception about modernity as a distinct period – this bias influences both the first images that pop into our head when we say the word as well as those ideas that are so deeply entrenched in our minds that they subconsciously shape our worldview.

A Great Wall divides the ancient from the modern in our minds (after Restall 2005: xi). The greatest strength of the wall is its unobtrusiveness – it's so deeply embedded that we forget that it is there. Before we can really talk about potential ancient globalizations, we need to tear this wall down. In *The Theft of History*, Jack Goody argues that the Western world had unfairly claimed the invention of democracy, capitalism, romantic love, universities, and other institutions of modernity (2006). In denying the existence of these ideas in other periods and regions, he argues that the modern world is seen, and skewed, through a Western lens. Goody does not consider globalization in his book, but globalization just might be the greatest theft of history. By defining globalization (and let's not forget love) as a Western creation of the last five hundred years, we needlessly divorce the modern from the premodern and warp our understanding of the world that we live in today.

In Goody's book, he shows how various academics over the years have reinforced the divide between modernity and antiquity. This shouldn't come as much of a surprise. All humans have a concern about their place in history. There seems to be a cross-cultural desire to contrast ourselves to those who have come before us, and this desire leads to a tendency to break up time in terms of distinct earlier eras. The Incas of the Andes, for example, believed in a period when gods walked the earth and humans were still yet indistinguishable from animals (Zuidema 2002: 240), and the legends of the southern Andaman Islanders of the Pacific describe an earlier age of the *Tomo-la* when ancestral spirits formed the land that the islanders now inhabit (Radcliffe-Brown 1964: 191). In the West, we have achieved this divide between our era and the past by the construction of the Great Wall.

Towering, yet somehow transparent, the Great Wall that separates modernity and antiquity is reinforced by the disciplinary boundaries that determine to a great extent what side of the wall a scholar sets up her intellectual tent. We go to our own conferences, read our own journals, and use jargon that can sometimes be difficult for the uninitiated to penetrate. These disciplinary divides limit the conversations between disciplines (and even within them – I've visited many anthropology departments where the archaeologists and cultural anthropologists barely talk to each other because they think they have nothing to share). An occasional salvo is sent over the wall from either side but usually quickly forgotten as people returned to the "serious" scholarship that defines their discipline. This divide, of course, is not confined to academia. Bookstores and libraries reinforce the Great Wall in how books are organized, websites tend to cleave to this division, and our casual conversations maintain this separation.

As I did, most people reading this book grew up in a society steeped in Western tradition. "Ancient" and "modern" are core concepts in this tradition and are so deeply entrenched in our way of thinking that they have become part of our subconscious (Bourdieu 1977: 164; Sahlins 1996: 395). Similar to the way that you don't think about breathing or walking, core concepts like the "ancient" seem to implicitly guide us during the course of daily activities (Giddens 1979: 59). These concepts are often remarkably durable, surviving political, economic, and social upheavals over hundreds of years (Geertz 1980: 134; Sahlins 1981: 17, 1996: 421). The Great Wall was first erected almost a thousand years ago when people started to think of a modern era. Before we can take this wall apart, we need to understand how this wall was constructed over time and how globalization came to fall on one side of it.

"Ancient" and "modern" come from the Latin words, *antiquus* and *modernus*, and were first used to describe distinct periods in the Middle Ages. Writing during the fourteenth century, for example, Petrarch described three eras in world history – antiquity, the dark ages, and modernity. He felt that antiquity was a golden age and that he was writing on the cusp of the new age of modernity that would bring the world into a second age of enlightenment. The boundaries of the modern period and their relationship to antiquity would change through the next centuries as the concepts were integrated into romanticism, rationalism, and other intellectual movements. In most cases, authors sought to link modern developments with ancient precedents. This changed, however, during the eighteenth century when philosophers believed that they were breaking completely from the past to form a true Age of Enlightenment, a new era of freedom, democracy, and reason. By the middle of the nineteenth century, modernity was commonly conceived in Europe as a split from earlier stages of Western history (Calinescu 1987).

The mid-nineteenth century was a period of incredible social, political, and economic change in Europe. Far-flung colonies allowed unprecedented wealth to flow into much of Europe, and millions of Europeans sought their fortunes overseas. Capitalism became the dominant economic system and its imposition was transforming lives in both the cities and the countryside. There was still widespread faith in science and progress during this period, although frustrations were beginning to grow among a burgeoning working class that felt increasingly disenfranchised.

Most Europeans believed that they had entered a new modern era, and they desired an "imperial synthesis" to explain their newfound prosperity relative to other parts of the world (Trigger 1989: 110). This synthesis was supported by scientists through their research program in social evolution during this period. Following schemes that were already popular within Europe a century earlier, social scientists in the late nineteenth century attempted to organize cultures across space and time into a universal scheme of distinct stages of development.

One of the most influential books from this period was Lewis Henry Morgan's *Ancient Society* (1963 [1877]). Morgan thought that humanity progressed over time from a state of savagery to one of enlightenment. By gaining intelligence through new inventions and discoveries, people moved to higher stages of development that were marked by better subsistence patterns, religious beliefs, family structure, and political organization. He thought that all cultures moved through these stages, with some cultures being stuck in savagery and others having moved up the ladder of progress. The topmost rung of that ladder was modern Western society.

The grand evolutionary schemes of Morgan and his colleagues were being called into question by the dawn of the twentieth century as faith in the progressive nature of capitalism began to wane in many circles. Increased fieldwork around the world revealed an incredible degree of cultural variability through time that could not be pigeonholed into clearly defined stages; and researchers found that the people dismissed as savages by Morgan were just as intelligent as the researchers were (e.g., Boas 1989). In response to this cultural diversity, the study of culture broke into subdisciplines in order to better understand groups within their own cultural contexts. Archaeologists got the past and sociology and anthropology split the present. Although this division of labor effectively broke up the idea of a ladder of progress, it also ended up reinforcing the separation between the ancient and the modern.

The two decades after World War II brought a brief return to the ideas of social progress. Based in large part on how stimulus packages were helping economic recoveries of Europe and Japan, a modernization theory developed that argued that the adoption of Western economic, political, and social structures by recently decolonized countries would lead to their eventual prosperity. There was a renewed confidence in technological progress as a panacea and this was reflected by the return of evolutionary models in the social sciences (Trigger 1989: 289–90).

A new generation of scholars was radicalized in the political and social turmoil of the 1960s and 1970s. They rejected evolutionary theories, viewed modernization instead as a destructive wave of Westernization, and perceived the changes that were occurring in the non-Western world as the result of people's resistance to the spread of Western modernity (D'Andrade 2000). Although these scholars trumpeted the cultural diversity of the non-Western world, the nuances of Westernization remained largely unexplored.

By the 1990s, Westernization was beginning to be reconceptualized as a far more complicated process now called globalization (e.g., Appadurai 1990; Giddens 1990). Globalization scholars argued that many of the changes occurring in the world were a result of increasing interregional interactions. They traced back some of the connections to the European voyages of discovery in the fifteenth century and showed how a series of social transformations, driven by capitalism, massive urbanization, colonialism, and new communication technologies, provided the critical push that led to the globalized world of today (e.g., Castells 1996; Sklair 2002; Wallerstein 1979).

For the last 1,000 years in the Western world, time has been divided into the modern and the ancient. Over the last few decades, there has been a rush to understand our changing modern world and we now talk about such things as "modernity," "Westernization," and "globalization." Recent scholarship has undeniably provided us with a clearer sense of our world today. Yet, the unintended consequence has been to further reinforce the Great Wall by maintaining the tacit assumption that the world today is categorically different from what came before.

In this book, I argue that the divide between ancient and modern is an artificial one and suggest that we would be richly rewarded if we took down the Great Wall that separates ancient civilizations from modern globalization. If the processes could be linked, archaeologists and other researchers who study the past would be able to mine the rich globalization literature to better understand the dynamics of these pivotal periods of widespread cultural change in world history. Conversely, an understanding of ancient globalization would help us parse out those aspects of the world today that are unique to modern globalization from those that are more general features of a phenomenon that has occurred earlier in our history.

ASSAULTING THE GREAT WALL

Some readers might suspect that I am late to the game since the "intellectual assault of the Great Wall," after all, is well underway (Restall 2005: xi). Inspired by work like Fernand Braudel's three volume *Civilization and Capitalism* (1979) and Eric Wolf's *Europe and the People without History* (1982), scholars over the last two decades have unleashed a barrage of scholarship that has made the Great Wall increasingly visible by linking globalization to ancient civilizations (e.g., Ekholm and Friedman 1979, 1985; Hall and Chase-Dunn 2006; LaBianca and Scham 2006; Nederveen Pieterse 2004).

Scanning the titles of these books, like *The World System: Five Hundred Years or Five Thousand?* (Frank 1993) or *A Splendid Exchange: How Trade Shaped the World* (Bernstein 2008), one might certainly argue that the call for ancient globalization is almost old hat. I disagree. Although I am heartened by this upswelling of scholarship, I feel that most of the work being done on ancient globalization ultimately fails to really address ancient globalizations because this scholarship does not tend to allow for multiple periods of globalization to have emerged within unique cultural, environmental, and historical settings.

My concern might seem counterintuitive. Don't all of these approaches deal with globalization in antiquity? Yes they do, but they don't really get at ancient globalizations in the plural. Instead, these approaches tend to either trace the roots of modern globalization further back in time or project selected aspects of modern globalization on to the past. To make my point clearer, I have depicted how these conceptualizations of premodern globalization map on to heuristic line graphs of increasing interregional interaction over

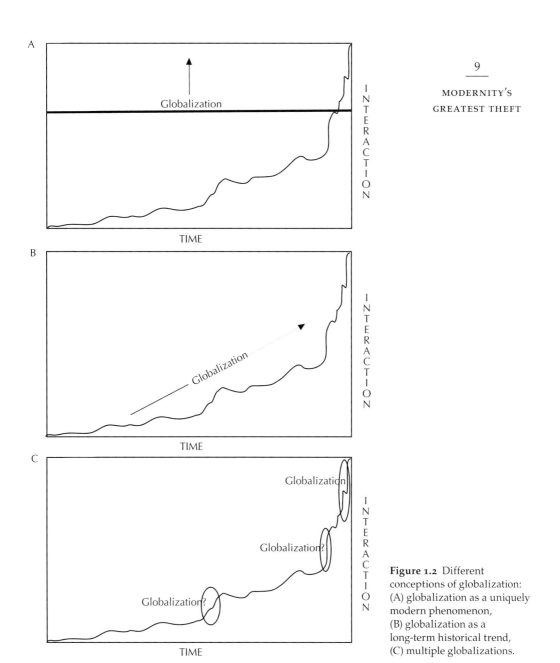

Figure 1.2 Different conceptions of globalization: (A) globalization as a uniquely modern phenomenon, (B) globalization as a long-term historical trend, (C) multiple globalizations.

time (Figure 1.2). Graph A shows the standard conception of globalization as a modern phenomenon. The bold line that cuts straight across the graph is the moment at which globalization begins – the Great Wall that forms when interactions increased dramatically during the last five hundred years. Where exactly this line sits depends on when the scholar feels the break between the globalized present and the unglobalized past begins.

The remaining two graphs acknowledge ancient globalization but in two very different manners. Graph B represents globalization as a gradual process that increases over the entire span of the graph, while Graph C shows globalization as discrete bursts in interaction and therefore identifies multiple periods of globalization that have occurred over time. These latter two major approaches that accommodate early globalization are what I call the globalization as long-term process approach and the world systems approach. Those who think of globalization as a long-term process tend to conceive of globalization along the lines of Graph B, while world systems scholars, of course, often think more in terms of Graph C.

The globalization as long-term process approach (Graph B) was developed over the last ten to fifteen years by historians who felt that ancient interactions were short shrifted in globalization studies. The historian William H. McNeil perhaps best captured this approach in his recent argument: "the world is indeed one interacting whole and always has been" (2008: 9). By looking at history from a long-term global perspective, scholars like McNeil see a trend toward increasing interaction over time.

Another of the more influential voices in this approach belongs to Jan Nederveen Pieterse. In his book *Globalization and Culture*, Nederveen Pieterse views globalization as the end result of increasing integration and hybridization that dates back at least to the origins of agriculture (2004). Other authors following the globalization as long-term process approach disagree with Nederveen Pieterse on when globalization first began – Robert Clark (1997) and Nayan Chanda (2007), for example, argue that it began with the dispersal of the first humans out of Africa, while McNeil (2008) traces globalization back to the control of fire – but they all suggest that globalization today is part of an acceleration of earlier trends. In the globalization as long-term process approach, history unfolds as a unified story, an "age-old process expanding the human niche in earth's ecosystem" (McNeil 2008: 8).

The world systems approach (Graph C) emerged in the 1960s out of work within sociology that modeled global capitalism as a system that locked poor nations into exploitative relationship with Western nations (Frank 1966, 1967). Immanuel Wallerstein's world systems model argued that the world could be divided into three major zones, a core, semiperiphery, and periphery, which are tied together by a world market of bulk commodities necessary for everyday life

(1974). The core contains strong governments and generally supports industry and wage labor, the periphery has weak states typified by coerced labor and monoculture, and the semiperiphery has semistrong states with limited industrialization. In the model, surplus wealth flows into the core from peripheral and semiperipheral nations.

Although Wallerstein suggested that his model could not be applied to understanding the precapitalist world (1974: 15–16), the model was embraced by many scholars interested in understanding the role that interregional interaction played in ancient societies (e.g., Blanton and Feinman 1984; Chase-Dunn and Anderson 2005; Chase-Dunn and Hall 1991, 1997; Kardulias 1999; Rowlands et al. 1987). Most of these scholars envisioned world systems in the plural – moments in world history when inter-societal relationships developed in particular regions. At one extreme, Christopher Chase-Dunn and Thomas Hall described a "very small world-system" that operated among the Wintu and rival hunter-gatherer groups in California's Sacramento Valley (1997: 121–48). At the other extreme, the world system approach was used to understand the relationship of the Roman Empire to northern Europe, the Middle East, and northern Africa (Nash 1987). Although these scholars do not tend to use the term "globalization," their vision of history falls into Graph C on Figure 1.2.

Both approaches drag globalization back into antiquity, but are the readers of these books really learning about *ancient globalizations in the plural*? I argue that they are not. The globalization as long-term process approach (Graph B) seems instead to extend modern globalization's adolescence. Those who read books advocating this approach will learn that world history is dotted with people who established new connections between regions and that great empires, world religions, and transcontinental trade routes connected large groups of people together. They will find out, as in the subtitle to Nayan Chanda's book (2007), how early traders, preachers, adventurers, and warriors shaped globalization. For Chanda and his colleagues, there is only one globalization because they define globalization as the trend toward increasing world interaction and integration over the course of human history.

The problem that I have with this approach is that the bursts of interaction that occur in world history become just part of the grand unfolding of history in the globalization as long-term process

approach. If globalization were personified, then the books following this approach would be her biographies. Past events – like the
corporal punishment meted out by a second-grade English teacher
or a long illness in Spain – are seen as formative to the person the
woman eventually becomes.

In a similar manner, the books advancing the long-term process
approach look back on the events that made modern globalization
possible. I applaud their scholarship, but this method necessarily
precludes the possibility of globalization in the plural. Interactions
in antiquity cannot be seen as true examples of *real* globalization
in this framework (there is only one globalization in their story).
Instead, earlier interactions are seen as *globalization-lite*, at best part
of a precocious adolescent that would blossom in time into the true
globalization of the modern world.

The world systems approach (Graph C) fails to get at ancient
globalizations for a different reason. Even though its proponents
consider earlier moments of globalizations in the plural, those who
adhere to the classic ideas of the approach have a tendency to rep-
licate the present in the past by peopling early civilizations with
modern capitalists. World systems was originally built to explain a
particular era, and after almost three decades of engagement with
the idea, there is a growing realization that ancient political economies could not work the same as modern ones (Kohl 1978, 1987, 2007;
Stein 1999; Upham 1986; Wells 1999; also see chapters in Cusik 1998
and Stein 2005a).

Past transportation hurdles were too high, city bureaucracies were
too weak, specialization was too shallow, and exchange networks
were too limited. Colonies and cities did occasionally control and
reshape outlying areas in a variety of ways, but the specific power
geometry of global capitalism did not exist in the past. Wallerstein
now appears to have been right – ancient societies could not sustain
across broad areas the kinds of political and economic relationships
that he saw in the world today (1974: 15–16). If you strictly follow
the world systems approach, then you are not really finding ancient
globalizations. Instead, you are imposing a modern structure onto
various ancient settings.

Most scholars working in antiquity have quickly recognized these
problems and have adjusted the world system approach to fit earlier
periods (Kardulias and Hall 2008; Schortman and Urban 1992, 1994).
Among other changes, they shrank the size of the system, made the

core less dominant, allowed a more active and varied peripheral zone, and diversified the types of connection between the two zones (Chase-Dunn and Hall 1997: 12–15; Denemark et al. 2000: xvi; Earle and D'Altroy 1989; Kardulias 1999, 2007; Parkinson and Galaty 2007; Peregrine and Feinman 1996; Schneider 1977; Stein 1999).

These adjustments, sometimes called the comparative world systems approach, have yielded perspectives that fit much more closely with available data. Yet, these authors have also transformed their models to such a degree that they no longer function like the world systems model used to explain modern interactions (e.g., Stein 2002: 27–8). These more recent world system studies of past interactions instead fit better into more acephalous, dynamic ancient globalization models like the one I offer later in this book (but see Kardulias and Hall 2008 and Chase-Dunn 2006 for a counterargument on the continued vitality of the world system approach).

FINDING THE "S" IN GLOBALIZATIONS

If we want to explore the possibility of globalizing moments in the past that had similar cultural consequences to those that we are experiencing today, then we need to look for globalizations in the plural. Neither the globalization as long-term process approach nor the world systems approach really does this. However, a new ancient globalizations approach can be built on the strengths of these two approaches. From the globalization as long-term process approach, we can borrow their general emphasis on how interaction and integration can occur within a variety of political, economic, and social structures, and from the world systems approach, we can take the view that globalization has occurred many times in the past (so I also argue for Graph C on Figure 1.2).

Yet how does one identify earlier periods of globalizations? Only a few eras of increased interaction might also be eras of globalization. To separate out globalizing periods from periods when this phenomenon did not occur, we need to take the definitional criteria for globalization used by many leading theorists and apply these same criteria to the past. Using these definitions for modern globalization, an earlier globalization era would have evidence for both (a) a significant leap in interregional interaction and (b) the social changes that are associated with the creation of a global culture (Figure 1.3).

This methodology, I hope, is straightforward. A mechanic goes through his checklist to find what is wrong with your motor; a medical doctor diagnoses a disease through her knowledge of the likely symptoms. In a similar manner, we can determine if a surge in interaction reached the threshold of globalization by identifying the social changes associated with a global culture that I will describe in the next chapter.

This is not to suggest that globalization is identical in every case. On the contrary, considerable variation occurs because cultural, environmental, and historic conditions make every era unique. This diversity has been highlighted by the research into interregional interactions that was sparked by the application of world system approaches. The examples in this book further outline this rich variation in the spread of early civilizations. Yet the examples in this book also show how people in the past sometimes reacted to increasing long-distance connectivity in ways that were broadly similar to the way that we are reacting to globalization today.

Since neither the globalization as long-term process nor the world system approach presents a strong case for ancient globalizations, it is easy for theorists to dismiss early examples of intense interaction and integration as not really being true examples of globalization. In a popular book on modern globalization, Thomas Hylland Eriksen, for example, readily admits that the Roman and Aztec Empires integrated large regions together but suggests that they should not be conceived of as true examples of globalization because they lacked "the existence of a global *discourse*, a shared (but not uniform) communication system" (2007: 5, emphasis in original).

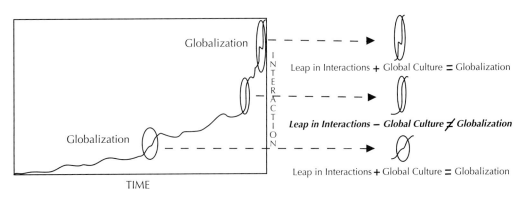

Figure 1.3 Determining if globalization has occurred by identifying a leap in interactions *and* the creation of a global culture. Note that globalization does not occur in the middle graph because a global culture fails to emerge.

Since my discussion of globalization later in this book discusses how global discourses and other widely recognized hallmarks of globalization were achieved when global cultures were created in antiquity, the possibility of ancient globalizations becomes more difficult for scholars to ignore when critically compared to the criteria that these same scholars use to define the modern era.

The potential success of an intellectual assault on the Great Wall by using a definition of globalization that stresses the social transformations that can occur with increased connectivity is hinted at in the pages of *Connectivity in Antiquity: Globalization as Long-Term Historical Process* (LaBianca and Scham 2006). This volume is one of the first books that I know of that brings together archaeologists and historians in a sustained engagement with the work of a leading theorist of the social dimensions of globalization.

The theorist, Manuel Castells, describes an emerging global social structure that is being driven by the technological transformations that have occurred in electronics, communications, and biology since the end of World War II. He calls this social structure the "network society" and wrote an influential three-volume work called *The Information Age: Economy, Society, and Culture* (1996, 1997, 1998). *Connectivity in Antiquity* challenged Castells's assertion that the network society was a product of the last fifty years by demonstrating the importance of network connections throughout much of the Old World from the third millennium B.C.

Castells wrote a response to the contributions that was included as the last chapter of the book. His response, which I quote here at length, is interesting because I think it demonstrates the potential fruitfulness of studying ancient globalizations as moments of surging interactions that were broadly commensurate with our experiences today:

> The argument put forward by the essays included in this book is a compelling one, and bears considerable theoretical significance: networks are fundamental forms of social organization throughout human history. Therefore, a network theory of society is a critical component of social theory, and it is relevant to all societies … when, in my own research, I limited the validity of my analysis of the social structure that I theorized as network society to our contemporary society, tentatively identified as the Information Age, I was wrong both empirically and

theoretically. Empirically: networks seem to have always been at the heart of social structure and social change … Networks did not have to wait for microelectronics to be a decisive tool in organizing production, trade, power and communication. Theoretically: a network theory of society is relevant, and indeed fundamental, for general social theory, without being dependent on a given technological paradigm. So, what this volume suggests is the need to decouple network theory and the empirical analysis of social structure and social processes in the Information Age. "Our" network society would be a specific form of the network society, as a trans-historic form. Thus, globalization is not new: under different forms, it appears to have happened not only in the 19th century of the common era, but thousands of years ago … In the last analysis, *there is nothing new under the sun*. There are only variations on the theme of the human experience. (Castells 2006: 158, emphasis in original)

Manuel Castells does not reject the singularity of the Information Age in his response (he spends the remainder of his chapter arguing why this age is unique), but his engagement with the authors in the volume spurred him to begin to untangle aspects of globalization from recent technological changes. In a similar manner, the archaeologists and historians in the volume were encouraged to divorce Castells's theoretical idea of a network society from the modern age that he thought created it. Our understanding of both the modern and the ancient worlds was enriched through the critical movement back and forth across the Great Wall.

Connectivity in Antiquity, however, did not go far enough. Like world system theorists, the authors in this volume have shown that periods of increased interregional interaction have occurred repeatedly in human history (see Figure 1.2). Yet, the existence of long-distance networks in antiquity in and of themselves will convince very few that globalizations occurred during these periods. You need, as others have begun to do (e.g., Hitchner 2008; Pitts 2008), to find more and more of the major characteristics of globalization in past cultures. In this book, I extend these efforts to breach the Great Wall by using the approach sketched out in Figure 1.3 to present what I hope is a compelling case for globalization eras in the ancient world. Although I see the first strong evidence for globalization occurring with urbanization and the spread of some early civilizations, there are hints of possible earlier globalizing moments from the move-ment of Venus figurines to the exchange of Lake Van obsidian that I hope other scholars will pursue.

Interestingly, globalization may be easier to demonstrate archae-ologically in the spread of these earlier civilizations than in the spread of empires and world religions. The extension of religions and empires was usually mediated through the expansion of well-developed states. State structures have a tendency to try to limit interregional connectivity by exchange restrictions and the leveling out of local differences through centralized planning (Scott 1998; also see Yoffee 2005). In a similar manner, some scholars think that glob-alization has become a more widely recognized phenomenon over the last few decades because a decline in state power has opened up a wider variety of interconnections between people (see chapters in Friedman and Chase-Dunn 2005). The inability of city dwellers to subjugate people in the countryside to their will during the spread of the world's first civilizations, especially as one moved further and further away from urban centers, should therefore make globaliza-tions during these periods more archaeologically visible.

Is the world different than what it was five hundred years ago? Yes, of course it is. Globalization has been happening over the past few hundred years – dense, deep interconnections between people now span the planet – and these connections have transformed our lives in ways that are unique to world history. A sense of the radi-cal difference of modernity prevails in our everyday lives. It is easy to think, just like Leo Colston in *The Go-Between*, that "the past is a foreign country" that is so very different than where we are now (Hartley 1953: 9). Yet we need to be wary of this sense of radical differ-ence. Although every age is indeed unique, people in each age have tended to accentuate the differences with the past and downplay the similarities (e.g., McNeil 2008: 9). The interregional interactions in the world today are "strikingly new" in many ways (Appadurai 1990: 295), but I argue that the general process of globalization is strikingly old as well. Thinking of globalizations in the plural will allow us to take the first steps toward a general theory of globalization.

THE FIRST GLOBALIZATIONS

To call something 'ancient history' is often used as a pejorative today. We tend to trace our history back only so far – to find the genesis of our world in the birth of the nation-state, for example, or in the introduction of capitalism. Excavations from Huari, Cahokia, Uruk, San Lorenzo, Teotihuacan, Harappa, and other early cities titillate us with exotic stories from the other side of the Great Wall, but we feel that the cultures that unfolded around these cities followed a logic alien to our fast-paced, hyper-integrated world. If the spread of the world's first civilizations were instead early examples of globalization, then we need to more seriously consider ancient civilizations of the world as germane to our lives.

We need to take down this Wall and begin to look with fresh eyes at how our present era compares with the grand sweep of human history. Contrasting the earliest globalizations with its most recent form may allow us to find those aspects of the phenomenon that are independent of the mechanisms of a particular period and region. We are well aware of the differences between ancient megaliths and MTV, but we are not used to trying to find the similarities between them. If we begin to think about globalization in the plural, we might gain some insights into the present and future of this current globalization era. Were there ancient globalizations? Modernity's greatest theft has been to remove this as a legitimate question to ask.

2

How to Pluralize Globalization

Asking if there were ancient globalizations is a question that might seem much easier to ask than to answer. The grand sweep of human history that awaits those who tear down the Great Wall separating modernity and antiquity is incredibly complex. One of the ways to deal with these intricacies would be to declare, like those who follow the globalization as long-term process approach, that *all* of these past interactions are the roots of modern globalization. Yet history has not unfolded along a well-trodden path of ever-increasing long-distance interaction from the first humans to the present (Wenke and Olszewski 2006). Instead, history unfolds in a more cyclical rhythm of expansions and contractions. Mesoamerican and Andean history, for example, is broken up into "horizons" of widespread cultural traits that are sandwiched between periods of regionalization (Rice 1993a), and Ancient Egypt's chronological sequence displays a similar pattern (Kemp 1989).

Archaeologist Joyce Marcus provides perhaps the best visual representation of these "peaks and valleys" of interregional interaction (1998) (Figure 2.1). Using case studies from both the Old and New Worlds, Marcus shows how various areas experienced similar "dynamic cycles of consolidation and collapse" over time (1998: 81). Although Marcus associates these cycles with the formation and dissolution of polities, other scholars have connected this pattern to the rise and fall of larger interaction networks (e.g., Frank and Gills 2000; Friedman 1992, 2005; Hall and Chase-Dunn 2006). Why this cycling occurs is an important question, but my main concern in this book is to gain a better understanding of particular peaks in interaction and determine if some of these peaks should be considered periods of globalization.

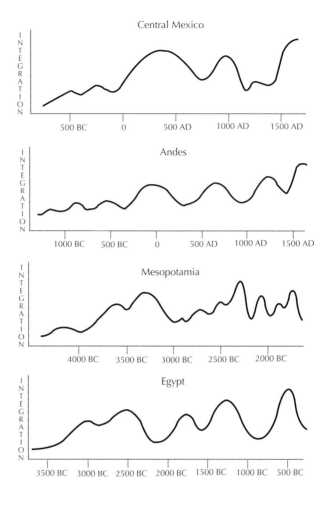

Figure 2.1 Interaction
cycles from different parts
of the world (adapted from
Marcus 1998).

The peaks in interaction in Figure 2.1 might seem paltry when compared to the scale, speed, and density of interactions in our modern globalized world. Yet we need to understand these earlier periods as best we can within their cultural context – earlier peaks may have been just as dramatic when seen through the eyes of a Maya farmer or Babylonian trader. Many social scientists have noted an array of substantial cultural changes that have occurred over the last few decades because of the creation and intensification of global networks.

If earlier peaks of interregional interaction caused similar transformations, shouldn't we also consider these peaks as earlier periods of globalization? An affirmative answer to this question would go far beyond semantics. A pluralized globalization would encourage us to reflect much more critically on how our current era compares to earlier periods of intense long-distance connections. Perhaps more importantly, work on earlier globalizations might provide some hints to the future of the current peak in interaction that we are experiencing.

IDENTIFYING GLOBALIZATIONS

Identifying earlier eras of globalization hinges on our ability to define when a period of globalization occurs. In Chapter 1, we discussed how many social scientists suggest that modern globalization is the consequence of the creation of dense networks of interconnections and interdependencies that link people together across regions (e.g., Ritzer 2007: 1). For these scholars, globalization occurs when the array of social changes driven by these networks come together to create a global culture. To determine if globalization occurred in a period, we will therefore need to verify that the interactions that occurred in a particular time period meet these same criteria. All globalizations should (a) be triggered by a surge in long-distance connections that (b) caused the specific array of cultural changes associated with the creation of a global culture. If a period meets these two criteria, then it is a period of globalization.

Before we plunge into earlier peaks of interaction, we need to better learn how modern globalization fits into these criteria. How was modern globalization spurred by a surge in interregional interaction? And how did this interaction then lead to the creation of a global culture? Answering these questions will allow us to better compare potential examples of earlier globalization to our own era.

A SURGE IN INTERACTION

The linking of globalization to surging interregional interactions should not come as a surprise to the reader. We are awash (drowning?) in a sea of globe-spanning interactions these days. I chat regularly with Peruvian friends on the Internet, watch the Hang Seng stock index with trepidation, and can guiltily admit that I have put ingredients from four continents into one salad. All of us have a few of these prototypical globalization moments each day, and we are all aware that our personal networks have increased in scale and complexity during our lifetimes. Globalization theorists also recognize that our networks are rapidly increasing, but there is considerable debate about when this surge in interaction began (e.g., Castells 1996; Ericksen 2007; Tomlinson 1999).

Most globalization theorists would rightly hesitate to give you a specific date to the "start" of modern globalization, but most would argue that globalization began earlier than the last couple of decades. The conventional wisdom among globalization theorists is to place the beginnings of globalization somewhere in the last six hundred years or so (Eriksen 2007: 13; Schäfer 2007). When exactly the current globalization era began within this time period is not important for our discussion. Yet it is important for us to understand why modern globalization is linked to a surge in the size, density, and depth of long-distance connections.

Summarizing the last six hundred plus years of global history is an imposing task, but thankfully understanding this era from a worldwide perspective has become an academic specialty in and of itself (e.g., Hopkins 2006). Two good books that offer brief summaries of modern globalization from the fifteenth century to the present are Alex MacGillivray's *A Brief History of Globalization* (2006) and Jürgen Osterhammel and Niels Petersson's *Globalization: A Short History* (2005). These books aren't without flaws – they tend to ignore the subwaves of global integration and contraction that occurred during this period (Arrighi 1994; Chase-Dunn et al. 2000) and tell the story of modern globalization from a Western perspective that often underemphasizes non-Western connections and achievements (e.g., Abu Lughod 1989; Frank 1998; Hopkins 2002) – but I use these books for the sake of clarity to construct the following summary of the surge in interaction associated with modern globalization. This brief history will allow us to tease out aspects of the phenomenon that we can look for in earlier periods.

The story of modern globalization begins in the second millennium A.D. At the beginning of the millennium, the most influential and richest societies in the world were found in places like China, India, and Mesopotamia. Ruled by powerful kings, these well-organized states derived most of their wealth internally. The states had far-flung exchange networks, but they lacked the "global intent" to increase interactions because they did not want to shoulder the unnecessary risks of explorations (MacGillivray 2006: 27; but see Abu Lughod 1989, Frank 1998, and others for a strong counterargument). In contrast to these regions, Europe was made up of a number of small, poor, fragmented states that were of little consequence to world affairs.

Europe lay at the western extreme of Asia's far-flung exchange network – the famous silk routes over the land and on the sea that linked the East's great powers. The trickle of goods from Asia, as well as from Africa, came to Europe at exorbitant prices. European leaders dreamed of finding a way to trade directly with Asia and Africa, and technological improvements in seafaring and cartography in the fourteenth century finally made this possible. The Portuguese began to explore the coast of Africa in the mid-fifteenth century, and Bartolomeu Dias rounded the horn of Africa in 1487. Five years later, Christopher Columbus sailed west with the support of the Spanish Crown and stumbled into the New World; in 1498, Vasco de Gama reached India. The European Age of Discovery had begun, and in 1494 Spain and Portugal divided up the world in the Treaty of Tordesillas.

The Portuguese set up a string of fortified trading posts around Africa and into Asia. They often faced considerable opposition from local groups around these forts, and they had to fight off Muslim and Chinese traders, as well as pirates, on the open seas. Nonetheless, a Portuguese fleet captured Malacca, the gateway to the Spice Islands, in 1511 and tried to monopolize the trade in cloves, nutmeg, mace, pepper, and other seasonings. Portuguese success in creating an Asian trade empire was limited by native resistance, and they were largely pushed out of the trade by Dutch, French, and English naval forces during the first half of the seventeenth century. The European incursions into the Pacific sent ripples of concern across Asia and led to the expansion of existing powers like the Ottoman Empire and Ming dynasty China. By the early eighteenth century, Europe controlled the Indian Ocean, but their territorial holdings were limited to a few captured islands and a handful of toe-holds on the continent.

The story was quite different in the New World. The Spaniards began to aggressively colonize Hispaniola (present-day Haiti/ Dominican Republic) the year after Columbus first landed on the island. Columbus was disappointed with the island's natural resources, but the island, like others in the Caribbean, was an ideal place for growing sugar. After the native Taino population was rapidly decimated by disease and mistreatment, the colony began to import African slaves in 1501 to work the crop. Sugar, as well as the institution of slavery, was rapidly exported to other islands and the Portuguese established plantations on the coast of Brazil.

By the early eighteenth century, hundreds of thousands of African slaves had been shipped to Spanish, French, and British colonies in the Caribbean. The sugar trade, however, was only of secondary importance to the Spanish in the New World. Spanish explorers had managed to conquer Mexico and Peru in the early sixteenth century, and soon after these colonies began shipping out tons of gold and silver from the New World. Much of this wealth ended up in India and China after being used to pay off Spanish debt and buy luxury items. The cultural effects of European colonization of the Americas were immense as depopulation, cultural collapse, slavery, Christianity, and colonial practices all radically transformed native lifeways. These effects were much greater than those occurring during this period in Africa and Asia since Europeans had made only a few inroads into these continents.

After about 1760, European states tried to strengthen their hold over their colonies and integrate them more completely into their respective imperial economies. In some cases, these actions led to revolts. In the New World, for example, the United States broke off successfully from the British in 1783, and the Spanish colonial holdings on the American continent crumbled by 1825. In other cases, colonial holdings were strengthened. The British, particularity aggressive in this period, wrested control of Canada from the French in 1763 and began their first campaigns to take over the Indian subcontinent.

Political consolidation went hand and hand with economic intensification. The sugar trade exploded during this period, and millions of African slaves moved across the ocean to the New World. In Europe, the Industrial Revolution began to transform both the cities and countryside by the end of the nineteenth century. Industrialization quickly altered global trade patterns – by the 1830s, for example, British factories were flooding the world market with cheap textiles – and led to three inventions, the steamship, locomotive, and telegraph, that would break down cultural and geographic barriers during the second half of that century.

European colonialism reached its zenith as the nineteenth century drew to a close. Africa was carved up by the European powers; China was defeated in the Opium Wars and forced open to greater trade; and Latin America, though nominally independent, was heavily influenced by outside interests. The global trade in exotic goods was dwarfed by the trade in raw material that was flowing into industrialized countries. At the same time, there was a surge in human migrations around the world during this period.

More than 25 million Europeans migrated abroad and more than 12 million Chinese left their country. In places like the United States, people came together from very different cultural backgrounds – some chose to abandon their previous identities, some chose to strengthen them, and some immigrants had new identities forced upon them by others. Urban elites had been embracing a pastiche of Western culture in different parts of the world for three centuries, but now more and more people were being exposed to European and other foreign ideas. Even as Western influence spread across the world, there was an increasing concern in the West about the negative impacts of industrialization, capitalism, and colonialism. Karl Marx's *The Communist Manifesto* in 1848, for example, was one of the earlier critiques of capitalism's treatment of workers, and the horrific lives of rubber workers in the Congo shocked Europeans in 1904.

As the twentieth century unfolded, communication and transportation networks were spreading across the world, exchange and production chains crisscrossed continents, and European power straddled the globe. World War I broke many of these global connections and ended Europe's world domination. The League of Nations, as well as other attempts at creating a new world order, failed following the war, and the globe fell into an economic depression that further weakened Europe's control over its colonies. World War II exacerbated these problems. Europe lay in ruins after 1945, and colony after colony declared independence in the decades that followed.

The destruction in Europe also allowed for new international institutions to emerge. The United Nations, International Monetary Fund, World Bank, and General Agreement on Trade and Tariffs were created in the years following the war. These institutions provided international forums that charted a new course of multilateral free trade and off-shore production that promised development to those impoverished nations that embraced political and economic reforms. The United States and the Soviet Union arose during this time as the world's superpowers. An "Iron Curtain" fell across Europe, and the world was dividing into two ideological blocs. The portable radio, rock and roll music, Hollywood movies, and satellite television were at the forefront of these polarized cultural encounters.

The collapse of the Soviet Union in 1991 left the world with a single superpower. The countries in the former Soviet bloc entered more deeply into the world economy, and trade over the last two decades has reached unprecedented levels. The advent of the computer has further sped up global transaction and increased the integration of world financial markets. The promise of development for the poorer countries of the world, however, has not been fulfilled. Although places like Japan have prospered in a global economy, one billion people in the world are living on incomes that are lower than those they would have received in 1500 A.D. The widening gap between rich and poor has led to international protests against unfettered globalization that began in the 1990s. Meanwhile, the Internet, as well as a surging international tourism market, is bringing people from different regions in greater contact with each other, and transnational corporations are increasingly trying to reach into untapped markets with high-profile advertisement campaigns. These increasing interactions have both contributed to the idea of a global culture and fueled unease about the loss of indigenous tradition.

This very brief summary of interactions over the last six hundred years touches on several themes that are particularly germane to our goal of identifying earlier periods of globalization. Most importantly, this summary demonstrates that a surge in interregional interaction did indeed occur. This is not to deny the importance of Muslim traders in ninth-century A.D. East Africa or to denigrate the famous "treasure ships" sent out in 1403 by Chinese Emperor Zhu Di to open up new commercial and diplomatic relations. These earlier interactions, however, pale in comparison to those that were occurring throughout the world by the end of the sixteenth century, and the pace, scale, and density of these interactions have continued to increase since then. This surge, of course, has not been a single, smooth, upward sweep. Armed conflicts, protectionism, and flawed international regulators have curtailed global exchanges at times, but there has been a clear linear trend toward greater and greater interaction (Chase-Dunn et al. 2000: 87).

Another important theme that can be drawn from this summary of interaction is that modern globalization began as a colonial expansion. In this case, European colonization was the unanticipated result of a blind bid to open up new trade routes to the fabled riches of Asia. Colonization was a major catalyst for increasing the size and density of interregional relationships, but it was far from the sole factor. The incursion of Portuguese ships around Africa and into the Pacific, for example, stimulated a wide variety of responses from a wide variety of non-European leaders, traders, priests, and other actors who forged new relationships with both the Europeans and each other. Many of the dense, long-distance networks that were created during the period were not directly connected to the European colonial system, and Europeans played little or no role in these interactions (e.g., Hopkins 2002).

A third theme in this summary that is of special interest to us is that the cultural consequences of increasing interaction were protracted and spotty. Spanish influence on the many aspects of courtly life in Mexico, for example, soon blurred the lines between colonizers and colonized (e.g., Rosenmüller 2008), while many other regions of the world remained largely isolated from broader global currents until the last few decades. This history shows that modern globalization was neither a simple, swift process nor synonymous with the Europeanization of the world. Europe, and later North America, was perhaps the most significant player, but there were many groups that exerted varying degrees of influence in different ways at different times on global networks. Although we will discuss the trends associated with global culture in the next section of this chapter, the history of modern globalization suggests that a global culture does not emerge all at once or remain constant.

A final theme of interest to us from our discussion of surge in interaction over the last few centuries is that some of the current global networks might be fracturing. Globalization's future is, of course, a controversial topic in globalization studies. To cite just one instance, *New York Times* columnist Thomas Friedman declared in his book *The World Is Flat* that trends in globalization over the last couple of decades like job outsourcing and the creation of the Internet have led to the leveling of the competitive playing field between countries and jeopardizes the role of the world's leading great cities (2005). In a swift response article entitled "The World Is Spiky" (2005), the urban studies guru Richard Florida argued that the world is instead becoming more and more dominated by a handful of innovator cities that will grow at the expense of other regions. Although these scholars offer different visions of the future of cities, they both would agree that the dramatic increase in the web of global interconnections over the last few decades has caused considerable global tensions and sparked the desire of a significant portion of the world's population to at least partially unplug from the grid. How globalization will play out over the next century is one of the more pressing questions of our era and a question that I will return to at the end of this book.

THE CREATION OF GLOBAL CULTURE

A peak in interregional interaction alone does *not* equal globalization (see Figure 1.3). Our definition of globalization posits that these interactions must also lead to the creation of a global culture. To understand what I mean by the term "global culture," we have to first better understand what the term "culture" means. We could spend an entire book trying to define culture (Alfred Kroeber and Clyde Kluckhohn spent over 400 pages trying to define the concept in 1952), but for our purposes we can get by with a popular textbook's definition of culture as "the system of shared beliefs, values, customs, behaviors, and artifacts that the members of society use to cope with their world and with one another, and that are transmitted from generation to generation through learning" (Plog and Bates 1988: 7).

Culture, as the definition suggests, is largely a local product learned through daily interactions with one's family and community. This is still very much the case – think of how much your loved ones have shaped your life – but culture was particularly localized in many parts of the world until fairly recently. A good example of this comes from M. N. Srinivas's moving account of life during the 1940s in Rampura, a village in the south of India (1976). The village, like many across India at this time, was insular. Life was focused on agriculture, and the rhythms of the season were tied to crops. Men in the village learned to work the land from an early age, grew up with their extended family, remained with their families in the same home after marriage, and inherited land within the village after the death of their father.

Globalization changes cultures by suddenly increasing the number, depth, and variety of connections between people across regions. This does not mean that nonlocal connections are absent before globalization occurs. The notion of fixed, insular, largely ahistoric cultures has justly been criticized (e.g., Abu-Lughod 1991; Gordon 1992; Gupta and Ferguson 2002; Wolf 1982). To return to Rampura, Srinivas notes in his book that the village was already connected to the outside world during the 1940s in many ways. Women, for example, married into the village from outside, men routinely went on religious pilgrimages that took them into cities, and a road near the village, though poorly maintained, allowed for the limited transport of people and goods to and from other places.

Yet surging interregional interactions in the second half of the twentieth century radically changed the way of life in Rampura and other rural villages in India. On the one hand, these connections exposed them to a wider diversity of ideas, people, and products. On the other hand, these connections were transformed by these villages whose members sometimes asserted long-held, or even invented, traditions because of the perceived threat of cultural homogenization. In many cases, people found themselves torn because they wanted to be both "traditional" and "modern" (e.g., Appadurai 1996; Eriksen 2007; Featherstone 1990; Robertson 1992).

In Rampura, Srinivas noted a more global village in the 1950s and 1960s during his return visits. Men were now investing money in property in the city instead of buying new lands at home, a government-funded hospital and school were constructed in Rampura, and hairstyles and clothes of the younger generation were beginning to match national and international trends. Yet, is this when we say that globalization first occurred in Rampura? When exactly this occurred is not particularly of interest to us. The pace of cultural change in Rampura accelerated in the 1960s – is this when these villagers became part of a global culture? Did it occur in India and elsewhere with the global turmoil of World War II? Did it begin with the British Empire or in 1498 when the Portuguese explorer Vasco de Gama landed in India at Calicut?

Global cultures are created through the dynamic tension between the global and local. The people of Rampura, like those living in many villages around the world, now find themselves enmeshed in long-distance interaction networks that are transforming their culture. Just because cultures change, however, does not mean that a global culture has formed. Social scientists recognize a series of social trends that are hallmarks of the formation of a global culture. To find earlier globalizations, we need to find these hallmarks in the past. In most cases, these social trends will fail to appear because the size, strength, and density of interactions during an earlier era did not exceed the globalization threshold.

With the reams of quantitative data available on the world today (Kudrle 2004), you might rightfully ask why I am using more qualitative indicators like social trends and global culture to identify if and when the globalization threshold was reached in the past. Yet numbers in and of themselves often fail to get at the heart of how increasing connectivity changes people's lives. The first bale of imported cotton, for example, has far different social implications on dress in a region than the one billionth bale of cotton. Sometimes significant cultural change can even happen when the global links to a region are severed as when Melanesian islanders dressed like soldiers and fashioned control towers and airplanes out of straw and wood only *after* foreign goods stopped flowing into the area after World War II.

I do not eschew numbers in this book, but my emphasis on the cultural dimensions is derived in large part from the globalization of culture approach, one of the most popular ways of studying modern globalization (Sklair 2006). Drawing in large part from this scholarship, I have identified eight closely related trends that are commonly associated with modern globalization. Since these overlapping trends are associated with the creation of a global culture, they should all be discernable during a period of globalization. Because I will discuss these hallmarks in detail in Chapter 7 when I compare the impact of early urbanization to globalization, I only introduce these ideas very briefly in this section.

The first of the trends is *time-space compression*, an acceleration of long-distance economic and social processes that shrinks one's experience of space and time. With time-space compression, the world feels smaller and smaller. The second hallmark of globalization is *deterritorialization*, the sense that many places seem unconnected to their local cultural context. This trend might best be illustrated by walking into a high-end shopping mall where much of the mall's decoration, architecture, etc., would be designed to signal that you have entered a space removed from normal life. *Standardization* is the third trend. Since globalization brings diverse groups together, there is a need to operate on a common footing through the use of shared language, economic structures, etc. The fourth trend in globalization is *unevenness*. Global networks are not the same across the world. Some places like New York City are highly connected, whereas other places have very few connections to the outside world.

Homogenization, the fifth trend, is perhaps the most well-known of changes occurring in globalization. Homogenization is the process through which foreign, often Western, goods and ideas are adopted by other groups. This process is often balanced by the sixth trend, *cultural heterogeneity*, as new ways of living are generated through the mixing of various global flows. Listening to the Swedish heavy metal band Opeth, for example, would give you a sense of how globalization leads to the creation of hybrid music styles. The *re-embedding of local culture* is the seventh trend seen in globalization. The social changes that occur because of global flows can be traumatic, and some groups react to these changes by returning to local traditions. This embrace of the past, often reimagined for the present, is sometimes explicitly done to reject foreign influence. *Vulnerability* is the last trend. As global networks connect people together in more numerous and deeper ways, groups become increasingly interdependent. When things go wrong, as they did during the global financial crisis that began in the fall of 2008, everyone is affected.

All eight of these trends can be found when a global culture has been formed. I should caution again that the term "global culture" is not meant to evoke for the reader only the trend toward cultural homogenization, the idea of Tibetan herders snacking on hamburgers or Brazilian fishermen arguing about their favorite Hollywood movie. Cultural homogenization does, of course, occur with the creation of global culture, but I use this term in this book to encapsulate all of the ways that people's lives are fundamentally transformed by the increased flow of long-distance goods, people, and ideas.

Social scientists are in broad agreement that these eight trends have occurred over the last few hundred years. But have global cultures emerged earlier? The ancestors of those living in Rampura, for example, were part of the Maurya Empire (321–184 B.C.), a great military power that stretched throughout India, Pakistan, and much of Afghanistan. The Mauryans introduced substantial social and religious reforms in their country and traded across much of India and Europe. Even further back in time, the Rampura ancestors would have found themselves on the fringes of the great Indus Valley civilization (2600–1900 B.C.), which is known for its extensive commercial networks, artistic achievements, and script.

The Rampura area may or may not have been globalized during these earlier periods. The only way that we could tell would be to test these various eras using the two criteria for globalization outlined in this chapter. Can we document (a) a surge in long-distance connections during an earlier period that (b) caused the array of cultural changes that are associated with the creation of a global culture? If we can, then we would have strong evidence for an earlier globalization era.

GLOBALIZING THE ANCIENT WORLD

Globalization is a complex phenomenon. On the one hand, flows of goods, ideas, and people erode the local social structures and behavioral norms that maintain group identities. On the other hand, these flows are often indigenized and lead to the strengthening or invention of local traditions. This dialectic leads to the creation of a life that is "suffused with the sense of the fleeting, the ephemeral, the fragmentary, and the contingent" (Harvey 1989: 11). For many, living in a globalized world is as terrifying as it is promising. It is terrifying because of the specter of a world freed from tradition – an unsettled, fragmented place that is lacking moral guidance and sanctuary. It is promising in that the breaking of tradition and the fragmenting of society could lead to the possibility of a rebirth of a shared, better humanity.

These ambivalent feelings about the world can easily be seen as a unique product of global modernity (Giddens 1999). There is much to be said for this position. Global modernity *is* unique in human history. The speed, amount, and worldwide extent of long-distance interactions are without parallel, and no previous period can match the pace and degree of global social change of our times. Yet there have been other eras of great social change that were triggered by surging interactions across large parts of the Earth. These earlier periods tend to be treated as preamble – faint foreshadowing of today's globalized world. Yet the feeling of being trapped on a runaway world may be nothing new. Feelings like these, along with other aspects of modern globalization, could have occurred during earlier eras.

Since we are left with only a scattering of bones, ceramic fragments, sculptures, seals, and other artifacts, it might seem that both of the criteria that I have outlined for defining a previous globalization era are hopelessly out of the reach of those who study early civilizations. Fortunately, this is not the case. One of the cornerstones of archaeology is finding evidence for interaction, and scholars have gotten quite good at tracking objects, ideas, and people across space and time. We can, for example, identify the sources of obsidian traded over thousands of kilometers, model widespread interaction networks, and trace migrations of people through their bones and teeth (e.g., Burger et al. 2000; Knappett et al. 2008; White et al. 2004). Although the details of these interactions are often unclear – as most things are when you talk about the world's first civilizations – the first part of this equation, a surge in interregional interaction, should be clear in the material record.

Documenting the cultural changes associated with complex connectivity is more problematic in early civilizations, but it may be just because those who study the past aren't used to thinking in terms of globalization. Scholars studying antiquity are often familiar with the modern globalization literature – they occasionally reference some of the theoretical insights that were derived, at least in part, from studies of globalization today – but they choose to borrow these ideas piecemeal. An archaeologist, for instance, might apply the concept of hybrid identities to the Olmecs of first millennium B.C. Mesoamerica, but hesitate to compare identity formation in today's Paris with the Olmec city of San Lorenzo. Yet, the reason why the archaeologist borrows the theory in the first place is that she *sees* evidence for hybrid identities in the material record of the Olmec (Clark and Pye 2006: 217; Lesure 2004: 74). The use of globalization literature hints at how archaeologists are finding similar cultural transformations in the past.

The most significant barrier to a study of globalizations in the plural, therefore, is likely *not* the paucity of the material record. Instead, it is the mental barrier of the Great Wall that separates modern globalization from the rest of history. To break through this barrier, we need to explicitly compare the social changes associated with modern globalization to those that occurred during some of the peaks of interaction that have occurred in earlier periods. Most of these periods will fall short of the globalization threshold since even the most dramatic of processes like a military conquest, mass migration, or the spread of a religion will not often create all of the social trends associated with globalization. A few of these epochs, however, may meet the definitional standards for globalization that have been proposed by most scholars.

Pluralizing globalization should be easy to do if we set our minds to it. We just need to evaluate evidence from earlier eras with respect to those definitions of modern globalization that are commonly held by scholars. One of these definitions suggests that globalization is

(a) a surge of intense long-distance interaction that (b) causes the social changes associated with the creation of a global culture. If an earlier period meets these two criteria, then these eras should also be considered as periods of globalization. In other words, we need to follow the rather blunt cliché in looking for earlier globalizations: if it looks like a duck, walks like a duck, and quacks like a duck, it might just be a duck. The first step in pluralizing globalization is to allow for the possibility of such "ducks" in antiquity.

I argue that the world's first globalizations occurred in association with the rise of some of the earliest cities. The swift growth of these cities caused waves of interactions that swept across broad swathes of the globe. In the pages that follow, I present a general model that shows how urbanization caused wide-ranging cultural change. We then examine three case studies of early cities in the North American mid-continent, Andes, and Mesopotamia, before finally returning to our definition of globalization in order to determine if we can use the term to describe the periods of interregional interaction that were detailed in our three case studies.

3

Cities and the Spread of the
First Global Cultures

It is difficult to imagine a world without cities. More people around the globe now live in urban rather than rural areas, and almost everyone has traveled to a city, seen cityscapes on television, or used goods manufactured in factories. Yet for most of human history there were no urban centers. Indeed, there were no villages until about 14,000 years ago, and up until a few decades ago the great majority of people lived in small communities. To determine whether the spread of some early civilizations were earlier moments of globalizations, we need to first appreciate what life was like in villages before cities emerged. Almost all the people you knew were neighbors, virtually everything that you owned or consumed came from nearby, and your ideas about how the world worked came from family traditions. The emergence of cities transformed people's lives by dramatically increasing interregional interaction. Who you knew, what you ate, and what you thought changed after the urban revolution.

The possible links between urbanism, interaction, and the spread of what has often been called civilization have been of long-standing interest within anthropology, sociology, and archaeology (Schortman and Urban 1998; Trigger 1989: 150–5). One of the earliest authors to make these connections was Emile Durkheim. In his classic work, *The Division of Labor in Society* (1984 [1893]), he argued that there were two extremes in social integration – mechanical and organic solidarity. He suggested that mechanical solidarity is common among hunter-gatherers whose solidarity is based in shared practices and beliefs. In contrast, he thought that the organic solidarity found in industrial societies is based on the mutual interdependence of individuals who often perform very different roles within a culture. He recognized the growth of cities as one of the fundamental driving forces toward organic solidarity (1984 [1893]: 201–5).

Durkheim's interest in the cultural changes associated with urbanization was very influential and informed the work of the next generation of scholars. The work of this group is perhaps best exemplified by *Man Makes Himself*, a book by the archaeologist V. Gordon Childe that argued that wealth accumulation and craft specialization in cities led to wide-ranging trade networks that spread urban culture outward (1951 [1936]: 121–2). Childe, like Durkheim before him, helped to set the agenda for future scholars and we are still striving to fully understand early urbanism's impact on the trajectory of human history.

This book's early globalization model builds on the now classic works of early urbanization, as well as more recent books that explore the origin and spread of some of the world's first civilizations (e.g., Algaze 1993a, 2008; Pauketat 2007; Yoffee 2005). I suggest that rapid urbanization, at places like Uruk-Warka, Cahokia, Harappa, and San Lorenzo, created new flows of goods, ideas, and people across the landscape. These flows caused many outlying groups to forge new relationships with other partners who, in turn, caused more flows by expanding their own interaction networks. Some of these new relationships were with city dwellers, many of them were not. The cascade of reactions to urbanization led to the creation of far-flung networks that sometimes achieved a degree of connectivity sufficient enough to breach the globalization threshold. Global cultures that were as tumultuous and fractured as the one that we live in today emerged when this threshold was crossed (Figure 3.1).

This chapter describes this globalization model in greater detail and takes us briefly through 200,000 years of history to show how the emergence of cities created a surge in connectivity. There is little in my discussion of sedentization (settling down in one place), urbanization, and interregional interaction that will be surprising to archaeologists and other scholars. The only major difference in this book is in how these themes are organized. For example, scholars have long talked about how more long-distance interactions are engendered by urbanization (e.g., Schortman and Urban 1998). Some authors have tended to emphasize the possible core-periphery relationships that occurred with early urbanism and have focused their attention on colonial outposts and the flow of goods moving in and out of cities (e.g., Algaze 1993b). Other scholars have focused on how cities were part of larger systems that formed as a result of increasing interaction between multiple exchange partners (e.g., Renfrew and Cherry 1986). The globalization model that I put forth in this chapter simply brings perspectives like these together under the umbrella of a dynamic model of global culture and the social changes associated with it.

SETTLING DOWN

For almost 200,000 years of our existence as anatomically modern humans, we lived as hunter-gatherers. People spent most of their time spread thinly across the landscape in small mobile bands of no more than a few dozen people. You knew everyone in your group (probably too well), had few possessions, and enjoyed no privacy. Shelters, if they existed at all, were expedient and ephemeral. For most of us, this lifestyle would seem to be incredibly arduous but Marshall Sahlin famously called mobile hunting and gathering groups the "original affluent society" because they easily fulfilled their subsistence needs by spending only three to five hours on

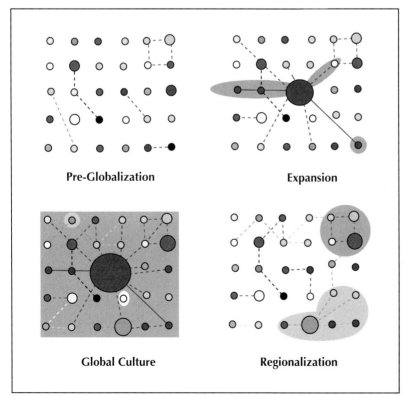

Pre-Globalization

Expansion

Global Culture

Regionalization

Figure 3.1 Model for the four phases of ancient globalization: the dots are communities and the dot near the center is a growing city. The lines represent flows of people, objects, or ideas between communities with the solid lines representing direct colonial links. This model is, of course, a simplification; in reality there would be many more lines, and each community would be broken up into families and even individuals engaged with different intercommunity flows.

food-related tasks each day (1972). Although this time estimate is likely too low (Kaplan 2000), it is nonetheless true that hunter-gatherers spent a lot of time visiting with friends and family.

Hunter-gatherers spend a lot of time socializing in part because they want to minimize risks – food sharing, for example, ensures that giraffe meat is given to each family in the band and having a friend forty kilometers away allows you to go there if times are tough in your particular locale (Lee 1984; Wiessner 1996). Social relationships are often sealed by exchanging gifts and through this mechanism goods like salt, obsidian, and ochre can move across distances of several hundred kilometers or more. The movement of goods in these gifts exchanges in the past, when combined with people crisscrossing the landscape on visits to friends, resource zones, and annual gatherings, would have created intense interaction networks outside of one's band (e.g., Chase-Dunn and Hall 1997: 121–48; Johnson and Earle 1987: 28–9). Yet, these were largely *regional* networks created with one's immediate neighbors.

The introduction of agriculture in and of itself does not significantly change the hunter-gatherer lifestyle and the size of social networks. The first clear evidence for agriculture comes from the Near East around 12,000 B.C. (Byrd 2005), but some of those people who adopted agriculture did not settle down into permanent villages. Like other regions of the world (e.g., Buckler et al. 1998), many hunter-gatherers just added a few agricultural products to their wide range of preexisting food choices. The ambivalence to becoming a full-time, sedentary agriculturalist is understandable since the lifestyle entails a lot of work for limited rewards (Hard and Merrill 1992; Winterhalder and Kennett 2006; K. Wright 1994). Why thresh, winnow, and grind the tiny seeds found in ancestral wheat, when you could go out and spear a gazelle?

A combination of environmental and population pressures may have driven groups in different regions of the world to make the choice to settle down in one place to exploit a particularly rich resource zone rather than take their chances ranging from one location to another (Rosenberg 1998). Sedentary humans, however, are generally quite demanding on wild food sources (e.g., Anderson 2002) – they kill off most of the animals and strain plant resources. To live for long in most places, groups have to adopt agriculture as one of their primary means of survival. The more people rely on agriculture, the harder it is to abandon it. Agriculture allows you to increase the amount of food available locally; a larger family allows you to farm more efficiently; and a bigger family eats more agricultural products (Kramer and Boone 2002; Rindos 1980: 755). This feedback loop led to the establishment of the first villages and a shift in the organization of interaction networks.

Village life was a critical change in human history – houses create neighbors, walls provide opportunities for accumulating food and wealth, and accumulation provides the possibility of status competition and resentment (Alden Smith et al. 2010). One of the biggest changes was that it was no longer as easy to vote with one's feet since you would have to leave your house, crops, animals, and most of your possessions behind (Banning 2003: 5). These and other "emergent properties" of village radically altered social interactions (Yoffee 2005: 201).

The biggest change may have been that personal interactions maintained over long distances tended to collapse into village relations as people became more concerned with pooling risk and easing conflict at the local level. When this trend was combined with families turning increasingly inward because of their ability to accumulate personal possessions and store their own agricultural products (Banning 2003; Minnegal and Dwyer 1998), it led to increased vulnerability and smaller interaction networks.

Despite internal pressures to expand in size and social complexity, villages in the ancient world usually remained quite small and largely undifferentiated because that is how people wanted it. Living in larger groups causes problems in terms of rising inequality, and people tend to zealously guard against threats to the status quo in status positions. Bigger villages also have increased communication problems, subsistence stress, and disease. These detriments seem to swamp any perceived benefits of staying together, and most villages split apart once the population exceeded a few hundred people (e.g., Bandy 2004). In fact, there seems to be a cross-cultural natural limit to how big a settlement can grow without significant social changes (Fletcher 1995; Friesen 1999; Johnson 1982).

These natural limits did not prevent the rare village from growing quite large. In the Near East, for example, the town of Jericho grew to about 2.5 hectares by 8000 B.C. (Naveh 2003: 83) and the site of Çatalhöyük was a "remarkably dense settlement" of 13.5 hectares by 7000 B.C. with as many as 8,000 people (Hodder 2007: 106). Yet there was considerable effort to maintain long-standing village dynamics at these sites by leveling out social differences and devoting considerable time and resources to rituals that downplayed individuals and celebrated community membership (Blitz 1993; Hodder 2007; Kuijt 2008; Lewis-Williams 2004).

These larger sites certainly had interaction networks that were wider than smaller villages – Çatalhöyük residents routinely traded with groups that were more than seven hundred kilometers away – but there was little driving people to radically expand their interregional connections. There may have actually been considerable pressures to minimize interregional interactions in most cases. Just as in smaller villages, people could have hypothetically stockpiled more than just crops and cooking pots. Those who sought higher status may have been tempted to hoard desired raw materials and exotica from outside of the region. Yet those who acquired goods from afar were also likely to be under considerable pressure to obtain only what was perceived to be beneficial to the community as a whole.

As George Orwell noted in *Animal Farm*, it is a small step from "we are all equal" to "some are more equal than others" (1996 [1946]). As population expanded, a few villages seem to have decided that the best way to deal with the social stresses of increased settlement size was *not* to fission apart or invest heavily into leveling status differences, but instead to organize more horizontal and vertical divisions within the community (Fletcher 1995: 189).

Why a group decided to make these changes despite their steep initial costs remains a pressing question in archaeology (e.g., Price and Feinman 1995), but the genie can't be easily put back in the bottle once new social positions are created. A shift toward organic solidarity (i.e., Durkheim 1984 [1893]) causes two major changes. First, settlement growth is encouraged because specialization is most effective when it is spread across larger and larger groups. Second, organic solidarity provides the motor for enlarging interaction networks because a metals expert needs steady access to copper and a priest's position might be based on continued access to foreign knowledge.

The decision to embrace a greater degree of social heterogeneity appears to have changed the rules of the game – shattering the ceiling on settlement growth and opening up various ritual, social, economic, and political pathways to urbanism. Although people had interacted across great distances for thousands of years, most relationships that people had were with those who lived within a few kilometers. The birth of cities would create an unprecedented surge in interregional connections. This surge, the first criterion we use to define a period of globalization, would dramatically transform people's lives across vast regions.

THE BIRTH OF CITIES

Where and when the first cities emerged in the world is a matter of considerable debate in archaeology largely because there is no commonly held definition of what a city is. For example, George Cowgill gives an exhaustive definition of a city as a "permanent settlement … considered home by a significant number of residents whose activities, roles, practices, experiences, identities, and attitudes differ significantly from those of other members of the society who identify most closely with "rural" lands outside such settlements" (2004: 525). Glenn Storey meanwhile suggests that "we know it [a city] when we see it" (2006a: 2), and Linda Manzanilla nicely ducks the question of what a city is altogether by defining instead an "urban society" that presumably encompasses both cities and the surrounding countryside (1997a: 5).

Following Louis Wirth's classic definition, I define cities as permanent settlements that have (1) a large population size, (2) dense population nucleation, and (3) high heterogeneity in the social roles of inhabitants (Wirth 1938: 8). Cities in this definition are defined relative to other settlements within a particular cultural context because the considerable worldwide variability in site organization does not allow for a set urban threshold like a population of twenty thousand people or a density of five thousand people per square kilometer (Wirth 1938: 3–8; also see Childe 1950). In comparison to many Mesopotamia sites, for example, the population densities of Maya centers like Tikal were quite small (Rice 2006). Yet, I define Tikal as a city because it was substantially bigger, denser, and more heterogeneous than most Maya sites.

The transition from a big village to a city occurred in a variety of ways. Some cities seem to have emerged in large part from the intentional plans of religious and political leaders, while others developed more organically as inhabitants adapted to increasing numbers (e.g., Manzanilla 1997b; M. Smith 2003a; Storey 2006b; Ucko et al. 1972). However cities may have emerged in different places, they tended to emerge very quickly. While the transition to sedentism took a few millennia in most regions, cities usually grew exponentially over the course of a few hundred years (Cowgill 2004: 534). Eretria in Greece, for example, developed from a "scattering of huts" to a hundred-hectare site from 850 to 700 B.C. (Morris 2006: 37), and the city of Teotihuacan in Mexico ballooned from a large village to a city covering eight square kilometers from 150 B.C. to A.D. 1 (Blanton et al. 1993: 120). A woman born and raised in one of these cities would have seen big changes in her lifetime and these changes were likely discussed across living generations and enshrined in oral histories.

The spectacular growth of Mumbai, Dakar, Lima, and other cities in today's developing world provides a sense of how the transition to early urban life was experienced (Gugler 1997). The flood of rural migrants over the past few decades has far outpaced the ability of these cities to provide basic services. Many people live in shantytowns that are only slowly being incorporated into urban infrastructures, and the experience of new migrants to the city is often confusing, dangerous, and downright miserable. We know little about the first decades of the earliest urbanization in the ancient world since these occupation levels are buried deep under the detritus of later occupations. Yet in those places where such evidence can be found, it appears that urbanization was initially just as ad hoc and chaotic as the early growth of most cities today (Cowgill 2003: 48; Shen 2003: 304–5).

People likely came to the earliest cities for the same reasons that people now move to cities. Many people move because of the perceived economic opportunities that a city provides. In the turbulent era of urban growth, most newcomers to earlier cities would become porters, servants, beggars, prostitutes, and farmers (though with a longer commute), but a few would become administrators, judges, police, traders, or craft specialists. Success, however limited, would encourage others to move to the city. People also come to the city because of the excitement that the city offered. Early cities were often arranged around temples and plazas where great ritual performances were held with parades, costumes, music, and sacrifices. The safety of city walls would have also drawn people to the city in some instances, while others were coerced into moving by the loss of their lands or the threat of violence (Cowgill 2003: 51).

Like today, there were also considerable disadvantages to living in a city. One of the biggest challenges of early urban life might have been dealing with the physical demands of so many people living together in one place. In cities, agricultural products and domesticated animals become the dominant part of the diet, as wild foods all but disappear. The crush of human (as well as animal) flesh leads to problems with sanitation, garbage, and disease that can only be partially overcome through changes in behavior (Cowgill 2003: 48–50; Storey 1992). Since basic services likely lagged behind the needs of the growing population, people must have initially struggled to carry out group activities, conduct economic activities, or simply move from one side of the city to the other (M. Smith 2003b: 19–23). People would have also seen their living spaces shrunken and reorganized in order to fit more houses into tightly confined urban spaces (Bafna and Shah 2007).

The biggest challenge to urban leaders would have been to instill a sense of community in city dwellers. As the city increased in size and heterogeneity, preexisting ideas of community would have rapidly broken down. The mechanical solidarity that Durkheim saw in hunter-gatherers emerged from the shared experience of a small group living together and doing the same things (Pauketat 2001: 12; Yaeger and Canuto 2000: 4–6). Settling down in one place did not radically transform this solidarity. You changed what you did, but there remained little specialization and a person knew at least the faces of the few hundred people living in the village. The growth of cities, however, made mechanical solidarity impossible. There were too many people doing too many different things. Beyond the possible powerful psychological effects of loneliness and depression, anonymity likely led to increases in crime and concerns about the maintenance of public order (Cowgill 2003: 48–50). A new sense of community needed to be forged.

In his recent book *Chiefdoms and Other Archaeological Delusions*, Timothy Pauketat argues that changes in traditions and the sense of community were the "X factor" in the development of cities and civilizations (2007). As people came into the city from many different places, Pauketat argues that there was "a grand negotiation of divergent political and cultural interests, conflicting cultural memories, and alternate kin and supra-kin allegiances form the inside out and outside in" (2007: 163). Since each person came to town with different customs, aspirations, and ideas about city life, the "grand negotiation" envisioned by Pauketat might have occasionally seemed more like a melee. From these chaotic beginnings, new cosmopolitan ways of thinking would have formed, and some of these ideas would have been championed by elites and other urban factions.

The most important of these ideas were often religious. Cities tended to emerge as holy sites with elite power often resting in large part on their access to the sacred. As the city grew, elite conceptions of the world were increasingly materialized in the decorations on temple walls, statues, and pots (DeMarrais et al. 1996; Manzanilla 1997c). A sense of community emerged as people moved through the cityscape together, gazed upon statues, danced at feasts, and passed each other on the street. This is *not* to suggest that the community was united. Many groups felt disenfranchised and resisted elite demands (Joyce 2000, 2004); and most retained some traditions from their native lands (Janusek 2002). Nonetheless, the cosmologies developed in the city often made sense to city dwellers because these ideas were based in large part on a mélange of preexisting beliefs.

THE REVERBERATIONS OF URBANISM

The urban revolution also caused the birth of the countryside (Yoffee 2005: 60–1). As people moved into the city, the surrounding area was often depopulated. At one point between 80 and 90% of the people in the Basin of Mexico lived in Teotihuacan (Cowgill 2003: 38), and a similar shift can be seen in the Lake Titicaca Basin after the founding of Tiwanaku in Bolivia (Browman 1997: 237). As cities like these grew, they quickly outstripped the abilities of urban residents to provide for themselves (Johnson and Earle 1987: 247; Schwartz and Falconer 1994: 3). The area around cities therefore became the countryside – a breadbasket region that was increasingly dedicated to agriculture and herding.

The countryside was radically transformed to meet urban subsistence needs. Workers constructed new roads, irrigation canals, store houses, corrals, and agricultural systems. Farmers and herders made decisions on breeding, fallow periods, and fertilizers that favored increased yields over long-term sustainability. Village economies shifted to focus more narrowly on the surplus production of a few animals or crops, and farmers made fields out of the wild lands that people had traditionally reserved for hunting, fishing, and other activities (e.g., Bandy 2005; Hastorf 1993; Zeder 1991).

Food, of course, was not the only thing flowing into the cities from the countryside. Rural households also concentrated more on the surplus production of other goods like pottery, scraped hides, stone tools, and metals (Adams 2004; Hayden 1994). A village around a local chert source might increase production and create tools specifically for the urban market (e.g., Hester and Shafer 1994), and new labor regimes would have been put in place to better exploit stone quarries and drag architectural elements into the city (e.g., Janusek 2002: 134–245). Since changes in rural life to meet urban demands led villagers to adopt more risky subsistence strategies – more time making cloth or growing corn means less time to invest in planting a broad range of plants in a variety of locations, those people living in the countryside found themselves tied more and more closely to the city. The growing regional economy became the farmer's safety net when things went wrong.

The rural transformations caused by urbanism would have been less acute as one went further from the cities. Since many foods, like greens, uncured meats, and milk, spoil quickly and most foods are bulky to transport, much of the food consumed in cities came from only a few hours away (Earle 2002: 193; Zeder 2003: 160). Some of this food could have been generated by the many people who lived in early cities and also maintained fields on the outskirts of town. The costs of such an urban-based subsistence system, however, would increase with every kilometer a field was removed from the city (Stein 1999: 59). For a metropolis to survive, the people living there also had to actively nurture connections with people living within a day or so walk.

City dwellers' concerns about maintaining relationships with the countryside should not be underestimated. As it is today, rapid urbanization was a logistical nightmare. There were too many people, too many activities, and too many local customs to control. City officials would have been unable to impose a structure on urban life in these formative years (Yoffee 2005: 94), and many, if not most, of the economic, political, and cultural interactions that occurred between the city and countryside were initially on an ad hoc basis (Adams 2004; Oka and Kusimba 2008: 356–7). A shrine, for instance, could have been supplied with offerings by a believer who lived outside of town; an urbanite might exchange stone tools for milk with her cousin who is a nomad; a neighborhood leader's position in the city was likely backed by the strength that his family has in the village.

Some of the earliest states likely emerged from the efforts of officials to regularize and simplify the interactions between the city and neighboring villages and nomads (Yoffee 2005: 17). Since there were considerable logistical difficulties of acting over distances in the ancient world, the reach of the state was often limited to the city's breadbasket region and a few more distant colonial outposts (Goldstein 2004; Stein 1999: 55–64). Yet many of the goods, people, and ideas that moved in and out of cities came from the areas that cites and emergent states could not control (or at least could not control for long). The city's longer-distance flows are of greatest interest to us because they link the city to a much wider part of the world. On occasion, these interactions were the initial catalyst for sweeping social, economic, and political changes that spread across vast areas.

THE LONG-DISTANCE MOVEMENT OF GOODS

As cities grew, the creation or extension of roads, trails, and waterways enlarged the breadbasket region. These improvements cut travel times and allowed porters, boats, wheeled transport, and pack animals to bring products from much greater distances than was initially possible when a city was founded. Well-maintained paths allowed for semiperishable foods like maize and wheat to be transported over dozens of kilometers (a human porter carrying a 50 kilogram pack can regularly travel 150 kilometers in four to five days [Malville 2001]), and longer-lasting foods, such as grains, and dried or smoked meats, fish, fruits, and seaweed could travel further still. Dried seaweed, for example, was carried by llamas 3,000 meters up the Andes mountains to the Inca capital of Cuzco (Hyslop 1984), and salt is known to have traveled across continents (Andrews 1983). Improved transportation networks would have also been appealing to pastoralists who could drive their animals hundreds of kilometers to town in order to provide residents with meat, sinew, wool, milk, and cheese (Zeder 1991, 2003).

There was more than just food being transported into the cities from far away. Cities also had a vociferous demand for raw material to fulfill basic subsistence needs and support the activities of an increasingly heterogeneous society. Some raw material imports are obvious – the shells for beads that came from distant oceans, the obsidian for blades that was quarried in a remote quarry, and the copper for bronze tools that was mined and smelted on another island (e.g., Knapp 1990; Miller 2007; Torrence 1986). Yet even objects that one might think were locally obtained, like the firewood needed for firing ceramics (Arnold 1993), the dyes used to color textiles (Boytner 2006), and the bitumen used as a sealant and adhesive (Stein 2001), were sometimes acquired from sources that were hundreds of kilometers away. As important as food to the survival of the city, raw materials were often imperishable and could be obtained over a greater distance.

Prestige objects also joined the flow of goods moving into the capital. Status differences continued to grow in most cities, and these status positions needed to be supported and legitimated (Brumfiel 1994; Brumfiel and Earle 1987; Earle and D'Altroy 1989). One of the more common ways to meet this need was to accumulate goods that could be offered as gifts and used for ostentatious displays (D'Altroy and Earle 1985). Goods that came from far away were likely prized in and of themselves for being exotic and difficult to acquire (Helms 1988). The feathers on a leader's headdress, for example, were a spectacular display of her reach across great distances, and the green obsidian knife that she wielded was a clear signal of her connections to foreign groups. Many of these prestige goods arrived into the city ready to use, but in other cases raw material from different locations were transformed into finished products by the growing number of artisans in the city.

The flow of goods coming into the city was paralleled by goods rushing out of the city. With increasingly large and specialized populations, cities allowed for more efficient labor organizations that could produce huge surpluses (Stanish 2004: 14). Urban workers often mass-produced goods from locally available raw materials and from raw materials coming in from outside areas (e.g., Bennett 2007; Miller 2007). These goods, ranging from stone hoes to gold masks (Pauketat 2004a; Shimada 1995), were then shipped off as gifts, used as payment by elites for incoming goods, and made available in markets where people from various places exchanged local and foreign products (e.g., Adams 2004; Feinman et al. 1984; Smith 1976). Some producers may have even tried to "brand" their goods to assure distant consumers of their quality and provenience (Wengrow 2008).

Goods in the city were attractive to people living in rural areas because the city provided goods that could either not be found locally or were of a higher quality because they were made by urban artisans. Yet the most attractive aspect of an urban product was likely that it was from the city. Salt, obsidian, and a few other goods available in town were essential for life, but villagers had survived just fine for generations without many of the objects. They didn't *need* a fancy bowl or stingray spine. The most important lure of most urban products was rather their symbolic associations (e.g., Sheets 2000). The swirling figures on a ceramic vessel or the raised relief of the sculpture would have been attractive ascetically to people living in the countryside, but more importantly the iconography would have linked the eventual owner of these objects to the beliefs and ritual practices of urban temples.

THE LONG-DISTANCE MOVEMENT OF PEOPLE

Most of the people going back and forth through a city's gate lived nearby. Yet, an array of archaeological techniques – such as dental traits, skeletal pathologies, ancient DNA, and the percentages of different chemical isotopes in human bone (Larsen 2002) – reveal that long-distance population movements were common during periods of urbanization (e.g., Kellner and Schoeninger 2008; Knudson 2008; White et al. 2004). Some of these people, like the sacrificial victims buried at the temple of Quetzalcoatl at Teotihuacan (White et al. 2002) or the foreign lord buried at the Maya city of Altun Ha (White et al. 2001), reflect the kinds of population movement that one might expect when reading stories of the past populated by warriors, priests, and princesses. Yet people from many other walks of life were also on the move.

Many people came in and out of cities to exchange goods. On any day, you might have seen farmers bringing their crops in carts, docked barges filled with lumber, and a long caravan of donkeys leaving the city's gates laden with wine amphorae. The bulk of the exchanges would have come from the agriculture core surrounding the city or from regularly contacted places further afield that contained important resources (Brown 1984; Flad 2007). Yet, cities were also always searching for untapped or underutilized markets. Aztec traders from the city of Tenochtitlan, for example, went across much of Mesoamerica seeking prestige objects for elites. They exchanged breech cloths, jewelry, feather work, and other objects that were manufactured in Tenochtitlan for jade ornaments, exotic feathers, cacao, and other goods that were only available in far-off places (Hirth 1984: 299).

People also came into and out of the city looking for other kinds of opportunities that were not available in their native lands (e.g.,

White et al. 2004). Some of these people moved permanently to the city, but many people likely stayed for only a short period (see Weyland 1993 for a modern example). A woman might come into town to buy textile dyes and then return to her village a week later, while a young man might spend two years as an apprentice metalworker before deciding to open his own shop back home. These migrants would return periodically to the city during their lifetimes, and their successful trips likely emboldened their neighbors to make similar voyages. Since the cities were made up of people from many different regions, migrants would often look toward urban compatriots to help them navigate the cityscape, find work, and procure a place to stay. The continued influx of groups often created ethnic enclaves that were similar in many respects to those found in many large cities today (M. Smith 2003b: 21).

Some people's movement away from the city would have been more permanent (Stein 1999: 69–73). They might be part of officially sanctioned colonial outposts set up by the city for a variety of overlapping purposes. These colonial outposts acted as trading outposts, religious missions, and/or extraction sites that were closely linked to the urban political economy (see chapters in Stein 2005a). Other people might be on the road out of town because they were fed up with city life, fleeing from persecution, or because greater opportunities could be had in another location. Some of these migrants likely retained contact with family and friends in the city, and they would have often still maintained many aspects of their urban lifestyle in their new homes (e.g., Owen 2005; Van Gijseghem 2006).

People would also have gone in and out of the city on pilgrimages. A city's temples, stadiums, and plazas attracted thousands of people (Inomata 2006; Jennings 2008; Manzanilla 1997b). Many of the attendees were from the city, but some of those at the spectacles came from the countryside in order to reinvigorate their religious faith or just be entertained. These visitors took in the sights of the city during their brief stays, picked up a few souvenirs and gifts for family and friends, and then returned home to talk about their experiences to kinsmen. Likewise, urbanites would have had a similar experience in reverse when they left the city on pilgrimages to rural sacred sites. If modern pilgrimages can serve as a guide (e.g., Sallnow 1987), annual treks to sacred sites were important rites of passages that most people completed at least once in their lifetime.

THE LONG-DISTANCE MOVEMENT OF IDEAS

The flow of people and goods between the city and countryside also led to a flow of ideas. In the earliest phases of urbanization, people came into the city from across a broad region and brought with them their customs, possessions, and cuisine. These immigrants not only created the physical form of the city with their labor, but they all contributed to the cultural construction of the metropolis (e.g., Pauketat 2004a: 34–5). This cultural construction was an ongoing process as people in the city changed their views of the world through time as different political, economic, social, and religious factions redefined aspects of city life (M. Smith 2003b). The city was also reconstructed by the countryside on an ongoing basis. Traders, pilgrims, migrant laborers, and visiting dignitaries constantly came into the city with new ideas and products. Most of the time foreign ideas were ignored, but occasionally an idea took hold and became an important part of the city's social fabric (e.g., Topic 1991).

The cultural reconstruction that began in the city swept into the countryside. Ideas were likely the most powerful of early urbanization's flows since areas with no direct contact with the city could still be reached by the ideas that were forged there (Sherratt 2004: 79). The return of a family to a distant village from the city, for example, must have been a moment of great excitement in a village. The travelers would talk about their experiences, the marvels that they saw around them, and perhaps pass around some of the souvenirs that they acquired from their journey. The stories of these travels would have quickly spread across the village, and as people came through the village they would have heard the tales of the city and taken the stories with them to other places. The details of the stories, of course, would change in each telling. The notions that spread would not have been just embellished tales of temple rituals but new ideas that impacted how people build their houses, stored their harvests, feasted together, and buried their dead (e.g., Cobb and King 2005; Goldstein 2003; Hole 1999; Kuijt 2008). If all of this was possible from the experiences of a single family, imagine the impact of thousands of travelers telling their tales.

We cannot trace the spread of ideas from the first cities directly by reading texts from the countryside. Writing systems developed hand in hand with some of the earliest cities, and they were initially used by only a small percentage of the population for bookkeeping, devotion, and elite propaganda (Schmandt-Besserat 1996; A. Smith 2003). Fortunately, we can track the spread of ideas indirectly through other aspects of the material record.

The iconography on a textile conveys a rich cosmology, the decorations on a bowl give considerable information to the person who receives it, and there are many ways that the body can be used to mark gender, ethnic, and community identities (Boone 1994; Bowser 2000; Knudson and Stojanowski 2008). The major indicator of the sharing of ideas during early urbanism is found in the wide geographic spread of ideologically charged motifs that were found on carved megaliths, pots, figurines, textiles, and other artifacts. Some of these objects were traded from the city, but most were made elsewhere by rural people who had grown familiar with these motifs. Instead of trying to make exact replicas, local artisans often crafted objects that mixed urban and regional ideas into new pastiches (e.g., Lesure 2004: 74).

FLOWS BEGET FLOWS THAT BEGET FLOWS

As cities quickly swelled in size, administrative systems would have been hard-pressed just to maintain internal order and fill resident demands. Projecting power over the countryside was spotty and sporadic, and as ideas, people, and objects moved away from the city, many would have swiftly entered into networks that were far beyond the city's control. Could the city, for instance, dictate whether a farmer passed on one of its obsidian blades to a cousin or restrict a migrant laborer from using a new kind of wall construction that he saw in town? Urban culture (in terms of the ideas, goods, and even people generated in these settings) could quickly become disentangled from urban–rural flows and beget strictly rural–rural flows used by people who were reacting to the new opportunities and challenges that urban culture created (see Figure 3.1). These new strictly rural flows in turn could create still more flows, and a chain reaction could occur that moved further and further beyond the limits of the networks that were originally created between the city and the countryside (Kohl 2007; Sherrat 2004).

Archaeologists have tended to focus on the city and its agents when investigating the broader impact of urbanization (e.g., Algaze 1993a; Cusik 1998; Stein 1999, 2005a), but these eras cannot be boiled down to just interactions with the city itself (Jennings 2006a).

Although colonial outposts, trade diasporas, and other networks that extended to and from the city were very important as catalysts for social change, they made up only a small part of the interregional interactions during these eras. A few archaeological examples can help illustrate how the emergence of cities led to a surge in inter-regional interaction that created networks that were (a) beyond the control of the city and (b) contained connections that often bypassed the city.

The precursors to the first cities in China emerged by at least the second millennium B.C. (Liu 2006; Shen 2003). These sites, like Yenshi and Zengzou, were massive walled compounds that were more than two hundred hectares in size. The sites were dominated by palace and temple complexes occupied largely by royalty and their courts. Population aggregation and economic specialization in these compounds led to the creation of the first cities in the eighth century B.C. (Shen 2003: 290–2). These sites swiftly became important market centers, and people flooded into the cities to live, trade, and worship. While officials controlled some production and commerce, many transactions occurred outside of city or elite control (Shen 2003; Underhill and Fang 2004). More often than not, villagers were in control – they decided who they were going to interact with in the city and under what terms.

Excavations at the salt production site of Zhongba provide an example of the dynamic relationship between early cities and the countryside in China (Flad 2007). In the third millennium B.C., people at Zhongba began converting brine into salt through an evaporation process that involved a variety of different storage containers. Around 500 B.C., salt production increased dramatically at the site in response to rapid urbanization that was occurring elsewhere along the Yellow and Yangzi Rivers. Before A.D. 500, salt producers had worked independently and sunk ceramic-lined evaporation holes willy-nilly across the site. After this period, an organized grid of channels, holes, and pots were used to streamline the process and increase production.

Salt extraction was likely now run by emerging local elite, whose nearby tombs sometimes contain ceramic models of the local brine wells. Oracle bones and other artifacts suggest that these elites identified closely with a cosmopolitan lifestyle, but they allied themselves with different groups. Some of the elite tombs closely emulate the tombs from the distant Chu state in terms of architecture and funerary assemblages, with some of the objects from the tombs perhaps being carried up the river by Chu traders. Yet, other local elite had connections with other groups like the Ba and Western Ha, and the tombs of these local elites emulated these foreign styles. These data indicate that cities did not control salt production at Zhongba. Instead, urbanization created a greater demand for salt production, and that demand led to changes in social stratification and the organization of production at the site. Even though many of Zhongba's elites chose to align themselves most closely with the Chu, the elites interacted with a wide array of other regions depending on their own self-interest.

A second example of how most interactions were not dictated by the city comes from the Tiwanaku culture of the Lake Titicaca Basin in Bolivia. Around A.D. 500, the site of Tiwanaku grew rapidly into a city that would soon cover six square kilometers (Janusek and Blom 2006: 240). The site was likely an important pilgrimage center that hosted events in the massive plazas, courtyards, and pyramids that dominated the city's center. The Tiwanaku art style, a blending of long-held Andean notions of ancestor worship, sacrifice, and the living landscape (Isbell and Knobloch 2006), seems to have been a compelling one to visitors, and the style and associated religious practices quickly spread thanks to the llama caravans that connected the city to near and distant regions (Janusek 2008: 105). Although earlier archaeologists spoke of a Tiwanaku Empire, it now appears that the city only established a few colonial outposts (Browman 1997).

One of the places where Tiwanaku influence was strongest was the Cochabamba Valley of eastern Bolivia. Cochabamba's local ceramic styles were deeply influenced by Tiwanaku by around 800 A.D., and goods likely manufactured at Tiwanaku, such as feather mantles, snuff tablets, metalwork, and ceramic vessels, also appear in Cochabamba graves (Browman 1997: 232; Oakland 1986: 245). These imports were likely carried into the region by llama caravans led by Tiwanaku traders, a few of whom may have settled into the region (Janusek 2008: 228). The extension of east–west caravan routes through Cochabamba from Tiwanaku stimulated great social changes. Yet there is little evidence to suggest that Tiwanaku controlled the valley.

People sought to capitalize on this trade by affiliating with Tiwanaku and adopting aspects of the city's ideology. Many, for example, emulated Tiwanaku drinking patterns of reciprocal hospitality at the household level (Anderson 2009; Goldstein 2003). At the same time, Tiwanaku influence led to an "explosion of exotic goods from more distant regions" as villagers also reached out to other groups from other mountain valleys and the jungle (Janusek 2008: 28). Just as in the Chinese case, urbanization led to increased interaction and significant social change in the countryside, but these interactions were occurring both between villages and the city and between these same villages and other places.

Our final example of the impact of urban flows comes from the site of Kurban Höyük in southeast Turkey (Wattenmaker 1994). After an earlier episode of urbanization and interregional interaction in the fourth millennium B.C. in Mesopotamia (I discuss this period at length in the following chapter), there was a second period of rapid urbanization in northern Mesopotamia in the mid-third millennium B.C. (Stein 2004). Sites like Chuera, Titriş, and Leilan grew into cities of forty to one hundred hectares, and the development of these cities was paralleled by increasing economic specialization and status hierarchies both in the cities and in the surrounding countryside (Schwartz 1994; Wilkinson 1990; Zeder 2003). Some of the changes in the countryside reflect a response to the city's economic needs for staple and prestige goods, but the changes were also the result of new interactions that were largely independent of the political economies of the cities (Hole 1999).

When urbanization began in northern Mesopotamia, the site of Kurban Höyük was a sleepy agricultural village that had sat on the bank of the Euphrates River largely unchanged for over two thousand years (Wattenmaker 1994). The site grew from one to six hectares in the middle of the third millennium B.C., and specialization and status hierarchies increased at the site during this time. The site was not controlled by a city, at least not directly, but Kurban Höyük was enmeshed in a wide-reaching exchange system that included cities and other places. The village specialized during this period in decorated wheel-made pottery that was made for export, and it imported a wide variety of products from different regions.

The most striking development in Kurban Höyük was that both elites and non-elites at the site "manufactured goods for their own use if such goods were of minimal significance for bearing social messages" but obtained "goods of greater social significance through exchange" (Wattenmaker 1994: 118). They made their own cooking pots and stone tools, but they obtained their ceramic cups, copper pins, and garments from other producers. Some goods came from a city; most of them did not. These publicly displayed items would have signaled the participation of Kurban Höyük in an interaction sphere that far exceeded any urban network and stretched across northern Mesopotamia.

ANCIENT URBANIZATION AND GLOBALIZATION

It is important to underline the chaotic frenzy of rapid urbanization. Although archaeologists tend to model their understanding of this phenomenon from the studies of long-established ancient cities (e.g., Manzanilla 1997a; M. Smith 2003a), these places have had hundreds, if not thousands, of years to work out the kinks. The realities of mid-nineteenth-century London or late twentieth-century São Paolo are better examples of what life would have been like. City and countryside grew up together with little oversight, constant conflict, and seeming unending change. If life can be turned upside down by recent instances of rapid urbanization, then I would imagine that the experience of living through the birth of the world's *first* cities would have been at least as turbulent.

People had been interacting with each other across great distances for over 200,000 years, but early urbanization caused a burst in interregional interaction that reached unprecedented levels. In a few cases, I will argue that the web of people, ideas, and goods moving across the landscape was large enough and thick enough to exceed the globalization threshold and cause widespread social change. City elites were some of the biggest players in these webs, but for the most part the geography of the web and the cultural changes that occurred were the result of a plethora of urban and rural individuals making decisions based on their perceived self-interest in a variety of local, cultural, and environmental settings (e.g., Rauch 2002). The changes that occurred in the wake of these flows had the potential to create global cultures – "civilizations" to use the parlance of early archaeologists (Yoffee 2005: 17) – that were as fractured, dynamic, and shaped by local conditions as the global culture that exists today.

The birth of cities unleashed a dizzying movement of people, goods, and ideas across wide regions. If a global culture were created as a result of these interactions, then a family of farmers who had never set foot in the city would have felt that their lives were changing significantly because of it. How they planted their crops, socialized, and prayed could have been impacted, and they would have felt more connected to the city and other places than ever before. The family likely would have had some misgivings about these changes, but they were all caught in a web of interactions that could be manipulated by them but not fully controlled. They were part of a global culture.

Many of the models that we commonly use to understand periods of early urbanization only capture a small part of the complex realities of these periods. Did early urbanization create core-periphery interactions like the ones argued by the world systems theorists? Yes, there were many interactions of this type. Were there peer-polity and other co-evolving relationships between relative equals? Of course, these kinds of relationships also developed. Were there ideas that diffused from place to place? Yes, this was happening too. All of these kinds of relationships are found overlapping in our current global culture, and they can all be subsumed under a globalizations model. In the three chapters that follow, we will explore three cases where I think globalization occurred as a result of the far-flung interaction networks spawned by the urbanization of Uruk-Warka, Cahokia, and Huari. These networks set off a chain reaction of responses by other groups that eventually breached the globalization threshold to create a global culture.

4

Uruk-Warka

In the final weeks of 1932, R. Campbell Thompson's mood was turning increasingly glum. As the long-time director of the Nineveh excavations, he had spent the last few years at this northern Mesopotamian city searching for Assyrian buildings and inscriptions on behalf of the British Museum. His assistant for the 1932–3 season, Max Mallowan, had convinced Campbell Thompson to dig a deep sounding from the highest part of one of Nineveh's mounds down to sterile soil. Campbell Thompson knew that the sounding would produce the first chronological sequence for the northern Mesopotamia, but it was a dangerous endeavor that was taking workmen away from the historical levels of the site that most interested him and the museum (Gut 2002: 18). His mood darkened as the sounding went deeper and deeper into cultural fill. The daily march of buckets out of the black hole finally ended in the first days of 1933 when diggers reached sterile soil thirty-one meters below the surface (Thompson and Mallowan 1933: plate 73).

Campbell Thompson's frustration with the blasé artifacts coming out of the hole reached a crescendo midway through the sounding. As his workers dug through almost twelve meters of fill dominated by thousands of mass-produced, undecorated bowls, he despaired in a letter that "if these miserable bowls represent all that is to be found" then he would have trouble finding future sponsors for his excavations (quoted in Gut 2002: 20). The same "miserable bowls" were showing up throughout Mesopotamia in other deep soundings that were being conducted in the first decades of the twentieth century (Figure 4.1).

In a Baghdad conference in 1930, scholars decided to name the period associated with these bowls after Uruk-Warka, a large site

Figure 4.1 Bevel-rim bowls from the site of Hamoukar (image courtesy of Clemens Reichel).

located some six hundred kilometers from Nineveh in southern Mesopotamia (Pollock 1999: 20). Although of little interest to scholars of Campbell Thompson's generation, the Uruk Period (4200–3100 B.C.) is now widely recognized as a critical period of rapid urbanization and social change in the greater Mesopotamian world.

Uruk-Warka is one of many ancient massive mounds situated along the Tigris and Euphrates River in modern Iraq. Occupied for five thousand years, the site grew during the Uruk Period from a small town to one that covered 250 hectares – in comparison Athens was only half the size of Uruk-Warka when this Greek city reached its height three thousand years later (Nissen 1988: 72). No other fourth millennium site in Mesopotamia rivaled Uruk-Warka in size and monumentality (Boehmer 1991: 467–9; Pollock 1999: 57–8), and the increasing social stratification, craft specialization, and bureaucracy during this period in Mesopotamia was likely spurred in large part by Uruk-Warka's emergence (Johnson 1973, 1975, 1978; Neely and Wright 1994; Wright 1977, 1981a; Wright and Johnson 1975, 1985). The mass-produced bowls that Campbell Thompson disparaged have become emblematic of this pivotal period in world history. Known today as bevel-rim bowls, the vessels were likely used to distribute food rations in a centralized economy (Nissen 1988: 84–5).

The urbanization of Uruk-Warka stimulated social changes in three continents. Uruk style artifacts have been found from Egypt to Pakistan, and the movement of ideas, people, and objects out of southern Mesopotamia in the fourth millennium, often called the

Uruk expansion, had reverberations down the line in Eastern Europe, West and South Asia, and northern Africa (Sherrat 2004). One of the most influential explanations of the Uruk expansion was first outlined by Guillermo Algaze (1989, 1993a). He suggested that the spread of Uruk artifacts was the result of a colonial expansion out of southern Mesopotamia that created an ancient world system within which imported raw materials from the periphery were exchanged for exported finished products. The publication of Algaze's model caused quite a stir in Mesopotamian archaeology and much of the work on Uruk over the past twenty years has been geared toward addressing the nature of interregional interaction during this period (e.g., Postgate 2002; Rothman 2001a; Stein 1999).

The research generated in the wake of Algaze's world systems' model has revealed a far messier fourth-millennium reality that varied considerably between sites and across time. In some places, southern Mesopotamian colonists created outposts, while other sites are littered with the remains of hybrid styles that combine southern Mesopotamia attributes with those from other regions. In still other places, the period is marked by a seeming rejection of almost anything that could be classified as Uruk material culture. Since these new data do not fit comfortably within the world systems model that Algaze originally conceived, he has attempted to adapt his model to Mesopotamian realities in subsequent work (2001a, 2001b, 2005, 2007, 2008). Other scholars, however, have used these new data to argue that Uruk-Warka and other sites in southern Mesopotamia were just a few of the many regional players connected through trade and shared cultural practices (Frangipane 2001, 2002; Oates and Oates 2004; Rothman 2004; Ur i.p.).

Both of these viewpoints on the fourth-millennium Near East can be correct. The complicated mosaic of social change across this broad region cannot be explained by southern Mesopotamian colonization alone. Yet, the period also cannot be explained without the growth of Uruk-Warka. Colonization, along with cultural diffusion, prestige goods exchanges, migrations, and regionalization all operated on groups at once during the era. In this chapter, I suggest that the Uruk civilization can be best conceptualized as an early period of globalization that began with the rapid urbanization of Uruk-Warka. The flow of goods, ideas, and people coming in and out of the city caused social changes that rippled far beyond the networks initially created by the city's emergence.

URUK-WARKA AND THE URUK EXPANSION

Although the term "Mesopotamia" traditionally refers to the land between the Tigris and Euphrates, I will follow other scholars in using the term more broadly to describe the area within the basins of the Tigris, Euphrates, Karkeh, and Karun Rivers (Figure 4.2). This area, encompassing modern-day Iraq, eastern Syria, southeastern Turkey, and southwestern Iran, can be divided into four environmental zones. The first zone is the southern alluvium around Uruk-Warka, a region of fertile soils and marshlands, but little rainwater. The second zone is the northern plain where sites like Nineveh can be found. Higher and wetter than the southern alluvium, the northern plain allowed for rain-fed agriculture, but the rolling hills and deeply incised rivers of the region made irrigation more difficult.

The high plain was surrounded to the north and east by the foothills of the Zagros and Taurus mountain ranges. Despite the mountains' challenging topography, this third environmental region was a valuable source of metals, stone, hardwoods, and other resources.

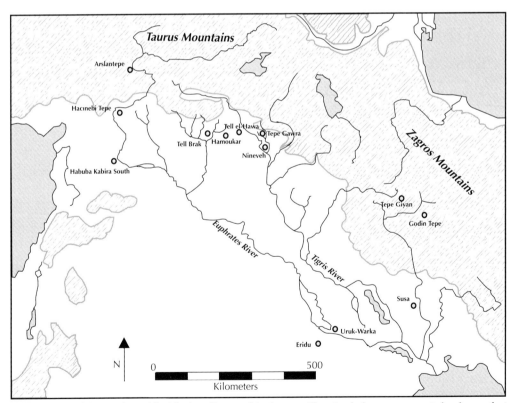

Figure 4.2 Map of the Uruk world with sites discussed in the text. The stippled area represents land 3,000 feet (914.5 m) above sea level (base map redrawn from Rothman 2001c: 6).

Table 4.1. Uruk chronology

Period	Time Range	Globalization Phase
Ubaid	5800–4200 BC	Pre-Globalization
Early Uruk	4200–3800 BC	Expansion
Middle Uruk	3800–3400 BC	Global Culture
Late Uruk	3400–3100 BC	
Jemdet Nasr	3100–3000 BC	Regionalization
Early Dynastic	3000–2334 BC	

Finally, the regions to the east and west of the Tigris and Euphrates were a mixture of river oases, desert, and semiarid zones. Even though most people in Mesopotamia lived close to arable land near the major rivers, people living in this fourth region tended flocks of animals that were essential for all (Postgate 1994: 3–18).

A stretch of desert between the southern alluvium and northern plain long served as a physical barrier between northern and southern Mesopotamia. This cultural barrier broke down during the 'Ubaid Period (5800–4200 B.C.) (Table 4.1). 'Ubaid sites across Mesopotamia had broadly shared beliefs, ceramic styles, and architectural forms (Stein and Özbal 2007: 331). Most 'Ubaid sites in Mesopotamia were small (Adams 1981: 58), but a number of larger towns of up to fifteen hectares had developed by the end of the period (Stein 1994: 38; Wright 1981b: 324). Farmers during this period boasted the full corpus of Mesopotamian domesticates. They cultivated wheat, barley, lentils, and vetch and took care of herds of sheep, pigs, and cattle (Charvát 2002: 58–9; Pollock 1999: 66).

There are hints in the larger towns of growing social complexity. Some of the sites boasted public temples, evidence for craft specialization, and large homes that contained administrative artifacts (tokens and seals, which I will discuss later) and stockpiled goods (Jasim 1988; Pollock 1988; Roaf 1988; Stein 1994; H. Wright 1994). These growing social differences, however, were masked by 'Ubaid people in death since standardized burials were used to stress community allegiances (Hole 1988: 180; Pollock 1999: 195). Although long-distance exchanges were certainly occurring during the 'Ubaid Period (e.g., Carter 2006; Esin 1985; Yoffee 1993), there is no evidence for significant migrations during this period. Instead, 'Ubaid is perhaps best conceived of as "the gradual, peaceful spread of an ideological system that was translated into a variety of different local schemes" (Stein and Özbal 2007: 342).

The trend toward greater social complexity continued during the Early Uruk Period (4200–3800 B.C.). The best evidence for social changes in this period comes from the town of Susa in the Susiana plain in southwestern Iran (see Figure 4.2). Founded around 4300 B.C., the town quickly grew to a size of ten to fifteen hectares. The center of the town was dominated by a massive platform that was more than ten meters tall and boasted a temple, storage facility, and residences (Pollock 1988: 284–6). As many as two thousand people were interred around the platform, and most of these people were buried with a "more or less" standard set of pots (Pollock 1988: 286).

A closer inspection of the burials around the Susa platform reveals that the mortuary-leveling mechanism used in the 'Ubaid Period was starting to break down as copper axes and mirrors were placed in some burials. Quite rare in this period, copper was an exotic item imported from the mountains at least two hundred kilometers away. The burial evidence, when combined with data from excavations of the platform, suggests increased social stratification, and it appears that Susa's rising elites managed to build a political economy based on the contributions of labor and goods by surrounding villages (H. Wright 1994). This arrangement appears to have been unstable. Susa's platform was destroyed once, then rebuilt, and then destroyed a second time when the site was abandoned around B.C. 4000 (H. Wright 1994: 79).

Susa's rise and fall in the Early Uruk Period was likely paralleled in other parts of greater Mesopotamia. Evidence for increasing specialization, bureaucracies, and status differentiation, for example, has come out of sites like Tell Brak, Nineveh, Hacınebi Tepe, and Arslantepe in northern Iraq, Syria, and Turkey (e.g., Frangipane 2001; Oates and Oates 2004; Stein 1999, 2001; Ur i.p.). The general impression that one gleans from the data is that towns across Mesopotamia were growing during this period, and that emerging elites were likely pursuing a wide variety of strategies to gain and maintain power (Wright 2007). Many of these strategies seem to have been designed to better organize the collection, storage, and redistribution of local products.

The best evidence for emerging bureaucracies comes from the increasing use of stamp seals. Since at least the beginning of the 'Ubaid Period, seals stamped on to moist clay had been used to tag or close objects in combination with modeled clay tokens that stood for different classes of goods (Schmandt-Besserat 1996). Stamp seals in the Late 'Ubaid and Early Uruk Periods were often more diverse than earlier examples with complex forms perhaps suggesting higher levels of bureaucratic control (e.g., Wright and Johnson 1975: 273).

The trends toward greater social complexity continued across much of Mesopotamia into the Middle Uruk Period (3800–3400 B.C.). A few sites began to grow quickly during this period. These sites, like Tell Brak (at least 130 hectares), Nineveh (about 40 hectares), and Tell el-Hawa (at most 50 hectares) (Algaze 2005: 138–139; Ur et al. 2007), were dominated by central temple–palace complexes and the sealings and tokens found in these areas attest to a continued interest in managing local resources (Pittman 2001). Yet, elites were increasingly looking outward as well (Oates and Oates 2004: 182). At Tell Brak in northeastern Syria, for example, there is evidence for the importation of gold, silver, shell, and other material brought to the site from "considerable distances" (McMahon and Oates 2007: 155; also see Emberling and MacDonald 2002).

The largest sites at the beginning of the Middle Uruk Period were in northern Mesopotamia, and the interregional connections that ran through these sites were bringing together the political economies of this area with Anatolia, Iran, and other regions (e.g., Gensheimer 1984; Gibson et al. 2002; Matthews and Fazeli 2004; Mellink 1989; Reichel 2002; Steadman 1996; Ur i.p.; Ur et al. 2007; one should note that the Uruk-Warka's survey maps that suggest the site reached 100 hectares by this time are deceptive since the text that accompanies these maps suggests that the site was likely much smaller [Finkbeiner 1991: 191–2]). While northern Mesopotamia seemed to be on the cusp of urbanization and intense interregional interaction, southern Mesopotamia remained a relative backwater (Algaze 2008; Oates and Oates 2004). This changed with the rapid expansion of Uruk-Warka.

THE CITY OF URUK-WARKA

Today's environment around the ruins of Uruk-Warka bears little resemblance to the landscape of 5000 B.C. The shoreline of the Persian Gulf extended as much as 250 kilometers into present-day Iraq at the time (Wilkinson 2003: 80), and the land around Uruk-Warka was composed of sediment deposits, marshes, and river channels (Algaze 2008: 40–4; Pournelle 2007). The rich, ever-changing landscape of the region provided a great wealth of marine and terrestrial resources for hunters and gatherers, but it seems to have also stymied the growth of villages until the 'Ubaid Period. As the alluvial environment dried and stabilized during the fifth millennium, large tracts of newly exposed arable land allowed more agriculture to be added to existing subsistence strategies (Pournelle 2007: 59). By the beginning of the Early Uruk Period, a number of permanent settlements were flourishing. One of these was Uruk-Warka.

Uruk-Warka was made up of two distinct fifteen- to twenty-hectare architectural clusters at the time (Finkbeiner 1991: 191–2). Workers expanded a small 'Ubaid Period public building in one of these clusters during the Early Uruk Period, and Uruk-Warka's first evidence for administrative tokens comes from Early Uruk levels (Postgate 1994: 24; Charvát 2002: 99). Other sites, like Eridu to the south, boasted similar public building complexes, and may have competed with Uruk-Warka for settlers (Postgate 1994: 24–5). This competition, if it existed, was over by the Middle Uruk Period (3800–3400 B.C.) when Uruk-Warka began to grow dramatically.

Despite being one of world's most important archaeological sites, we know very little about the Early and Middle Uruk Periods at Uruk-Warka. The site was excavated extensively by German teams from 1928 to 1990, but only for the last ten years of this span was it under the direction of a Near Eastern archaeologist (Boehmer 1991). Previous directors had been historians and architects, and they were primarily interested in reconstructing the architectural sequences of the more monumental sections of the site (Nissen 2002: 3). Most of our knowledge of Uruk Period levels of the city comes from two deep soundings in the Eanna district of the site (Sürenhagen 1986, 1987). These 1930 excavations, when combined with survey and excavation work elsewhere at the site, provide us with only a tentative glimpse into the city's early history.

The Eanna sounding revealed a series of superimposed construction levels dating back to the 'Ubaid Period. Although the complex stratigraphy and poor preservation in the sounding took decades of subsequent analysis to fully interpret (Strommenger 1980: 480), it appears that large public buildings were in place in the precinct by at least the Middle Uruk Period. The only remains of these earlier structures are "extensive heaps" of clay cones in the precinct that were left behind after a Late Uruk (3400–3100 B.C.) building project (Nissen 1988: 96). The Late Uruk complex of monumental buildings was decorated with colorful mosaics and covered an area of eight to nine hectares. Like the earlier buildings at Susa, the buildings in the precinct likely served multiple ritual, economic, and public functions (Nissen 2001: 154–5).

The Early and Middle Uruk deposits in the Eanna precinct and elsewhere hint at increasing craft specialization and long-distance exchange. The first evidence for metal tools, for example, appears at the end of the Early Uruk (Charvát 2002: 99–100). Specialists were also beginning to fashion more and more tools out of imported chert and obsidian, and new relationships were likely being forged with nomadic pastoralists as Uruk-Warka weavers began working with wool (Algaze 2008: 77–92; Charvát 2002: 99–100; McCorriston 1997: 518).

The most important shift in terms of specialization may have been the move from flax to wool-based textiles. Wooly sheep are not native to southern Mesopotamia and were introduced from the north by the beginning of the Uruk Period. Wool has several advantages over flax in terms of functionality and appearance. Wool garments took dyes more easily – a critical advantage when people were likely using clothes to signal emerging social differences – and wool is far less labor intensive to produce (Algaze 2008: 78–9). Texts from the Late Uruk Period at Uruk-Warka point to the importance of the wool industry, and it is likely that scores of workers were dedicated to producing wool textiles for export by at least the Middle Uruk (Algaze 2008: 81).

The city's rapid growth, combined with escalating craft specialization, rising trade, and increasing status differences, must have put considerable pressure on the existing political, economic, and social structures at Uruk-Warka. City elites responded with two Middle Uruk bureaucratic innovations, cylinder seals and bevel-rim bowls (Charvát 2002: 99–100). The more complex images on the sealings could carry more information to track goods as they circulated through the economy (Schmandt-Besserat 1996), and the bowls when filled with grain or bread could serve as payment for services rendered to employers (Chazan and Lehner 1990; Millard 1988; but see Nicholas 1987; for a slightly different interpretation).

Uruk-Warka would continue to prosper during the Late Uruk Period, even as sites in northern Mesopotamia stagnated or collapsed. The city grew to a size of 250 hectares (Finkbeiner 1991: 194), and the trends toward greater status differences, craft specialization, and long-distance exchange continued (Nissen 2001, 2002). The Late Uruk complex in the Eanna Precinct was a "very large economic unit" with its hands in agriculture, animal husbandry, craft production, and trade (Nissen 1988: 83). The mix of activities chock-ablock at Late Uruk sites suggests that elites were intimately involved in recruiting and organizing the laborers flowing into the city (Pollock 1999: 97–8). Since formal palaces do not make their appearance in Mesopotamia until the mid-third millennium, elite power was likely maintained at Uruk-Warka through a shifting balance of religious, political, economic, and social structures (Pollock 1999: 178). The site reached its greatest size during the Early Dynastic Period (3000–2334 B.C.) but began a slow decline after.

THE URUK EXPANSION

The rapid urbanization of Uruk-Warka during the Uruk Period must have sent shockwaves across the southern alluvium. By the Middle Uruk Period, the site's 100-hectare footprint was already ten times larger than any other site in the region and the city would more than double in size during the Late Uruk Period (Adams 1981; 60–81; Pollock 2001: 189, 196). The 50,000 people packed on the Uruk-Warka mound was a logistical nightmare. The city's frenetic growth would have quickly overwhelmed the exchange relationships that had previously supplied the towns of the southern alluvium, and the city's inhabitants would have had to increasingly rely on outside producers for food and other resources (Pollock 2001: 196). A boisterous, informal economy likely formed; it would have brought agricultural products, animals, labor, spun wool, and other rural products into the city in exchange for exotic goods, copper tools, cloth, heavenly favor, and other urban products (Adams 1981: 81). Some of the towns closest to the city may have been tied to the site by tribute obligations at an early date, but it is likely that most populations living outside of the city were initially connected much more tenuously to Uruk-Warka through trade partners, family ties, cult allegiances, and other relationships (Adams 1981: 81; Pollock 2001: 219; but see Johnson 1980: 249; for a different reading of the settlement data).

The city's growth created a surrounding countryside of increasing specialization as surrounding villages jockeyed with each other for positions in the emerging regional economy. Some households, for example, concentrated on making clay sickles, while others dedicated much of their time to knapping stone tools (Adams 1981: 78; Pope and Pollack 1995). Specialization may have been a response to the flow of exotic goods coming into the southern alluvium since these goods were being used to buttress the elite positions that were emerging at even the smallest of sites (Adams 1981: 78–80). Uruk-Warka's privileged access to these goods is hinted at in the ritual disposal of cultic material in the Reimchengbäude, a building in the Eanna precinct (Charvát 2002: 102–3). The structure was

> literally brimming with imported exotic goods, including several wooden chests with elaborated inlays of precious and semi-precious stones; small fragments of what would have been life-size stone and copper statues; mirrors and other implements made of copper; fragments of jewelry made of copper, silver, and gold; and various tools and weapons made of copper, copper-silver alloys, obsidian, and rock crystal. (Algaze 2001a: 35)

The hoard of goods, transported from locations that were as much as a thousand kilometers away, demonstrates the reestablishment, strengthening, and extension of some of the nascent interregional trade networks of the 'Ubaid Period that had collapsed by the Early Uruk Period (Oates 1993: 410).

The imports coming into the southern alluvium were not just prestige goods, but also daily necessities like timber, metals, and stone (Algaze 2001a: 51). These goods traveled to the city on boats, sledges, and the backs of porters (Algaze 2008: 56–7; Wright 2001: 127). These traditional means of travel were joined in the Middle Uruk Period by the introduction of donkeys. Donkeys, likely first domesticated in Africa (Rossel et al. 2008), could be organized into pack trains and sent across steep mountainous terrain (Oates 1993: 417; Wright 2001: 217). Wheeled transport, first seen in Late Uruk pictographs at Uruk-Warka (Bakker et al. 1999: 778–9), was another transportation innovation.

The desire to maintain the flow of goods into the southern alluvium was likely the catalyst for a colonial expansion of southern Mesopotamian settlers along key routes deeper into the Zagros Mountains and up the Tigris and Euphrates Rivers (Algaze 1989; Stein 1999, 2001b, 2005b). Beginning in the Middle Uruk Period, this expansion would result in a series of outposts spread across an area of approximately 5,500 square kilometers (Stein 1999: 91). Outposts can be identified in the archaeological record by their thoroughly southern Mesopotamian character in architecture, artifact assemblages, dietary choices, and other characteristics.

Some of these outposts were small trading enclaves placed in preexisting settlements. The best documented of these enclaves is Hacınebi Tepe in Turkey, a colonial outpost of a few dozen people who were able to "tap into the preexisting southeast Anatolian copper-exchange network" and also procure "lumber, gold, and semi-precious stones" (Stein 1999: 156–7). Other outposts were far more substantial free-standing colonies that might date to slightly later in the Uruk sequence. One of these colonies, Habuba Kabira South, was built in Syria along the Euphrates River. The colonial outpost covered at least eighteen hectares, and a large portion of it was surrounded by a fortification wall (Schwartz 2001: 248).

Although the roots of the Uruk expansion can be found in the urbanization of Uruk-Warka, the city did not organize the colonial network. The expansion was an outgrowth of competition among Uruk-Warka and other centers as "each scrambled to lay claim" to exchange partners and transportation routes (Algaze 2001a: 71, 2008: 64–6; Wright 2006; also see Rothman 2004: 96). The city may have had no rivals in the southern alluvium, but Uruk-Warka administrators could not impose their will on towns outside the city. The Susiana towns in southwest Iran, for example, were aggressive traders that sat at the terminus of an array of trade routes leading across the Zagros Mountains (Algaze 2005: 12). By the Middle Uruk Period, they secured trade connections to the west, especially with groups living near Iranian copper deposits (Matthews and Fazeli 2004: 71), and in the Late Uruk Period established an enclave in the heart of the site of Godin Tepe (Weiss and Young 1975). Susiana merchants were also involved in transactions in other regions – some of the seals used at Hacınebi Tepe, for example, were made from Susiana clay (Stein 1999: 43).

The competition between rivals that generated the Uruk expansion would have also made exchange networks unstable. As more and more people became involved as producers, consumers, and traders, these relationships would have become unwieldy (Algaze 2008: 65). This instability may have been a factor in what appears to have been a significant shift in elite strategies at Uruk-Warka during the Late Uruk Period. Settlement data suggest that the area around the city became more tightly integrated during the Late Uruk Period (Adams and Nissen 1972: 11; Johnson 1980: 255). In contrast to the Early Uruk landscape of isolated settlements evenly dispersed along watercourses, Late Uruk villages around Uruk-Warka were placed in accordance with an overarching irrigation project that maximized agricultural production (Adams and Nissen 1972: 11–12).

Tablets found at Uruk-Warka also suggest that the city was attempting to reorganize its relationship with the surrounding countryside. The earliest writing in the world, these Late Uruk tablets focused almost exclusively on the organization of local economic matters (Green 1980; Nissen 1986). Uruk-Warka's move to consolidate the surrounding region makes sense within the context of the grand sweep of Mesopotamian history. In later years, foreign trade was of *secondary* importance to cities relative to the management of local flocks, fields, and craft specialists (Postgate 2003). Writing, when combined with improving administrative technology and transportation networks, may have made effective management of the countryside possible for the first time. With a feasible alternative, Uruk-Warka's leaders could begin to move away from a more tenuous political economy that was premised on large influxes of imported goods.

Uruk-Warka's bid to control the alluvium did not go unchallenged for long. Larger towns were emerging throughout southern Mesopotamia by the end of the Late Uruk Period and visual representations of violence between towns are seen for the first time during this period (Pollock 2001: 218). Settlements around Uruk-Warka were short-lived, perhaps a reflection of repression and the fleeing of outside groups from increasing tribute demands (Pollock 2001: 218). The emerging tension in the area could have even brought violence to the city itself – seal impressions from the Late Uruk Period show both prisoner scenes and that the city was surrounded by a great wall (Boehmer 1991: 469).

Some of the southern Mesopotamian outposts in northern Mesopotamia might be better conceived of as refugee settlements of people who pulled up stakes in the southern alluvium to live permanently elsewhere (Johnson 1989). This second Uruk expansionary wave would have further destabilized interregional networks and sent another pulse of southern Mesopotamia people, ideas, and objects across a broad region. The increasing instability of north-south connection seems to have also led leaders in other towns to follow in Uruk-Warka's footsteps. They turned away from a political economy driven primarily by external relations and moved toward one driven more by the administration of local resources (Frangipane 2001: 342–3).

URUK GLOBAL CULTURE

The Uruk expansion resulted in much more than just the establishment of a few trading outposts and, perhaps, refugee colonies. There were sweeping changes that occurred throughout Mesopotamia that struck at the heart of how people lived their lives. For example, there was a "radical departure from age-old veneration of the dead" with its status-celebrating burials containing prestigious funerary objects to a mortuary practice that disposed of almost all individuals without a trace in the archaeological record (Charvát 2002: 152). The ubiquitous bevel-rim bowl was part of wholesale changes in labor organization, and the circulation of metal weapons revolutionized how people waged war. These and other aspects of Uruk culture were not solely the fruits of Uruk-Warka's urbanization – metalwork was first introduced in northern Mesopotamia for instance – yet the city provided the initial push that extended interregional interaction to unprecedented levels.

The interaction networks that formed carried more than just objects and were beyond the control of any one site. People, from traders to colonists, migrant workers, and marriage partners, circulated through these networks, and these people brought with them ideas that were eagerly discussed from settlement to settlement. The most gripping set of ideas likely had to deal with changing social relationships at growing sites like Uruk-Warka, Nineveh, and Tell Brak and the means through which these relationships were organized. How would a full-time potter find a way to feed her family? How would you ensure that the contents of a boat load were not pilfered during its journey down the river? What was the relationship between the gods, priests, and metal production? The organizational and technological solutions to these and other questions were created at Uruk-Warka and other large sites, but they were of interest to almost everyone living in the Middle East and beyond. This interregional dialogue, combined with all of the other ways in which these groups interacted, created what I would call an Uruk global culture.

The best way to understand this global culture is through a series of case studies that gets at how people's lives were impacted through these interactions. We begin these case studies by returning to the central Zagros Mountains that sit to the east of Susa in southwest Iran. As I mentioned earlier, a small group of Uruk colonists from the Susa area established a small enclave at the village of Godin Tepe during the Late Uruk Period. Built in the center of the site, the enclave was housed within an oval enclosure of buildings arranged around a central courtyard. There are tablets, cylinder seals, and sealings that link the colonists to trade with the southern alluvium, and about half of the pots used in the enclosure were made in the Uruk style (Weiss and Young 1975). The central focus of this enclosure was a well-made building with large niches and a central fireplace. The building was likely a public one that was used to entertained guests from the village and surrounding area (Weiss and Young 1975: 4–5). The degree of interest in things Uruk in the rest of the village is hinted at in the ceramic assemblages where about 20% of the pottery was made in the Uruk style (Weiss and Young 1975: 6).

Uruk influence was widespread throughout the central Zagros Mountains by the Late Uruk Period. People were on the move during this time as some decided to relocate into small farming villages, others took up herding animals, and still others jumped into long-distance trading (Henrickson 1994: 98). Although these population movements were caused by an array of factors, the most important of these factors was likely the economic opportunities provided by developments in the southern alluvium. Uruk ideas seem to have spread with the movement of copper, stone, sheep, and other products on the mountain trails. Some sites near these trails like Tepe Giyan and Ghabritan boasted the full corpus of Late Uruk wares, and likely had extensive contact with traders from the Susa region and elsewhere (Henrickson 1994: 89). Most other sites were further from these major trails, but still have at least a smattering of bevel-rim bowls or other Uruk-style pots, and the local ceramic styles of the region often reflect strong Uruk influence (Goff 1971: 145; Henrickson 1994: 88–9).

The embrace of Uruk influence in the central Zagros Mountains stands in contrast to what was happening in the Tepe Gawra, a village of about two hundred people on the edge of the northern plain near Nineveh. The site sat amid rich agricultural and pastoral lands and had easy access to mountain resources (Rothman 2002a: 7–8). Despite its small size, the site seems to have been an administrative center that served "many more people" than the residents of the village (Rothman 1994: 107). Residents of Tepe Gawra engaged in a wide variety of export-oriented crafts like cloth making, woodworking, and bead manufacture, and leaders in the community initially vied with each other to "garner influence and establish control" (Rothman 2002b: 58). Over time, there is evidence for increasing economic centralization as craft production moved into workshops and a main depository was built alongside a new temple (Rothman 2001b: 387). With Nineveh (the site where Campbell Thompson found his miserable bowls) just twenty kilometers down the river, one might suspect that Tepe Gawra's increasing centralization was the result of its incorporation into the town's infrastructure. This does not seem to have been the case.

The residents of Tepe Gawra appear to have been independent brokers that reacted to the new economic opportunities created by the growth of towns in the Early and Middle Uruk Periods by coming together into a collective to streamline production. Centralization was the result of increasing social stratification at the site and the adoption of new administrative techniques that were developing during the initial fluorescence of the Uruk sphere (Rothman 2002b: 59). Tepe Gawra, however, largely rejected other elements of Uruk culture. Most seals and sealing, for example, were made with local clays and none of the imported seals come from nearby Nineveh (Rothman 1994: 116). Uruk-style pottery is rare, and there are a variety of 'Ubaid Period pottery designs that reappear in the Middle Uruk Period (Rothman 2002b: 60). People also continued to be buried in large numbers at Tepe Gawra, and the contents of the tombs from gold to turquoise and electrum were used to mark the prestige of the deceased (Rothman 2001b: 391).

Although the people of Tepe Gawra profited off the flow of goods and ideas during the Uruk expansion, their general response was to return to an idealized past that was "known, remembered, and associated with local culture" (Rothman 2002b: 60). This response was not shared by all in the region – Nineveh may have welcomed a group of Late Uruk colonists from the alluvium, and there are many sites in this corner of the northern plain that embraced Uruk ceramic styles (Algaze 2001a: 44–5). As southern Mesopotamian influence continued to intensify in the Late Uruk, the site of Tepe Gawra was abandoned for unknown reasons. Perhaps they were outmaneuvered economically, or simply decided to pack their bags and leave for a less "Urukized" place.

The Uruk era unfolded differently at Tell Brak, a large town in Syria that rivaled Uruk-Warka in size at the beginning of the Middle Uruk Period. Sitting amid rich agricultural lands and dominating a major trade route into the mountains (Oates 2002: 120), Tell Brak was "a pivotal point in the relations between north/south and east/west" (Pittman 2001: 432). One of the mainstays of Tell Brak's economy seems to have been the manufacturing of a great variety of objects that were then exported to trade partners. Excavations of the Red Building, for example, revealed "massive" quantities of raw material that were used to make shell inlays, flint tools, disks of ground obsidian, and other objects (McMahon and Oates 2007: 151). Tell-Brak's export economy was already well developed before the Uruk expansion, but this network expanded further during the Middle Uruk Period as locals took advantage of new trading opportunities, administrative technologies, and religious ideas (Oates and Oates 2004: 182–3).

People from the southern alluvium moved to Tell Brak during the Late Uruk Period. These settlers brought with them the full range of southern ceramics, architecture, and administrative paraphernalia, and there are some hints that this colonization led to a slight shift toward production of objects most desired in the south (Oates 2002: 120–1). The ubiquity of southern pottery across the site might indicate a "large-scale takeover" of Tell Brak (Emberling and McDonald 2003: 10), but there is no evidence that the arrival of the settlers had any significant impacts on the local economy and social organization (Emberling et al. 1999: 29; Emberling and Macdonald 2003: 26; Oates 2002: 121). Tell Brak's lack of restructuring in the wake of southern colonization might suggest that the population movement was not part of a colonial project orchestrated by an alluvial center. Instead, the settlers may have chosen to migrate to the city in order to pursue new opportunities and flee increasing southern violence (although evidence from the nearby site of Hamoukar suggests that they may have brought some of this violence with them [Lawler 2006, 2007]).

Another site that can help us illustrate the spread of Uruk global culture is Arslantepe. In the mountains of central Turkey, the site was another settlement that was prospering before the Uruk expansion. During the first half of the fourth millennium, Arslantepe had become an important town in the region and emerging elite were trying to buttress their positions through the acquisition of prestige goods and the distribution of staple goods (Frangipane 2001). These elites drew on greater Mesopotamian ideas – as manifested in objects like seals and ration bowls at the site – but development of the site was largely an endogenous process fueled in part by its geographic position between resource zones (Frangipane 2002: 129).

The relative isolation of Arslantepe and other sites in the region further eroded during the Late Uruk Period when there seems to have been a shift toward greater metals production for export. Although Arslantepe maintained some kind of relationship with the southern alluvium (Frangipane 2001: 339–40; Pittman 2001: 441), the site's inhabitants interacted much more with other groups like the Transcaucasian nomads to the north (Frangipane et al. 2001: 134).

The communities in this mountainous region beyond northern Mesopotamia participated in a "capillary and intense" interaction network that extended across a broad region. This network developed in response to the rapid urbanization of Uruk-Warka (Frangipane 2002: 130), but the city was only one of many nodes of interaction. When southern connections collapsed at the end of the Uruk Period, Arslantepe reoriented its external economy to the north and welcomed new forms of pottery and metallurgy (if not people) from Transcaucasia (Frangipane 2001: 342; Frangipane et al. 2001).

The Uruk expansion also had a significant, but highly variable, impact to the west of the Euphrates. The Cilicians of south-central Turkey, for example, had been trading with northern Syria for almost two millennia before the Uruk expansion brought sites from this region like Tell Brak into new interaction networks with the southern alluvium (Steadman 1996: 147). Instead of embracing Uruk culture, the region of Cilicia "fortified itself, turned its back on north Syria, and developed new contacts to the north" (Steadman 1996: 154).

Uruk culture was also rejected in the southern Levant but for different reasons. Since Uruk material shows up in Egypt, it is likely that Uruk networks passed through the Levant. The intensification of olive oil production, for example, suggests that the region was participating in the wider exchange networks of the period (Gibson and Rowan 2006: 104), but the only possible evidence for Uruk influence are locally made bent spout vessels that may have derived from Uruk forms (Philip 2002: 225). The lack of interest in the Uruk cultural package in the region likely relates to the region's low level of political complexity. As Philip suggests (2002: 224):

> In the absence of complex economies and self-aggrandizing elites, features of Uruk material culture which were intimately connected with elite lifestyles and consumption, and structures of bureaucratic control, would have been of little relevance.

In a final example of the spread of Uruk global culture, Uruk ideas and objects were embraced in Egypt. By the last half of the fourth millennium, Egyptians were coming together into a few regional centers, and elites at these centers were "engaged in a concentrated programme of status demarcation and status display" (Wilkinson 2002: 238). Uruk global culture provided the Egyptians with both prestige goods and pragmatic solutions to their administrative problems, and they seem to have chosen eclectically from the Uruk corpus of ideas and objects based on their own tastes and needs.

Some Mesopotamian iconographic themes, such as winged griffins and serpent-headed panthers, were incorporated into Egyptian art (Joffe 2000: 115), and a few imported Uruk-style four-lugged jars, spouted jars, and cylinder seals were placed in Egyptian graves (Wilkinson 2002: 238–42). After Uruk Period networks collapsed, however, Egyptian elite turned inward for elite legitimization, and they jettisoned Mesopotamian themes from their artwork.

The collapse of the Uruk networks around 3100 B.C. was likely the result of a number of factors beyond the southern alluvium. Encroachment of Transcaucasian nomads in the north, for example, may have disrupted caravans in the Taurus Mountains, and the proclivity to build fortification walls across other parts of Mesopotamia suggests that growing warfare may have made long-distance interactions increasingly dangerous (Collins 2000: 66). Yet the most important factor in the collapse of the Uruk networks was likely the information systems that were being transmitted along these networks by the end of the Late Uruk Period.

The system of writing, more complex seals, and new bureaucratic structures that developed in Uruk-Warka and elsewhere were allowing settlements to better manage their local economy and rely less on long-distance connections that were becoming increasingly jeopardized by violence and competition (Algaze 2001a: 76). These ideas, spread through migrants, traders, laborers, and diplomats, enabled the creation of a post-Uruk political landscape of balkanized centers with exchange networks that were more regional in scale (Matthews 1992). Like Uruk-Warka, many of the sites that prospered during the fourth millennium continued to do so in the succeeding centuries because they were able to successfully retool their political economies. The size of the Uruk Period interaction network, however, would not be rivaled until the expansion of the Babylonian Empire in the middle of the first millennium B.C.

REIMAGINING URUK

One scholar has called the Near East in the fourth millennium a "melting pot of ideas" (Wilkinson 2002: 245). The words "melting pot" bring me back to debates in middle school about the metaphor of the United States as a melting pot or a salad bowl. The answer given to us then was that we did not live in a melting pot that fused together cultures, but instead in a salad bowl of cultural diversity. Both metaphors were actually good descriptions of what was happening in America during the twentieth century. Theorists recognize that there is both greater homogeneity and heterogeneity during globalizing eras. The debates on the fourth millennium in the Near East remind me of the melting pot vs. salad bowl debates.

Guillermo Algaze's *The Uruk World System* revolutionized Mesopotamian archaeology by recognizing the connections between the southern alluvium and social change across a broad swath of the ancient Near East (1993a). His vision of Uruk, however, can tend toward the melting pot side of the debates in treating Uruk as a unitary cultural phenomenon. The response of Joan Oates, Marcella Frangipane, and others has tended toward the salad bowl explanation by stressing the diversity of cultural experiences during the era (Frangipane 2001; Oates and Oates 2004). Both sides of the debate are correct because trends toward greater homogeneity and heterogeneity were occurring at the same time during the Uruk Period. Yet Uruk was neither a melting pot nor a salad bowl, but rather a melting salad (a vegetable stew?) triggered by a rush of interregional interactions that began in the Middle Uruk Period. To better understand Uruk civilization, we need to turn toward a globalization model.

The rapid urbanization of Uruk-Warka in the Middle Uruk Period created immense logistical hurdles that could only be overcome by the creation of new exchange networks into the mountains and northern Mesopotamia (Algaze 2008). Uruk-Warka likely established a handful of outposts outside of the southern alluvium, and in some cases people living around these sites might have been compelled by force to work for colonists. Yet, most of the networks that brought goods, people, and ideas to and from the city were outside of the control of city administrators. Most people embraced these new relationships on their own accord because of the perceived benefits that these relationships offered (Stein 1999).

The connections linking the city to the rest of Mesopotamia, however, were only a small part of the networks spawned by the Uruk expansion. Individuals also looked elsewhere, and most of the interactions that occurred likely circumvented Uruk-Warka altogether. The end result of the expansion was the creation of a global culture that developed through the intense interregional interaction of people throughout the Near East. Many people shared ideas, some people combined new ideas from one source with those from another, and still others tried to check out of the game entirely by embracing local traditions.

5

Cahokia

In 1811, Henry Marie Brackenridge walked up the Cahokia Creek in search of ancient mounds. Brackenridge lived in St. Louis – a town known for years as Mound City – and had been told that the biggest mounds in the area could be found on the grounds of a Trappist monastery on the other side of the Mississippi River. After walking for about four miles into the floodplain, he found himself in front of the largest earthen mound ever constructed north of Mexico (Young and Fowler 2000: 3–5). Two years later, he described this moment in a letter to his good friend, the former president of the United States Thomas Jefferson (1962 [1814]: 187):

> When I reached the foot of the principal mound, I was struck with a degree of astonishment, not unlike that which is experienced in contemplating the Egyptian pyramids. What a stupendous pile of earth! To heap up such a mass must have required years, and the labor of thousands.

Brackenridge spent the remainder of that day exploring the dozens of mounds that made up the site. He found flint, animal bones, and pottery littering the surface and concluded that "if the city of Philadelphia and its environs were deserted there would not be more numerous traces of human existence" (1962 [1814]: 186).

Henry Marie Brackenridge was perhaps the first European American to recognize the significance of Cahokia and its related sites in the St. Louis area. Unfortunately, his enthusiasm for the sites was not shared by many of his countrymen. Mounds, albeit usually smaller that those found at Cahokia, were a common feature throughout the eastern United States. Most people thought that the

Table 5.1. Mississippian chronology

Period	Time Range	Globalization Phase
Late Woodland	500–900 AD	Pre-Globalization
Terminal Late Woodland	900–1050 AD	
Mississippian	1050–1600 AD	Expansion
Cahokia's Peak	*1050–1300 AD*	Global Culture
SECC's Peak	*1300–1500 AD*	Regionalization
Colonial Period	1600–1763 AD	

mounds were either natural phenomena or the relics of an ancient group of mound builders, perhaps Aztecs, Toltecs, or even Israelites, who had been displaced by Native Americans by the fifteenth century. At their core, these alternative explanations were racist attempts to deny Native American social complexity that legitimized the manifest destiny of a precocious nation (Pauketat and Loren 2005: 8–9).

There is still considerable ambivalence regarding Cahokia and its role in North American prehistory. The site is now widely recognized as an important site of the Mississippian Period (A.D. 1050–1600) (Table 5.1) and the largest Pre-Columbian site in the United States. A handful of scholars share Brackenridge's vision of Cahokia as a prehistoric Philadelphia. Most do not. Few scholars consider Cahokia a real city (Pauketat 2004b: 3), and many have seen the site as the head of just one of the period's many independent Mississippian chiefdoms (Milner 1998; Smith 1978, 1990; Steponaitas 1986). In this view, Cahokia is not qualitatively distinct from Moundville, Etowah, Obion, Kincaid, Shiloh, and the dozens of other Mississippian Period mound centers across the southeastern United States that held sway over a collection of nearby communities.

Recent work at Cahokia and other Mississippian sites has quashed the more outlandish claims for Cahokia. The site was *not* the capital of a massive state or empire (contra Conrad 1991; O'Brien 1991; but see Holt 2009, for a reworking of the state model), and its political control seems to have been limited largely to the St. Louis area (Mehrer 1995; Milner 1990, 1998; Schroeder 2004a). Yet, Cahokia's creation started an era of incredible social change throughout the central and eastern United States – a "Big Bang" that sent ripples of change across much of the mid-continent (Pauketat 2004b: 65). Chiefdoms rose with "somewhat startling rapidity" after Cahokia's founding (Cobb 2003: 63), and a suite of objects exploded across eastern and central North America. These objects, ranging widely from supernatural icons like the Long-Nosed God to gaming pieces called chunkey stones (Pauketat 2004b: 10–11), were markers of the spread of a broad cultural horizon that changed people's ideas about how to worship, play, build their homes, and bury their dead.

The Mississippian was much more than a time period, and Cahokia was the source of many of the ideas, artifacts, and even people who helped to create Mississippian ways of life (Anderson 1997; Cobb 2005; Emerson 1997; Pauketat 2004b). Yet, the sweeping cultural changes led to as many differences as similarities. There was a great degree of variation across space and over time, and this variation was based in large part on each group's distinct historic, social, and environmental settings (Anderson 1994, 1996; Beck 2006; Cobb 2003; Muller 1997; Smith 1978, 1990; Steponaitas 1986; Wilson et al. 2006). How can we provide an explanation for *both* the substantial local diversity and widely shared characteristics of Mississippian societies?

Scholars have attempted to resolve this seeming tension by various archaeological models that pivot on how people responded to increasing interaction across political and geographic boundaries (e.g., Brown et al. 1990; Emerson 1997). Some of these models stress trade, others religion, and still other political ideology. This work has deepened our understanding of particular Mississippian relationships but suffers from too narrow of a focus. What is missing is an overarching model that encapsulates these various interaction mechanisms. The tension between the local and global seen during this period makes perfect sense if we think in terms of a global culture. If we envision the Mississippian era as a period of globalization, then we would expect to see a wide variety of social mechanisms operating at the same time as groups adjusted to a surge in the flow of goods, people, and, most importantly, ideas across the mid-continent.

In this chapter, I apply the model developed in Chapter 3 to describe Mississippian civilization as the consequences of the rapid urbanization of Cahokia. My writing draws considerably on Timothy Pauketat's work on understanding the relationship between Cahokia and the Mississippian era (2004b, 2005, 2007; also see Cobb 2005). Although I believe that he has overestimated the degree of Cahokia colonization and hegemony, the following pages owe a considerable debt to his work (he even ponders, albeit in a single phrase, the possible link between ancient civilizations and globalization [Pauketat 2007: 18]). Following his lead, I argue that Cahokia was the largest and earliest of the Mississippian sites and that the creation of the site was the catalyst for the Mississippization of the American mid-continent (Pauketat 2004b: 171; also see Stoltman 1991: 351). Mississippization was not the result of Machiavellian machinations of a Cahokia elite bent on regional dominance. Instead, it was a messy, stochastic, acephalous process that was caused largely by local responses to the challenges and opportunities that were created by the city's rise and fall. Like the Uruk Period in greater Mesopotamia, the Mississippian era might be best understood as another example of an earlier period of globalization.

CAHOKIA AND THE MISSISSIPPIZATION OF THE NORTH AMERICAN MID-CONTINENT

The story of Cahokia begins with the story of the Mississippi River. One of the largest river systems in the world, the Mississippi is perhaps the most dominant feature of the central United States. The river was much more that a ribbon of water flowing into the Gulf of Mexico. It was a transportation corridor, resource zone, and symbol of nature's power for Native Americans that was likely important to the first humans that came into the mid-continent at least 13,000 years ago (Adovasio and Pedler 2005). The river's floodplain supported creeks, oxbow lakes, marshes, swales, and natural levees that boasted rich soils and teemed with wildlife. The Mississippi watershed also provided access to a wide variety of resources, such as the hardwood of the forests of the Ozark uplift, the seashells of the Gulf Coast, and Lake Superior copper (Pauketat 2004b: 28–36).

Cahokia was founded in an area of the Mississippi River called the American Bottom, the floodplain of the river in southwestern Illinois (Figure 5.1). As rich a resource zone as any in the drainage, the area was likely first occupied by big game hunters before 11,000 B.C. (Adovasio and Pedler 2005). Nonetheless, the people living in the American Bottom were bit players in North American prehistory before the Mississippian era. While the America Bottom was home to small, dispersed groups of hunter-gatherers and horticulturalists (Fortier 2001: 192), for example, people were building the three-square-kilometer site of Poverty Point in Louisiana around 700 B.C. The site boasted earthen mounds and bird-shaped effigies and

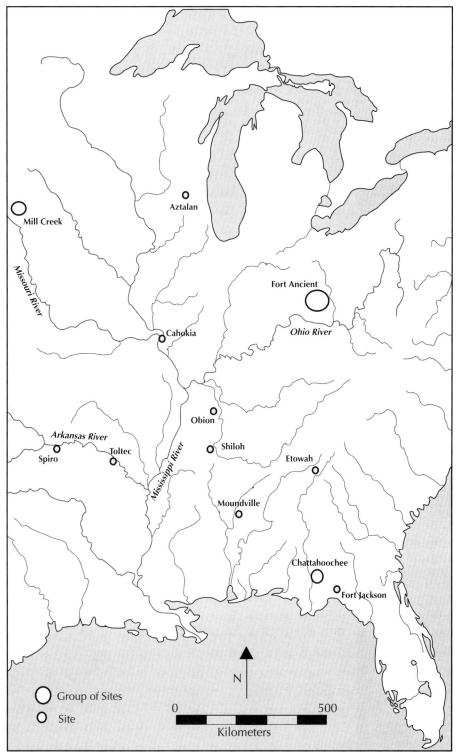

Figure 5.1 Map of the Mississippian world with sites discussed in the text (base map redrawn from Pauketat 2004b: 2).

contained objects from as far away as the Great Lakes and Appalachia (Sassaman 2005: 93). People in the American Bottom also remained on the sidelines during the Hopewell Interaction sphere from about A.D. 0–400. The nature of this interaction remains under debate (Carr 2006) but is marked by the spread of a suite of artifacts, new mortuary traditions, and the construction of geometric earthworks across much of the central and eastern United States (Dancey 2005).

The American Bottom's relative isolation to the broader currents of mid-continental history started to break down at the beginning of the Terminal Late Woodland Period (A.D. 900–1050) when maize joined native domesticates like squash, goosefoot, and sunflowers in the diet of many groups in the region (Chilton 2005: 140–4; Pauketat 2004b: 7–9). Like the rest of the central and eastern United States, this era was a period of agricultural intensification and settlement growth in the American Bottom. The social tensions of living in larger, more permanent settlements led to fissioning of communities across this broad region during the Terminal Late Woodland Period. With people increasingly on the move, innovations, such as crushed mussel shell for pottery temper, a new chipped stone hoe type, and red-slipping technique for vessels, spread with them to different parts of the mid-continent (Pauketat 2004b: 8–10; Stoltman et al. 2008). Since the American Bottom offered abundant exchange opportunities and rich soils to migrants, more and more people began coming into the locale by A.D. 900 (Pauketat 2004b: 59).

Most American Bottom communities at the beginning of the tenth century were formed together into hut compounds that were organized around a courtyard that boasted both communal storage and a central pole (Kelly 1990a, 1990b). Although most sites boasted only a few households, some villages grew during this period by adding parallel groups of huts, courtyards, storage, and poles as they expanded (Mehrer 1995: 140). By A.D. 1000, there may have been several large villages in the region that vied for new settlers by constructing their own earthen mounds (Emerson 1997: 57; Schroeder 2004a: 814; Stoltman et al. 2008: 334). One of these competing villages was Cahokia (Dalan et al. 2003: 69–71).

THE CITY OF CAHOKIA

Around A.D. 1050, Cahokia suddenly changed. In a concentrated building effort, the large village was quickly turned into a ceremonial center of massive proportions by the construction of Monk's Mound and the Great Plaza (Dalan 1997: 98). The nineteen-hectare Great Plaza was a *constructed* feature formed by flattening out a rolling landscape, and Monk's Mound would quickly grow to thirty meters in height and cover seven hectares at its base (Dalan 1997: 98; Pauketat 2004b: 69, 76). Both of these features were largely completed by A.D. 1100 (Dalan 1997: 98). If the Cahokians managed to build only Monk's Mound and the Great Plaza during this time span, it would have been impressive. Yet, they also built dozens of plazas and mounds during this fifty-year period. By A.D. 1100, there were 10,000–15,000 people living in Cahokia proper (Pauketat and Lopinot 1997: 118). If we include the populations of the immediately adjacent East St. Louis and St. Louis mound groups in this estimate then Cahokia's population would have likely exceeded 20,000. There are over 200 Mississippian Period mounds in the East St. Louis, St. Louis, and Cahokia complex – some 120 of these are found at Cahokia (Pauketat 2004b: 71) – and almost all of them were built in the frenzied first decades of occupation.

Despite its population size and monumentality, there has been a tendency by many archaeologists to avoid calling Cahokia a city (Pauketat 2007: 139–42). When compared to sites in Mesoamerica and the Andes, Cahokia does not seem particularly large and the site lacks evidence for the extreme status differences and intensive craft specialization found in these other places. Yet placed within the context of the North American mid-continent, Cahokia was worlds apart from other sites. Nothing before, during, or after the Mississippian era came close to rivaling Cahokia in size and monumentality – the next largest site, Moundville, was ten times smaller and contained approximately ninety fewer mounds (Pauketat 2004b: 71; 2007: 140). There is also clear evidence at Cahokia for densely occupied neighborhoods, craft production areas, and the negotiation and expansion of social roles (Alt 1999; 2001; Pauketat 2003; 2004b: 78–84; Pauketat and Alt 2004; Yerkes 1991). If we evaluate the site using the criteria laid out in Chapter 3, Cahokia was a city.

Like other cities, the central challenge at Cahokia was to create an urban identity that transcended the kin-based identities that had formed in the hut compounds of the previous period. This seems to have been done in part by building upon preexisting community based rituals (Pauketat 2004b: 84–7; Pauketat and Alt 2005). The poles placed in the center of hut compounds during the Terminal

Late Woodland Period, for example, had been routinely placed and replaced in community building rituals. At Cahokia, these rituals were recapitulated with massive posts to create a greater Cahokia community that nested above the kin-based ones (Pauketat and Alt 2005: 228–9).

The most important means of creating a Cahokia identity was undoubtedly the construction and maintenance of the mounds. Mounds were built in multiple stages, and it is likely that thousands of people got together annually to move earth, stabilize surfaces, and the like (Dalan et al. 2003). This work was likely organized around temple renewal rituals that were linked to large-scale feasting. The refuse of some of these feasts was found in a borrow pit adjacent to Monk's Mound in 1965. A reanalysis of this material revealed a wide variety of foods, broken pottery, and thousands of tobacco seeds (Pauketat et al. 2002). Participants in the labor feast likely left the feast with full bellies, a tobacco high, and perhaps a ritually charged keepsake from the ceremony (Pauketat and Emerson 1991).

Evidence suggests that status hierarchies in the initial decades of Cahokia's rise were initially muted and grew out of competition between largely egalitarian kin groups (Trubitt 2000; also see Knight 1990). The best evidence for status changes comes from Mound 72 at Cahokia (Fowler et al. 1999). Like other mounds in the American Bottom, Mound 72 seems to have begun its life as an ancestral monument. The mound was built on top of the charnel house and central poles of a preexisting hut compound, and the first burials in the mound seem to be orientated to these communal features (Watson 2000: 231). Less than halfway into the mound's construction, however, a man was buried on top of a cape or platform decorated with shell beads. The "beaded burial" would become the focal point of the mound's ritual activity. Rituals stressed the importance of outside links. There were sacrificial offerings of four groups of young women, for example, who had dental traits and bone chemistry that suggested that they were born outside of Cahokia (Ambrose et al. 2003; Rose 1999: 81–2). Other offerings were bundles of goods, like mica crystals, copper tubes, projectile points, and shell beads, that seem to have also been used to signify long-distance connections and the coming together of diverse groups into a single place (Goldstein 2000; Pauketat and Alt 2003; Porubcan 2000).

The shift toward greater differences in social ranking coincided with the peaking of the city's population in its first fifty years from

A.D. 1050 to 1100 (Pauketat and Lopinot 1997: 121). Although elites seem to have been created by the success of Cahokia's ideologically driven construction project, elite status was subsequently maintained through prestige good exchange, warfare, and craft specialization (Beck 2006: 33–4; Kelly 2006: 255–6; Trubitt 2000: 680–1). The seeds of Cahokia's eventual collapse appear to have been sown in the widening distance between the elite and non-elite. Mounting tensions between classes and factions divided the population, and these tensions were likely exacerbated by decreasing rainfall (Benson et al. 2009: 478). After A.D. 1200, palisades were thrown up around Cahokia and other sites in the American Bottom as cooperation across kin communities broke down (Pauketat 2004b: 147). Cahokia was in steep decline by A.D. 1300 (Pauketat and Lopinot 1997). After the initial burst of mound building, the population began a slow process of decentralization and dispersal that left the site virtually abandoned by A.D. 1400.

CAHOKIA'S EXPANSION

Like other cases of rapid early urbanization, Cahokia's rise led to both the creation of an agricultural heartland that supported the city and an out-migration that included the creation of far-flung colonies. Cahokia's urbanization occurred in one of the most fertile areas of the mid-continental United States. Although it was once thought that the city's occupants lived on a maize-dominated diet, we now know that they had a varied diet that included fish and venison (Buikstra and Milner 1991; Yerkes 2005). The mix of wild and domesticated foods in the Cahokia diet could only have been maintained through relationships with outside producers. The change in settlement patterns that occurred in the northern American Bottom around A.D. 1050 seems to reflect a shift toward agricultural intensification that may have been encouraged by the leaders of the groups who were nucleating at Cahokia and other settlements (Pauketat 2003: 56). New single-household farmsteads were scattered across the floodplain, and villages were constructed in the uplands about a day's walk from the city (Mehrer 1995).

The political relationship between these settlements and Cahokia is still under debate (compare Mehrer 1995 to Pauketat 2003). The people in these settlements were clearly aware of what was happening at Cahokia – they owned goods from the city and some of them may have migrated out of the city. The strongest evidence for Cahokian control over farmers is some evidence that the emerging elites at Cahokia had access to choice animal parts (Pauketat 1998:63) and "much more access" to animal protein (Ambrose et al. 2003: 217). Yet, there is also considerable evidence for local autonomy and some unease, if not resistance, to the social changes that were occurring at Cahokia. A change in how houses were constructed, for example, occurred at Cahokia around A.D. 1050. The old way of building a house began with setting individual posts into the ground. The Cahokia innovation was a wall trench that allowed a prefabricated wall to be raised (Pauketat and Alt 2005: 223–4). Some villagers in upland communities adopted wall trenching quickly, while others took several generations to do so. Some houses mixed wall-trenching and single-set posts, while others had "faux wall trenches" that hid single-set postholes (Pauketat and Alt 2005: 223–6).

The most likely explanation for the early Cahokia's political economy may be that the settlements in the northern American Bottom were tied to the city through kinship ties and that people regularly visited the city with animal and plant resources in order to participate in feasting, mound building, and other ritual events. When these activities began to decrease in the city due to increasing factionalism, people stopped coming. City and countryside could not survive unlinked, and by A.D. 1150 health was declining in the city, and the upland communities were widely abandoned (Pauketat 2003: 58; Trubitt 2000: 682). The city slowly lost inhabitants as they began to nucleate around smaller sites with chiefs whose legitimization no longer depended on the success of Cahokia's magnetism.

The city's rise also led to colonization and the wide dissemination of Cahokia-style objects. The nature and degree of Cahokia-driven colonization remains controversial. Many sites in central and eastern North America have at least a few Cahokia-style objects like chunkey stones, arrowheads, masks, and shell beads, and the people living there often adopted some Cahokian ideas like wall trenching and mound building. Although most of these sites likely obtained these items and knowledge through direct or indirect exchanges, other sites have wholesale changes in artifacts and settlement organization that suggest that the entire site was either a colonial outpost or a local site that boasted an enclave of Cahokian settlers (Kelly 1991a, 1991b; Stoltman 1991).

The clearest evidence for Cahokia colonists comes from late eleventh- and twelfth-century sites to the north in present-day Illinois, Wisconsin, Iowa, Missouri, and South Dakota (Pauketat 2004b: 124–6). One example of a likely colonial outpost is the site of Aztalan in southern Wisconsin. Settled around A.D. 1050–1100, the site is a radical departure from the surrounding settlements of the Late Woodland traditions. A planned community of some three hundred people, the site was organized around a central ceremonial space that contained two plazas and nine mounds. Artifacts and lifeways at Aztalan closely resembled those of the American Bottom, and the site was abandoned, like most other possible northern colonies, as Cahokia's influence waned between A.D. 1200 and 1300 (Birmingham and Goldstein 2005).

Although it is harder to demonstrate, a similar population dispersal may have occurred south of Cahokia (Pauketat 2004b: 131). In the second half of the eleventh century, there was a southern extension of Cahokia-style objects and ideas that paralleled the northern expansion. Sites like Shiloh and Obion in Tennessee have artifacts made in the American Bottom in their earliest levels, many of the walls at these sites are wall trenched, and their mound and plaza organization is similar to that found in and around Cahokia (Pauketat 2004b: 136–7). While these sites might have been Cahokia colonies, they may have also been local sites that were heavily influenced by contact with the American Bottom. In contrast to the northern expansion, Cahokian influence did not wane after the city declined. Instead, the development of these southern sites inaugurated a period of Mississippian chiefdoms that would continue for five centuries.

The reasons for colonization undoubtedly varied, but it was likely fueled in part by the desires of Cahokia's elites to gain regular access to goods like lead, mica, copper, seashells, deer meat, and hides that had long been valued in the American Bottom and elsewhere for their utilitarian and symbolic value (Kelly 1991a, 1991b). These goods would have been exchanged for specialized, finished products from Cahokia like shell beads, Ramey-style pots, chunkey stones, and Long-Nosed God ornaments (Emerson and Hughes 2000; Yerkes 1989, 1991) (Figure 5.2). The spread of these "calling cards" from Cahokia (Pauketat 2004b: 120) has been linked to ideas of a Mississippian world system and the establishment of a *pax Cahokiana* (Pauketat 2005: 205–7; Peregrine 1992, 1996).

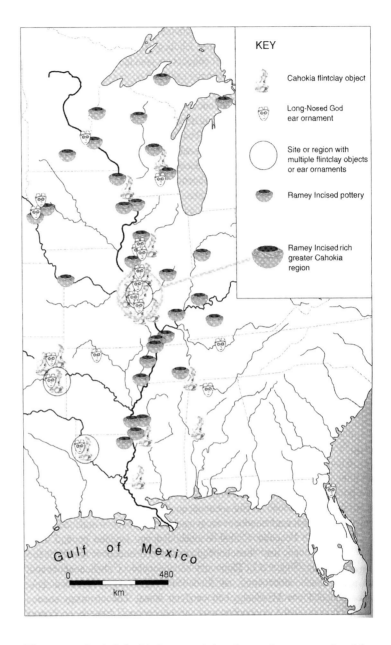

Figure 5.2 The spread of Mississippian artifacts (as seen in Pauketat 2004b: 122).

The spread of Cahokia's material culture, however, should not be taken as synonymous with the spread of a Cahokia-controlled network. Since there is little evidence that the city maintained widespread political, economic, or ideological control over its immediate hinterland, one would be hard-pressed to suggest that urbanites could significantly manage the actions of groups living further away. Cahokia's colonies were part of the first pulse of Cahokian culture outside of the American Bottom, but the city's colonial network lasted only a few decades, and many of the city's "calling cards" circulated only *after* political factionalism at Cahokia broke apart the site's nascent colonial network (e.g., Emerson et al. 2003). Perhaps paradoxically, the splintering of Cahokia and its colonies was likely integral to the creation of Mississippian global culture. This explosion of social relations led to greater flows of Cahokian ideas, people, and objects across the mid-continent and spilled over into those regional networks that had previously circumvented the American Bottom.

MISSISSIPPIAN GLOBALIZATION

Cahokia's emergence, colonial network, and near-collapse sent inter-action waves across the mid-continent. By at least the beginning of the thirteenth century, groups across the southeastern United States from northwestern Florida to eastern Oklahoma were linked together in a shared Mississippian civilization. The hallmarks of this global culture ranged widely from a reliance on cleared field corn agriculture to a shared iconography and town structure (King 2007a; Lewis and Stout 1998; Rogers and Smith 1995; Scarry 1996). This does not mean, of course, that all Mississippian people lived in the same way – as I discussed earlier there was considerable politi-cal, economic, and social variation across space and time (Anderson 1994; Beck 2003; Blitz 1999; Cobb 2003; Schroeder 2004b). Yet, each of these polities owed its emergence to participation in the wider Mississippian currents that had been stimulated by Cahokia.

The first generations of Cahokians left a rich legacy that subse-quent groups engaged with in different ways over the next six hun-dred years. One of the Cahokias' most significant achievements was its cutting of the Gordian knot of kinship ties that had stymied the emergence of status hierarchies. Mississippian chiefs were able to pro-claim to their followers, "I am the Cosmos," though each would have also needed to explain why they were more cosmologically significant than earlier chiefs and neighboring rulers (Cobb 2003: 78). The excesses of chiefly power also allowed other groups to turn the Cahokian logic on its head and suggest the priority of the group over the individual (e.g., Cobb and King 2005). The ongoing tension among chiefly, kin, and Mississippian identities led to a wide variety of changing social organizations across eastern and central North America.

Shifting social hierarchies were just one part of the rich Mississippian mosaic that shaped how people worked, played, and worshiped. Linked together in a variety of networks, the creation of a new art style, abandonment of a mound center, or other event could trigger changes over a vast geographic area (Cobb 2005). As with our Uruk case study, the best way to understand this mosaic might be through a series of case studies. These cases highlight not only the diversity of Mississippian cultures across space and time, but more importantly they demonstrate how these cultures were (re)transformed through a wide variety of linkages that were often independent of Cahokia.

We begin with Etowah, a famous Mississippian site in north-western Georgia that contains six mounds. The site, like many other centers during the era, has a complicated, punctuated history of settlement, abandonment, and reorganization (King 2003). Etowah was first occupied near the end of the Late Woodland Period and seems to have been one of several small fortified sites in the region that were locked together in endemic warfare (King 2003: 114). The villagers of these sites appear to have been seeking an end to this cycle of violence and found it through communal rituals that created a new universal identity that cross-cut previous allegiances. This new identity, forged through the building of wall-trenched houses, regular feasting, and mound construction, was a Mississippian one (Cobb and King 2005: 180; King 2003: 52–62).

Etowah's participation in the Mississippian civilization is perhaps best reflected in the changing style of shell gorgets (circular necklace pendants that were typically made from conch shells). Gorgets first appear at the site during the Mississippian era, and the earliest examples of these gorgets are in the cross and circle style. A symbol of fertility, purity, and renewal with deep roots in North America, the cross and circle gorgets may have been carved in an attempt to affirm the relationship of Etowah cosmology to other groups both within and outside of Georgia (Cobb and King 2005: 178–80).

Regional styles were added to the gorget corpus by A.D. 1200. One of the most common of these styles depicted paired turkey cocks. These cocks represented a clearer understanding of the Mississippian view of the cosmos as divided into an Above and Below World, but this vision was translated into the local idiom of turkey cocks that had greater resonance for the people of northwestern Georgia (Cobb and King 2005: 180). Just as this regional Mississippian identity was developing, however, the site of Etowah was abandoned for fifty some years (King 2003: 63).

Etowah reached its greatest size during the second occupation from A.D. 1250 to 1375. Settlers formalized the site's mound and plaza organization, built the bulk of Etowah's three largest mounds (Mounds A, B, and C), and fortified the site with a ditch and palisade (King 2003: 63–4). While the earliest occupation of Etowah seems to have been organized around a team-first, egalitarian ethos, the second occupation followed the changes occurring contemporaneously in Cahokia and placed a greater emphasis on individuals and social differences (Cobb and King 2005: 180–1; King 2006: 84–5). The groups associated with each of the three mounds were in competition with each other and distinctions between groups may have been broadcast through differences in how palisades, mound, and other structures were built (King 2003: 63–75). For the first time, people were buried in large numbers at Etowah with elites being placed inside mounds. Elites were buried with a fairly redundant set of marine shell, copper, and flaked stone artifacts that mimicked the depictions of supernatural beings found on the shell gorgets on embossed copper plates. The most popular of these supernatural beings was the Birdman, a mythic hero with Cahokian roots that these elites impersonated or became in death (Cobb and King 2005: 183–5).

Etowah was abandoned for a second time by around A.D. 1375. A smaller population returned to the site seventy-five years later, and the importance of the site seems to have largely been as a "symbolic referent to a potent past" (Cobb and King 2005: 187). The Birdman gorgets of the second occupation were replaced by gorgets that once again stressed universal themes. The rattlesnake of the regional Lick Creek style, for example, showed an open-mouthed rattlesnake forming a cross. This motif was associated with the Below World and referenced the first cross-and-circle gorgets made at Etowah two hundred years earlier (Cobb and King 2005: 184). Status hierarchies still existed in Etowah and the surrounding area; however, these differences were no longer supported with direct links to the supernatural. Instead, power was reinforced during this final occupation through appeals to tradition (Cobb and King 2005: 187).

The Chattahoochee chiefdoms on the border of southern Georgia and Alabama went through a broadly similar sequence of political and social integration. The Mississippian era began through the migrations of various groups into the Lower Chattahoochee River area between A.D. 1050 and 1200 (Blitz and Lorenz 2006: 126–8). These groups settled into a few small mound centers surrounded by Late

Woodland Period villages. Mound construction and status differentiation accelerated at the beginning of the thirteenth century, and the region was divided up into a series of small chiefdoms whose rise and demise over the next few centuries can be tracked, albeit roughly, through mound construction sequences and the spread of ceramic styles (Blitz and Lorenz 2006). The largest Chattahoochee mound sites are only slightly smaller than Etowah and have a similar complex sequence that suggests a relationship to broader Mississippian currents that changed over time (Blitz and Lorenz 2006: 35–42).

Like Etowah, the Chattahoochee chiefdoms peaked from A.D. 1200 to 1400. The most interesting thing about the chiefdoms for our purposes is their interregional relationships. Like many groups during this period, these chiefdoms participated in the Southeastern Ceremonial Complex. Often called the SECC for short, the exact nature of this religiously charged exchange network remains hotly debated, but it is defined by a series of related artistic styles found on elite objects (King 2007b: 250). This complex includes the Birdman motif at Etowah and seems to have been derived from a cosmology first developed at Cahokia (Brown and Kelly 2000). The difference in the SECC from one site to the next likely reflects local traditions and the specific network of connections that each site fostered.

For the most part, the Chattahoochee chiefdoms seem to have been minor players in the SECC exchange networks. The Chattahoochee River, however, was an important transportation corridor and a few spectacular artifacts, like a headdress of copper arrows from the site of Cemochechobee, demonstrate the area's links to sites as far away as Moundville in Alabama (Blitz and Lorenz 2006: 134). In parallel to their SECC connections, the Chattahoochee elites likely also fostered the development of a regional prestige ceramic style. The use of the incised bottles and beakers in this style crossed chiefdom boundaries and may have been used in libation ceremonies (Blitz and Lorenz 2006: 114–18).

The diversity in interaction networks in the area can be understood by comparing the Chattahoochee chiefdoms to the nearby site of Fort Jackson in southern Florida (Scarry 2007). The large mound site of Lake Jackson participated in the region's bottle-beaker style, and likely periodically controlled sites at the mouth of the Chattahoochee (Blitz and Lorenz 2006: 134). Lake Jackson had a far greater amount of SECC paraphernalia in its mounds than any other site in the area. The amount of prestige goods was not a simple reflection of the site's greater size. This material found at Lake Jackson, ranging from shell gorgets to limestone celts and embossed copper plaques, represents a limited range of material that seems to have been directly acquired from the site of Etowah (Scarry 2007: 146–8). While the Chattahoochee chiefdoms appear to have had interactions with groups across much of the southeast (Blitz and Lorenz 2006: 130), Lake Jackson's connections, and overall impression of the Mississippian world, came largely from its links to Etowah (Payne 2006: 103–5; Scarry 2007: 148).

Mississippian influence was also occurring to the west of the Mississippi. The middle and lower Arkansas River had been an area of precocious cultural developments at the end of the Late Woodland Period. Most people lived in small villages, and there were a few larger sites with a mound or two that served as local centers where people came to exchange goods and honor their dead (Nassaney 2001). The glaring exception to this pattern was the site of Toltec, one of the largest Late Woodland sites in the American mid-continent with eighteen mounds surrounded by a 1.6-kilometer-long embank-ment (Nassaney 2001: 164). Although it represented a more regional investment in labor, the Toltec's organization and architecture har-kens back to earlier mound building traditions that stressed relative egalitarianism (e.g., Bernardini 2004).

None of these mound sites on the Arkansas River "would have been labeled Mississippian by archaeologists" (Pauketat 2007: 111), and the core beliefs of those building the Toltec mounds would have been likely antithetical to the hierarchical and individualizing ideas that were being developed at that time in Cahokia. When Mississippian ideas swept into the region, Toltec, as well as other Arkansas mound centers, was abandoned around A.D. 1100. People appear to have rejected the new rules of the game (Nassaney 2001: 170) – the popu-lation scattered, and the only "Mississippian" trait that was widely embraced was shell-tempered pottery (Nassaney 2001: 169).

The Toltec response to Mississippian flows was not shared by the people living in Spiro, a small mound center further up the Arkansas River in Oklahoma. The area around Spiro was a resource-rich region and gateway to the west. Increases in interaction by A.D. 1100 led to the growth of Spiro, and the site began to compete with several other mound centers like Harlan, Reed, and Groseclose for both followers and access to the trade moving along the Arkansas

River. Each center housed a group of emerging elites who may have sponsored craft specialists who created prestige items out of exotic material (Rogers 1995: 87; 1996: 65). Although Cahokian imports came into the area during the twelfth century (Brown 2005: 120), the most important early Mississippian flow was the idea of hierarchy and how it might be maintained. Mississippian goods were treated largely like any other exotic item for decades.

Spiro's relative isolation from the Mississippian phenomenon suddenly changed around A.D. 1250 when people living at the site adopted a hybrid Mississippian identity, embraced intensive maize agriculture, and began a campaign of extensive mound building (Pauketat 2007: 111). The site became a paramount center with a trade network that included the American Bottom, but also accessed conch shells from Florida, pottery from Tennessee, stone stools from Kansas and Texas, copper from the southeast. An obsidian scraper from central Mexico was even found in the Craig mound at Spiro (Barker et al. 2002).

Spiro's elites were important players in the Southeastern Ceremonial Complex, and SECC material was both imported and locally made. There were strong Cahokian influences on much of Spiro's SECC material, but Spiro also likely led the development of the Craig regional style that reached into Texas (Brown 2007). Deep historical connections to a generalized Mississippian identity had become integral to elite status at the site by at least A.D. 1400. At around that time, elites were buried in the "Great Mortuary" with hundreds of prestige objects from across the American mid-continent (Brown 1996). Many of these items were in the SECC style, but they had been hoarded over more than two centuries and then placed together in the tomb as "one last vainglorious attempt to lionize their heritage" (Pauketat 2007: 111). There was little social capital left, however, in Mississippian associations. Mound building and high-status burials at Spiro would cease by A.D. 1450 as the population of the site declined dramatically (Rogers 1995: 89).

Most people enmeshed within Mississippian global culture, of course, lived far away from the handful of spectacular mound centers like Spiro, Moundville, Fort Jackson, and Etowah. Although well-defined hierarchical relationships are sometimes thought to exemplify the Mississippian period (Schroeder 2004b: 318), this was the exception rather than the norm. Smaller, often ephemeral, chiefdoms like the Chattahoochee chiefdoms were much more common, and the gulf between rich and poor was often slight (e.g., Anderson 1994, 1996).

Mississippian influence, for example, was extensive in Kentucky – there are wall trenches, small mound-plaza groups, and imported goods from Cahokia and elsewhere. Yet, craft specialization seems absent and elite control weak (Stout and Lewis 1998). The Kentucky assemblages drive home the critical point that most people were not elite with access to some of the more spectacular prestige objects of the era. Nonetheless, these people were full participants (whether they liked it or not) in the cultural upheavals of the Mississippian era.

The boundaries of Mississippian civilization should also be drawn to include areas to the north of Cahokia that have been traditionally excluded from the Mississippian sphere (Griffin 1967). The Oneota groups of the Great Lakes region and eastern Plains, for example, did not boast mounds, a marked hierarchical social structure, or a maize-dominated diet (Birmingham and Goldstein 2005: 43; Hart 1990; Theler and Boszhardt 2006). Yet, the Oneota were part of the Mississippian world through a myriad of connections. Colonists from the American Bottom established Aztalan and other colonies in the Oneota region (Birmingham and Goldstein 2005), and there is even evidence for pre–A.D. 1050 contacts between the two regions that were integral to the creation of Cahokia's cosmology (Salzer and Rajnovich 2000; Stoltman et al. 2008).

The Mill Creek groups of northwest Iowa also had a particularly strong relationship with Mississippian groups to the south. On the surface, there is nothing remarkable about the Mill Creek sites. People lived in small villages, had few status differences, and subsisted on a mixed economy of hunting, gathering, and farming. Yet, excavations at these sites have revealed marine shells, Long-Nose God masks, and locally made Ramey pots, which provide evidence for long-distance contact with Cahokia and other sites. The quality and quantity of goods in these sites far exceeds what one would expect in the area, and it seems that Mill Creek groups were a major supplier of bison robes, bird feathers, and hawk and eagle medicine bags to the Mississippian world (Fishel 1997).

The boundaries of Mississippian global culture should also be expanded to include the Fort Ancient culture of the Ohio Valley. While more complex than the Mill Creek groups, Fort Ancient people had minimal status hierarchies and even their largest sites had fewer than five hundred people (Griffin 1992; Nass and Yerkes 1995). Fort Ancient groups also made few mounds, ate less maize, and did not participate in the more spectacular artifact exchanges of the SECC (Schurr and Schoeninger 1995). Nonetheless, the region's ties with the Mississippian world are widely acknowledged (e.g., Schroeder 2004b: 316). Imported ceramics from Mississippian sites are found in the valley (Drooker 1999) and there is also evidence for small groups of immigrants entering the Ohio Valley from in or around the American Bottom (Cook and Schurr 2009). These interregional connections were likely driven by outside demands for the region's salt (Pollack and Henderson 1992).

Those who measure the extent of Mississippian civilization have tended to look for a suite of particular traits. If we think of civilizations as bundles of relationships, however, the boundaries of these civilizations often significantly expand. Groups like the Oneota, Mill Creek, and Fort Ancient rejected (or were unable to attain) aspects of Mississippian culture and transformed other aspects, but they were all enmeshed within the fractured landscape of a Mississippian global culture (e.g., Pauketat 2004b: 125).

If the peak of the Mississippian global culture was marked by the zenith of the Southeastern Ceremonial Complex from A.D. 1200 to 1400, then it occurred after fortunes had begun to decline in Cahokia. Cahokia's population had dipped to less than five thousand people by the end of the fourteenth century, and mound building was decreasing (Pauketat and Lopinot 1997: 114). The city (if we could still call it that) was suffering under the weight of chiefly demands, and the ties that bound Cahokians to each other and to the countryside were unravelling.

Other mound centers in the American mid-continent were following a similar trajectory. The region was becoming increasingly balkanized – chiefs hid behind massive palisades as warfare increased and buffer zones left chiefdoms increasingly isolated from their neighbors (Anderson 1994: 325; Blitz 1999: 589). The chiefly political economy that began at eleventh-century Cahokia was ultimately unsustainable and by the fifteenth century was largely exhausted (Muller 1997: 393–6). Cahokia itself was completely abandoned rather suddenly around A.D. 1400 (Pauketat 2004b: 153), and the populations of many other great centers melted away around the same time. By the time the Spaniard Hernando De Soto traveled up the Mississippi in 1541, many Mississippian towns were already abandoned or populated by squatters, and the rest would soon fall to the mass migrations, epidemics, endemic warfare, and general chaos of the post–contact period.

UNDERSTANDING THE MISSISSIPPIAN

The Mississippian era from A.D. 1050 to 1600 remains a subject of intense debate among North American archaeologists (Schroeder 2004b). Some scholars stress cultural diversity, while other stress broad similarities; some advocate for the local roots of groups, others support widespread Cahokian replacement of local traditions. These and other Mississippian debates are fueled in large part because there is a great degree of truth in these seemingly opposing views. Lifeways varied tremendously across this broad region, but these groups were drawn together culturally through interregional interactions with each other (e.g., Butler and Welch 2006; Meyers 2006).

The cultures of people living in places like the Etowah valley, Mill Creek, and the Tombigbee River were created through socialization with their family and friends, but life for them was also suffused with broader Mississippian currents that impacted how these groups cooked their food, tilled the earth, and looked to the heavens. This tension between the local and the global makes sense when one thinks of a Mississippian global culture (Cobb 2005).

As Timothy Pauketat has evocatively written, the urbanization of Cahokia around A.D. 1050 was the "Big Bang" that began the Mississippian era by setting off the first wave of people, goods, and ideas across the American mid-continent (2004b: 65). His metaphor gets at the rush of transformative changes that swept across the American mid-continent over the next fifty years. Cahokia, however, played only a partial role in the creation of Mississippian civilization. Unlike the Big Bang that began our universe, Cahokia's Big Bang did not expand outward from an initial condition into empty space. Instead, the Cahokia's Big Bang occurred within the complexities of a preexisting social landscape. By reconfiguring this landscape, Cahokia set off hundreds (if not thousands) of Little Bangs as different groups reacted to the city by engaging in interregional interactions of their own. These new or transformed networks often bypassed Cahokia, but they were just as fundamental to the creation of a Mississippian civilization.

A rich mosaic of interacting societies would develop and change during the six centuries of the Mississippian era. The fact that many, if not most, of these interactions occurred after Cahokia's decline should make one suspicious of models that posit a Cahokia state or world system. Yet, Cahokia's shadow was long and Mississippian interactions cannot be understood without its Big Bang and the reaction to this explosion by neighboring groups (e.g., Anderson 1997; Pauketat 2007). Mississippian lifeways were formed by the melding of the local *and* the global as identities were continuously being negotiated within chiefdoms and other political groupings that rose and fell across the American mid-continent.

To return to the more appetizing of the two metaphors that I used to describe globalizing eras in the last chapter, the Mississippian is another example of a vegetable stew because homogenization (the melting pot) and differentiation (the salad bowl) were both occurring at the same time. Although other models get at aspects of the Mississippian era, the dynamics of this period can best be understood through the lens of the model developed in Chapter 3. Cahokia's rise ultimately led to the spread of a global culture across the mid-continent. It was the first period of globalization that occurred in what is now the United States of America.

6

Huari

In 1931, archaeologist Julio C. Tello decided to use his vacation time to make a grueling trip from the coast to the Ayacucho Valley in the highlands of central Peru (Tello 1970: 519). He was going there in search of the source of what was then known as "Coast Tiahuanaco," a beautiful polychrome ceramic style that depicted gods, angels, plants, and animals in bold lines (Figure 6.1). The style, found at site after site on the coast of Peru, was reminiscent of that found on pots documented forty years earlier at the great ceremonial center of Tiahuanaco in Bolivia (Stübel and Uhle 1892). Even though many people believed at the time that these ceramics were evidence of the spread of a vast Tiwanaku civilization, Tello and other archaeologists thought the style was distinct enough to have developed independently.

Tello was the most famous archaeologist in Peru at the time. His lifelong goal was to prove that Peruvian cultures developed independently from those in Central America. He was keen on showing the importance of the sierra and jungle in Peruvian prehistory and was one of the few archaeologists of the period who regularly took trips into the mountains (Tello 1970: 520). When he got to Ayacucho, Tello was directed to the site of Huari, a sprawling site with monumental architecture. The ceramics on the site closely matched the Coast Tiahuanaco style, and his excavations confirmed the association of the style with some of Huari's most impressive buildings. Tello went on to dig at other sites after his visit to Huari, but he kept thinking about how the site might fit within the grand scheme of Peruvian prehistory. Some ten years later he would suggest that Huari was the source of the Coast Tiahuanaco style, as well as the capital of a Wari civilization (Tello 1942: 682–4).

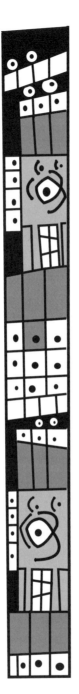

Figure 6.1 Wari-style pots from the site of Tenahaha.

Huari is now widely regarded by archaeologists as the principal site of a Wari civilization that swept across Peru during a period known as the Middle Horizon (A.D. 600–1000) (Table 6.1). Similar to the Uruk and Mississippian eras, there is considerable debate about the nature of this civilization. For most scholars, Wari was the first

Table 6.1. Wari chronology

Period	Time Range	Globalization Phase
Early Intermediate	200 BC–600 AD	Pre-Globalization
Early Middle Horizon	600–800 AD	Expansion Global Culture
Late Middle Horizon	800–1000 AD	
Late Intermediate	1000–1476 AD	Regionalization

empire of the Andes – a powerful state that expanded through military conquests to control a vast region (e.g., Isbell 1991a; Lumbreras 1974; Menzel 1977; Schreiber 1992; Williams and Isla 2002). Yet, I argue that the spread of Wari across Peru is better understood as another example of ancient globalization. This process, just as in the previous case studies, was shaped by the unique geographical and cultural parameters of the region within which the civilization emerged. Nonetheless, Wari shares with Uruk and Mississippian the basic pattern of urbanization, surging interregional interaction, and the creation of a global culture.

HUARI'S UNEXPECTED RISE

Taking a plane ride over Peru is a breathtaking experience. In less than two hundred kilometers, you can climb from the bone-dry coastal desert over the top of some of the world's highest snow-capped peaks and then down again into the sweltering jungle (Burger 1992: 12). This landscape of compressed environmental zones is daunting even from high above, and many travelers are shocked at the contrast between the severe climate and the grandeur of past Peruvian cultures. Yet the view from the air masks the great variety of natural resources available to the people of the ancient Andes.

Ocean and shorelines provided a rich bounty of fish, sea mammals, crustaceans, and guano; rivers and deserts yielded crops, game, and construction materials; the mountains provided metals, stone, and camelids (llamas and alpacas); and the jungle offered hallucinogens, exotic animals, and, on its western flanks, coca (Bawden 1996: 39–47; Burger 1992: 12–23). Since the patchiness of Andean resources makes it very difficult for a single group to survive in isolation, people of the area have long been linked through long-distance exchange across latitudes and elevations (Masuda et al. 1985).

These linkages between groups were especially important because the Andes are one of the most environmentally unstable regions in the world. Prone to earthquakes, volcanic eruptions, landslides, and, more rarely, tidal waves, Peru is most frequently destabilized by *El Niños* and *La Niñas* that devastate marine life and often cause torrential rainfall to occur on the coast and droughts in the highlands (e.g., Dillehay et al. 2004b; Moseley 1999, 2002; Philander 1990; Shimada et al. 1991). With resource zones scattered and prone to periodic failure, the maintenance of long-distance relationships was critical not only for daily subsistence but also as a social safety net for when things got bad in one locale.

The first people to come to Peru were big game hunters who followed the migration of mega fauna out of Siberia at least 13,000 years ago (Webb and Rindos 1997: 245–6). By as early as 8000 B.C., these groups were adding peppers, squash, beans, and other domesticates to their diets, and these foods were eventually followed by the domestication of maize, potatoes, guinea pigs, and camelids four millennia later (Dillehay et al. 2004a: 24–6). The increasing use of domesticates led to settling down in some places, and large ceremonial sites emerged around 2500 B.C. on the Peruvian coast (Haas and Creamer 2004; Quilter 1989; Shady Solís 2004, 2006; Shady Solís et al. 2001). The construction of these sites heralded a general trend toward population nucleation, resource intensification, monumental architecture, and social differentiation that culminated in the construction of Chavín de Huántar.

Located in the mountains of northern Peru, Chavín de Huántar was the most influential pilgrimage site of its time from 1200 to 500 B.C. (Burger 1992; Cordy-Collins 1977; Rick 2005). People from throughout northern and central Peru came to worship at the site's massive temple complex, and these visitors helped spread Chavín influence on art and architecture across this broad region (Druc 1998; Patterson 1971). More than just an art style, the spread of Chavín influence likely also marked the spread of a belief in the authority of priest-shamans, and the flow of goods and people into the site gave it considerable economic pull (Burger and Matos Mendieta 2002; Kembel and Rick 2004: 73). Chavín de Huántar's influence would be felt across Peru for centuries after the temple complex's precipitous decline around 500 B.C.

The subsequent Early Intermediate Period (200 B.C.–A.D. 600) was a time of increased fractionalization. People's horizons narrowed and most interactions only occurred between neighboring valleys. This fractionalization, however, did not stop the trend toward population nucleation, greater craft specialization, and increasing class differences in a few Andean regions. Some of the larger sites that developed during this time were not urban centers, but rather temple complexes with a limited support population (Silverman 1993). Yet on the coast and near Lake Titicaca, a few sites like Chiripa, Huacas de Moche, Pampa Grande, and Cajamarquilla had diverse populations that numbered in the thousands (Chapdelaine 2009; Hastorf 1999; Makowski 2008; Segura Llanos 2001; Shimada 1994; Van Gijseghem 2001). Each of these sites seemed to have been on the cusp of becoming the first great city in Peru at one point or another during this period (Makowski 2008), but that title would be claimed by Huari.

THE CITY OF HUARI

At the very beginning of the Middle Horizon, most people in ancient Peru would have been surprised to learn that a great city was being built in the Ayacucho Valley of the central sierra (Figure 6.2). The large sites that had developed elsewhere were found in areas with preexisting exchange networks that linked them to other trading centers and important resources. In contrast, the people in Ayacucho and the surrounding valleys had long been organized into small groups of herder-farmers whose contact with each other and other regions was limited and sporadic. While thousands were gathering under great platform mounds to worship in other regions of Peru, the people of Ayacucho seemed to have been content for most of the Early Intermediate Period to exchange for the occasional piece of obsidian, farm their fields, and care for their camelid herds.

The first inklings of change in the valley occurred as the Early Intermediate Period wore on. New imports and the creation of a new foreign-influenced ceramic style demonstrate that stronger connections were developing between the people of Ayacucho and other regions, especially the Nasca valley to the south (Knobloch 1976). New religious ideas were also coming into the valley, and these ideas were championed at several sites that competed against each other to woo worshipers with feasts, rituals, performance, and other activities (Isbell 2001b: 111–17; Leoni 2006). One of these competing

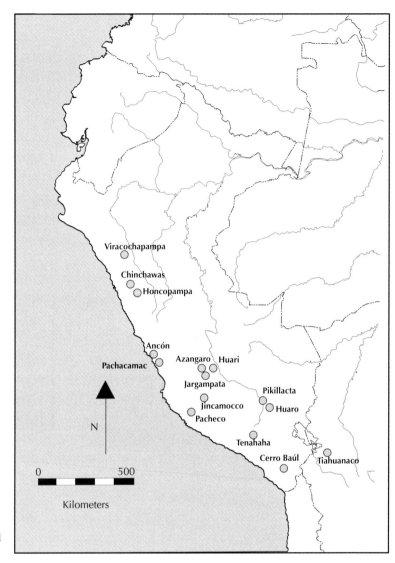

Figure 6.2 Map of Wari world with sites discussed in the text.

sites was Huari. Created when the population of a number of nearby hamlets came together to form a larger site around A.D. 400 (Isbell 1997a: 194), the site quickly rose to prominence around A.D. 550 when people began leaving rival sites and moving to Huari (Isbell 2001b: 117; 2009: 200).

Huari grew rapidly by "virtually inhaling" the surrounding populations (Schreiber 2005: 265), and the people just kept on coming. Although the site remains poorly studied, initial growth in the city appears to have been chaotic. There was little urban planning with immigrants constructing structures willy-nilly on land that they found available. As the city grew, the ritual complexes that initially attracted settlers to the site were being refashioned, and the focal point of the city became a series of monumental ritual and funerary complexes like Cheqo Wasi and Vegachayoq Moqo (Benavides 1991; Bragayrac 1991; Isbell 1988; 2001b: 127–35).

A new religion also emerged that linked cosmological figures to warriors and the elite (Isbell 2001b: 120) through an emphasis on sacrifice, ancestor worship, and trophy head taking (Arnold and Hastorf 2008; Cook 2001; Ochatoma Paravicino and Cabrera Romero 2002; Tung 2008). Although once thought to have been derived largely from the faith espoused at the site of Tiahuanaco in the Lake Titicaca Region (Knobloch 1983), recent research suggests that the religion was cobbled together from a wider variety of traditions (Haeberli 2006; Isbell 2001a; Isbell and Knobloch 2006).

Huari would become the largest prehistoric city ever in Peru in the space of a few generations. At its height in A.D. 700, the site covered almost fifteen square kilometers and housed as many as 70,000 people (Isbell 2001b: 106–7; Isbell et al. 1991: 24). Around this time, the 1.5-square-kilometer core of the city was largely transformed into a series of great rectangular compounds that housed the city's growing elite (Isbell 2009: 209–12; Isbell et al. 1991). The compounds were built in a new architectural style known as orthogonal cellular (Isbell 1991a), which was composed of repetitive modular units of long corridors and central patios. Platforms in these patios were likely used in rituals, and these rituals may have been associated with feasts where large amounts of food and alcohol were consumed (Cook and Glowacki 2003: 184–9; Isbell 2001b: 151). Like other ancient cities (Storey 2006b), there were also areas dedicated to craft production within Huari. Unfortunately, these areas have only been identified by surface collections and remain to be fully excavated (González Carré 1981: 94; Spickard 1983: 153–54; von Hagen and Morris 1998: 130).

THE WARI EXPANSION

Huari's growth from a small village to the largest city in the Andes in less than 150 years created a logistical nightmare (e.g., Hunt 1991). The needs of the city during the first decades of chaotic growth were likely met by a crazy quilt of kin networks, entrepreneurial traders, city residents working the fields, and other means (e.g., Oka and Kusimba 2008). Just as in Uruk and Cahokia, however, these ad hoc arrangements could not last as populations ballooned, and city dwellers increasingly demanded answers to a long list of daunting questions: How do we ensure a constant flow of food into the city? How can economic exchanges be monitored and recorded? How can we fund public works like roads and canals? The dedicated support of rural populations was also needed.

Huari's need for subsistence products was particularly acute because the valleys around the city have limited agricultural productivity because of their high elevation (2,500–3,000 meters above sea level) (Lumbreras 1974: 163, González Carré 1981: 88). To supply the city, the surrounding region was transformed through the construction of terraces, canals, and water storage systems that helped to increase both agricultural yields and camelid flock size (Browman 1999; Isbell 1977; Ochatoma Paravicino and Cabrera Romero 2001a; Raymond 1992; Raymond and Isbell 1969; Valdez and Valdez 1998; Vivanco and Valdez 1993). This area of intensive agricultural and pastoral exploitation may have been considerable. The Sondondo and Chicha-Soras valleys, for example, lie almost 150 kilometers away from the site of Huari, and research in these valleys provides considerable evidence for Middle Horizon economic intensification (Meddens 1991; Schreiber 1992).

The political relationship between these surrounding valleys and the city remains unclear since so little research has been done in this region. There is clear evidence for sweeping changes in some places that seem to have been orchestrated by Huari officials and some Wari iconography celebrates military prowess (Ochatoma Paravicino and Cabrera Romero 2001b: 458). In the Sondondo valley, for example, the Wari-style compound of Jincamocco was built, settlements were relocated to lower elevations, and the entire valley was massively terraced and irrigated (Schreiber 1992). Yet work in other valleys around Ayacucho suggests that Huari control was often indirect, largely ritually based, and heavily mediated by local leaders (Anders 1991: 194; Meddens and Branch i.p.). In aggregate, these data suggest that participation in the Huari sphere, at least during the Early Middle Horizon (approximately A.D. 600–800), seems to have been in part voluntary for many people in the valleys surrounding the city.

Huari control became more formalized in the Late Middle Horizon (approximately A.D. 800–1000) when efforts were made both to politically consolidate the lands surrounding Huari and to increase agricultural production in the area (Schreiber 2001: 89). New

Wari-style centers, like Jargampata and Azángaro, were built, and Jincamocco was expanded from 3.5 to 15 hectares (Anders 1991; Isbell 1977; Schreiber 2001: 90). Although these building projects should be seen as an indication of increasing Huari control over the valleys in the Ayacucho region, these efforts also suggest mounting concerns with regularizing the provisioning of the city.

All of the city's desires, of course, could not be met in the surrounding region. Huari also needed goods from outside of this region in order to meet the escalating demands of traders, elites, craft specialists, and other city dwellers. How Huari officials met this goal gets at the heart of the debate over the nature of the Wari civilization. We know that metals, obsidian, decorated ceramics, textiles, turquoise, and ritually important marine shell (spondylus and strombus) were all moving in and out of the city on the backs of llamas and human porters (Benavides 1999; Cabera Romero 1996: 88–91; González Carré et al. 1996: 100–2; Isbell 1985: 70; Pérez Calderón 1995: 85–6). To explain why this material was flowing in from across Peru (and in some cases beyond the nation's current borders), many archaeologists have argued that goods first came as tribute to regional Wari imperial administrative centers and then were sent off to the city (e.g., Isbell 1987; Isbell and McEwan 1991; Isbell and Schreiber 1978; McEwan 2005a; Schreiber 1992, 1999, 2001).

Over the last sixty years, scholars have identified dozens of sites as possible Wari administrative centers based largely on the presence of Wari-style ceramics and/or similarities with the orthogonal cellular architectural style found at Huari (Jennings and Craig 2001: 483; Schreiber 1999: 82). Many of the reported Wari sites, however, were not occupied by Huari settlers. Some of these sites pre- or postdate the Middle Horizon, whereas others seem to have been local emulations of Wari architectural designs (Jennings 2006b). One of the sites often discussed as a Wari administrative center, for example, was the massive thirty-two-hectare complex of Viracochapampa in the northern highlands, but it was abandoned before it could be completed (Topic 1991: 152). Other proposed Wari administrative sites, like Ichabamba and Pampa de Yamobamba, are known only from air photos or surface collections (Julien 1988: 292; Williams and Pineda 1985: 59). Removing all of the sites without clear evidence for housing Huari settlers leaves us with sites in only three areas outside of Ayacucho.

If Huari established sites in only three areas outside of the Ayacucho region (or even ten areas if some of the small, poorly studied sites turn out to be Wari installations), then one should be hesitant to agree with arguments that suggest that a Wari Empire controlled affairs across Peru. The argument for a Wari Empire becomes even weaker when we investigate the administrative reach of the three unequivocal Wari sites in greater detail.

One of the colonial outposts was established in the Cuzco region in the southern sierra. Huari settlers built a forty-seven-hectare site known as Pikillacta and completely transformed the surrounding Lucre Basin with roads, canals, defensive walls, quarries, and residences (McEwan 1991). Local groups remained in the basin and were integrated into what Gordon McEwan calls the "Greater Pikillacta System" (1991: 101).

The sheer size of Pikillacta's floor plan certainly smacks of imperial intentions, and these intentions are underlined by the hundreds of conjoined rooms with small, raised doorways that were likely designed as storerooms. Yet, the intentions of Pikillacta's architects were never fully realized. Only a fourth of the site was ever used, the majority of the site was under construction at the time of abandonment, and the storerooms ended up largely filled with ash and domestic refuse (McEwan 1996: 181–3; 2005b: 56–7). The site seems to have had little influence in adjoining valleys where only a few Wari ceramics are found (Bélsisle and Covey i.p.). Instead of Pikillacta serving as a testament of Wari imperial strength, these data emphasize how the site actually played a lesser than intended role in the region.

Pikillacta might not have even been the first choice for Huari colonists traveling to the Cuzco region. A second site called Huaro is located just seventeen miles away along a route to the Lake Titicaca Basin. Only recently discovered (Glowacki 2002; Glowacki and McEwan 2001), the site appears to have been a bustling settlement that grew organically to two hundred hectares and combined Wari architectural elements with constructions that were reminiscent of those coming out of Lake Titicaca traditions (Glowacki 2002: 267, 282). Although it has been interpreted as a regional administrative center (Glowacki 2002: 282–3; McEwan 2005d: 163), there is no compelling evidence to suggest that it functioned as such. Instead, the site might be better conceived as a frontier city that owed its prosperity to its close interaction with Tiwanaku settlements (Glowacki 2002: 267).

A second Early Middle Horizon colonial outpost was established in the coastal Nasca region. Huari settlers founded Pacheco, a site with an incredible amount of Wari ceramics, which was dug by Julio C. Tello before his fateful trip to Huari in 1931. While Tello's other digs had found the occasional Wari pot, Pacheco contained a series of adobe chambers filled with more than three tons of beautifully decorated Wari vessels that had been intentionally smashed and deposited in the chambers (Menzel 1964: 24–5). Although there is "extensive architecture, only faintly visible on old air photographs," that suggests that the site was large (Schreiber 2001: 88), the site was completely destroyed before other areas of Pacheco could be excavated.

The Huari colonial outpost was not particularly welcomed by the Nasca people. Most fled the land around Pacheco, and the only sites that remained were small villages perched in defensive locations (Conlee and Schreiber 2006: 100). Pacheco was abandoned before the beginning of the Late Middle Horizon, and Huari settlers appear to have left the lower portions of the Nasca drainage at that time (Schreiber 2001: 90). The only known Huari settlement in the valley during the Late Middle Horizon was the tiny (0.2-hectare) site of Pataraya located in upper reaches of the drainage (Schreiber 1999: 169) (a second small Wari settlement has recently been reported at a similar elevation but has not yet been published). Pataraya, perhaps built for the production of coca, is a poor candidate for an imperial administrative center. As in Cuzco, Huari seemed to have entered Nasca with imperial ambitions that were ultimately never met. By the Late Middle Horizon, the city's presence in Nasca was relegated to a small enclave(s) on the upper fringes of the drainage.

The most successful Huari colonial outpost was probably Cerro Baúl and its associated sites in the upper Moquegua Valley on the far south coast of Peru. Huari settlers founded sites on top of the massif of Cerro Baúl and on the nearby hills of Cerro Mejía and Cerro Petroglifo. Instead of building these sites as one great enclosure like Pikillacta and Viracochapampa, they instead constructed various compounds that held domestic, administrative, and ritual buildings. The upper valley was arid, and there were very few people living in this part of the valley at the time of Huari colonization (Williams 2002: 365). To sustain the colonial outpost, settlers built extensive agricultural terracing and established a large-scale irrigation system (Moseley et al. 2005; Nash 2002; Williams 1997, 2001). Through these enormous investments of labor, the sites were initially able to prosper.

By the Late Middle Horizon, however, Cerro Mejia was abandoned and Cerro Baúl was extensively remodeled with the construction of large plazas, more storage spaces, and two D-shaped temples (Williams 2001: 79). In general, the shifts in architecture seem to reflect a concern for bringing local elites into the political process (Nash and Williams 2005: 167). There are some indications that the site was becoming isolated from Huari – the colonial outpost seems to have lost its connections with obsidian coming out of Ayacucho, and the people living at Cerro Baúl were increasingly interacting with the Tiwanaku colonists who were moving into the valley (Nash and Williams 2005: 167–9). In short, the colonists of Cerro Baúl overhauled their political economy when they found that they were largely fending for themselves by the Late Middle Horizon.

Without the ample amounts of fertile lands that were available to the people of Cahokia and Uruk, it is likely that Huari was even more compelled than these other cities to push outward to sustain the city in an initial burst of interaction that sent priests, warriors, traders, and colonists out across much of Peru. Wari art is replete with images of warriors, and I suspect that warfare was a more important aspect of expansion than in our other two case studies. The millions of hours needed to build the massive compounds of Pikillacta and Viracochapamapa on opposite sides of the country are a testament to the city's ability to harness outside laborers (McEwan 2005c: 71–83).

Huari's dream of empire, however, failed to materialize. Conquest was not followed by consolidation, and the colonies that were initially designed to extract resources from the surrounding region were unable to do so beyond their immediate environs. The people living in Huari's few colonial outposts found themselves increasingly isolated from the city as the period wore on. Those colonial outposts that thrived, like Huaro and Cerro Baúl, did so by adjusting to this new reality and interacting more closely with their neighbors.

Yet without an empire, llama caravans laden with goods from throughout the central Andes still traveled to and from Huari. Huari colonial outposts still played important regional roles, and people still traveled widely. In fact, the interregional movement of goods, people, and ideas increased dramatically during the Middle Horizon (e.g., Burger et al. 2000; Lechtman 1980; Shady Solís 1982,

1988). Arsenic bronze, for example, was introduced and produced extensively across the country; flexed burial became more common; and the Quechua and Aymara languages likely became more widely spoken (Heggarty 2008; Lechtman 2003, 2005). These changes were associated with the widespread diffusion of Wari religious iconography, an architectural cannon, and a material culture package that included striped tunics, tall drinking cups, four-corner hats, and metal shawl pins (Isbell 2008: 738–9). Many people across Peru shared new ways of thinking about things like farming, metallurgy, and religion that were derived at least in part from activities in and around the city.

WARI GLOBAL CULTURE

Without empire, how can we explain the period's sweeping cultural changes that are associated with the spread of Wari artifacts and colonial outposts? The answer, I hope by now, is obvious. The urbanization of Huari caused a surge in interaction as city dwellers scrambled to meet burgeoning demands for food, raw materials, and prestige goods. The city seems to have foisted itself into the consciousness of many through its militancy and trading contacts, but Huari's greatest impact on the Andes was likely the religious beliefs that first came together in the city. The urban–rural flows created by the city caused a cascade of reactions by outside groups that would ultimately result in the creation of a global culture. People embraced some ideas, rejected others, and transformed still others to meet their own particular needs. Even while people were ignoring or avoiding the Huari and its colonial outposts, their understandings of the world were still undergoing fundamental change. As was the case in earlier chapters, the best way to document this global culture is to do so at the local level.

To begin our survey of the spread of Wari global culture, let us return to the Cuzco region of southern Peru. Site surveys in the Cuzco region show that the Middle Horizon was a period of great change throughout the region as population expanded, social stratification increased, and interregional exchange intensified (Bauer 2004; Bélisle and Covey i.p.). These changes were occurring as Huari settlers were settling at Pikillacta and Huaro (Glowacki 2002; McEwan 2005a); thus, it is usually assumed that these changes were associated with the imperial annexation of the region (e.g., McEwan

2005d: 162–4). Yet aside from Pikillacta and Huaro, there are no other confirmed Huari colonial outposts in the region and Wari-style or Wari-influenced ceramics are rare except in these two sites (Bélisle and Covey i.p.). Instead of Wari imperial dominance, the Huari colonial outposts seem to have been just one of many players in the region. Some local people interacted with the site, but most of the long-distance connections forged during the era were between non-Huari groups (Bélisle and Covey i.p.).

The local ambivalence toward the Huari settlements is demonstrated by excavations at Ak'awillay, an important local site located some fifty kilometers from Pikillacta. The site is surrounding by arable land and sits along what would have been a presumed trading route between Pikillacta and Huari. If a Wari polity sought to extend its control over other areas in Cuzco, then the lands around Ak'awillay would have been a good choice. Yet, there are few Wari sherds at the site, and excavations reveal that lifeways were largely unaffected by Wari. How people built their houses, cooked their food, and buried their dead did not significantly change in the period. This is *not* to suggest that Ak'awillay was isolated. The people of Ak'awillay were actively copying the ceramics of neighboring valleys during the Middle Horizon, and the presence of exotic goods, like obsidian and marine shells, suggest that they were developing longer distance contacts as well. They just seem to have ignored the Huari colonial outposts and focused their energies elsewhere (Bélisle and Covey i.p.).

There is, however, some Wari influence at Ak'awillay, and where this occurs is illuminating. Low frequencies of a regional ceramic style that was Wari-influenced were found in various contexts throughout the site. Although this suggests limited Wari influence in comparison to the higher frequencies of other regional styles, it also suggests that the people of Ak'awillay had knowledge of Wari styles and emulated them on occasion. More importantly, the few true Wari-style ceramics found at the site were associated with a large public building that was likely used for feasting and ceremonies. Most of the obsidian, the finest examples of ceramics in all styles, and most of the War-influenced sherds were also found in the building (Bélisle and Covey i.p.). This suggests that a degree of social and ritual importance was connected to the *Wari style*, even if the people of Ak'awillay (and the Cuzco region in general) were not interested in close associations with *Huari settlements*.

The changes that occurred during the Middle Horizon were even more dramatic in the sierra valley where I have done most of my fieldwork. During the Early Intermediate Period and first half of the Middle Horizon, the Cotahuasi Valley's population was settled in small, scattered villages (Jennings 2002). Although they had regular contact with outside groups – the local obsidian was traded widely before the Middle Horizon, and a few pots were imported – the people of the valley were content to make vessels in the same ways that they had for two thousand years (Jennings 2006a: 353). This pattern changed in the Late Middle Horizon when population in the valley significantly increased, agricultural production expanded, interregional exchange intensified, and social stratification began to emerge (Jennings 2002, 2006a).

All these changes came in the midst of a complete change in form, decoration, and manufacturing technique of local ceramics (Jennings 2002, 2006a, i.p.). Over the space of a few generations, Cotahuasi culture opened up to the outside world, and Wari was by far the strongest outside influence on Cotahuasi ceramics and other material culture. In short, by the second half of the Middle Horizon, many of the pots from the valley looked Wari, as did many of the metals and textiles. These changes were undoubtedly exciting for Cotahuasinos, but they would have been occurring during a time of considerable conflict as people negotiated changing relationships with each other, other villages, and the outside world.

When I initially began my research in Cotahuasi, I thought that the valley had been integrated into the Wari Empire (Jennings and Craig 2001: 487). Yet, almost all of the Wari goods in the valley were either locally made or imported from the surrounding region. There is no evidence for a Wari administrative center, and the sociopolitical changes that occurred seem to have been a reaction to new exchange possibilities and the introduction of new ideas and products (Jennings 2006a, i.p.). Without a valley-wide political hierarchy, Cotahuasinos came together at the ritual site of Tenahaha to eat, dance, and bury their dead in ceremonies where the Wari style and its associated ideas played a pivotal role (Jennings i.p.). Wari seems to have formed a kind of social glue that helped the people of the valley to understand their changing world and to relate to people in other valleys with whom they were coming into increasing contact.

The Central Coast was already changing dramatically hundreds of years before the spread of Wari global culture. During the

Early Intermediate Period, the population of the region increased, agriculture intensified, and social stratification became more marked. By the end of the period, large sites like Maranga, Pachacamac, and Cajamarquilla were likely powerful political centers that exercised control over the region and were beginning to control the trade routes leading up into the sierra (Kaulicke 2001; Marcone i.p.; Segura 2001; Seguara and Shimada i.p.). These centers continued to flourish during the Early Middle Horizon when their interregional connections significantly increased. Wari art styles were introduced at this time, as well as a local Wari-influenced style called Nieveria. Unlike in Cuzco and Cotahuasi, the use of Wari objects and Wari-related symbols was confined to elites who appear to have used Wari artifacts for their foreign cachet in order to reinforce their social positions vis-à-vis local non-elites (Marcone i.p.).

Earlier models of imperial rule of the Central Coast posited that a series of Wari administrative installations were founded in the region in order to placate a population clustered in urban centers. Yet we now know that the major political centers of the Central Coast were largely abandoned during the Late Middle Horizon and that the various candidates for Huari settler sites in the region have been disproved by more recent excavations (Segura 2001; Segura and Shimada i.p.; Valkenier 1995). The last possible site, Socos (Isla and Guerrero 1987), is known largely through surface remains, and its identification as a Wari administrative center is being increasingly challenged (Jennings 2006b; Marcone i.p.; Silva 1992). The Late Middle Horizon collapse was not the result of a Wari military incursion into the region. Instead, the population seems to have dispersed as local elites lost their legitimacy in the face of mounting environmental disturbances (Marcone i.p., Segura and Shimada i.p.; Shimada et al. 1991).

There was, however, increasing Wari influence on mortuary customs as the Middle Horizon wore on. Wari influence during the Late Middle Horizon on the Central Coast can perhaps be seen best from Ancón, a site containing spectacular burials that was first excavated by a pair of geologists in 1875 (Reiss and Stübel 1880–1887). The list of people who have dug at the site reads looks like a who's who of Peruvian archaeology, but unfortunately much of the work at the site remains poorly documented (Kaulicke 1997: 14–16; Slovak 2007: 42–9). Nonetheless, it is clear from what has been reported that mortuary traditions changed during the Middle Horizon. In the previous tradition, single individuals tended to be buried in extended position within shallow rectangular pits with little to no grave goods (Kaulicke 1997: 103). This tradition was largely replaced in the Late Middle Horizon by collective burials of people buried in a seated position with their knees drawn up to their chest and their hands placed on either side of their face. These burials were often accompanied by Wari or Wari-influenced artifacts.

Yet the changes that were occurring at Ancón were not limited to Wari influence. Many of the burials were wrapped with textiles and topped with a false head – a burial custom that may have been imported from the Nasca region – and there were also stylistic influences from North Coast cultures (Kaulicke 1997: 103). The variety of influences at Ancón might be also a reflection of increasing migration during the period. Nicole Slovak's isotopic research on thirty-five Middle Horizon individuals reveals that as many as four of these individuals may have lived significant portions of their lives elsewhere (Slovak 2007: 174). One of these migrants, a young woman who was 15–19 years old when she died, may have been from around Huari (Slovak et al. 2009: 163). Yet the other possible migrants, just like many of the artifacts, did not just come from the Ayacucho region. Ancón's stylistic pastiche was created by the wide variety of people, goods, and ideas that were passing through the Central Coast from Huari and elsewhere.

A final example of the impact of the spread of Wari global culture comes from the Callejón de Huaylas, a valley in the northern highlands. The people of the valley during the Early Intermediate Period were organized into a series of small competing polities that were linked by a shared Recuay tradition of distinctive kaolinite pottery, stone sculpture, and megalithic tombs (Isbell 1997a: 195–205; Lau 2006: 150–1; Ponte 2001: 222–8). Recuay groups were able to obtain exotic pots, obsidian, and other material from neighboring valleys in northern Peru; however, they seemed largely uninterested in these outside influences and maintained their "Recuayness" for more than five centuries (Lau 2006: 163).

Life in the valley changed considerably during the Middle Horizon when long-standing cultural boundaries became permeable. There was a surge in foreign influence, and the acquisition of long-distance goods reached unprecedented levels (Lau 2006: 162). Goods and influence came from Huari, but also from across much of northern and central Peru (Lau 2006: 162; Paredes et al. 2001: 286;

Ponte 2001: 229). Most aspects of mortuary traditions continued unchanged, but new types of tombs that mixed local and Wari influence were introduced (Ponte 2001: 245).

Recuay's changing relationship with the outside world during the Middle Horizon has been studied by George Lau at the village of Chinchawas (2005). In the Early Middle Horizon, the number of imported ceramics coming into the site increased more than a hundred-fold (from 2 imported sherds to 206 in his sample [Lau 2005: Table 1]), and the frequency of obsidian at the site "peaked sharply" (Lau 2005: 90). The pots came from across central and southern Peru, but Wari imports were becoming increasingly popular (they would make up 8.9% of the imported total between A.D. 700 and 850) and Wari influence was also seen on local ceramic styles (Lau 2005: 86). Lau suggests that the people of Chinchawas were intensifying local camelid production in order to acquire Wari pots and other exotic material as prestige goods (2005: 94).

Interregional interaction continued to increase in the Late Middle Horizon as more pottery from more places was coming into the site. Interestingly, increased interaction did not translate into increased desire for Wari objects. While villagers still desired Wari styles from the central highlands, they seem to have shifted their attention to the North and Central Coast where they now received 44.6% of their imports (Lau 2005: 89, Table 1).

Many of the Wari goods that were flowing into the Callejón de Huaylas may have been funneled through the site of Honcopampa. Occupied throughout the Middle Horizon, the site sits adjacent to an important pass leading into the valley (Isbell 1991a: 310; 1991b: 34). The architecture at the site includes D-shaped temples, patio groups, and other aspects of Wari orthogonal cellular architecture. Although the researcher of the site originally suggested that Honcopampa was an intrusive Wari imperial center (Isbell 1989, 1991b), he now suggests that the site was built by people from the valley because of the prevalence of megalithic door lintels and other local features (Isbell i.p.). The site likely served as a gateway community that controlled access to some of the exotic material coming into the Callejón from the central highlands (Jennings and Craig 2001: 494; Schreiber 2001: 91). The emulation of Wari architecture suggests that the residents of Honcopampa had perhaps a privileged knowledge of Wari cannons and the desire to affiliate closely with Wari ideas, but it is doubtful that the site was a Huari-controlled installation.

The unfolding of Wari global culture played out in a similar manner throughout the rest of Peru (e.g., Castillo 2001; Chapdelaine i.p.; Nelson et al. i.p.; Sciscento 1989; Shady Solís 1988). The Middle Horizon was a period of increasing interregional interaction, and Huari was often the most important player in these interactions. Wari, however, was *not* synonymous with the city of Huari. The roots of the civilization can be traced to the initial spread of people, products, and ideas out of Huari in the beginning of the Middle Horizon, but Wari global culture itself was the product of dynamic interaction between people in different regions. Some aspects of Huari's orthogonal cellular architecture style, for example, comes from the building traditions of the northern sierra (Topic 1991: 162), and Huari religion was a bricolage of important, long-standing ideas from throughout southern Peru and northern Bolivia (Isbell and Knobloch 2006). Wari global culture, therefore, emerged through interregional interaction and continued to change over time based on those interactions.

Wari global culture was different from place to place. Some people received Huari imports, others were influenced by Wari ideas, and still others seem to have been unaffected by the Wari phenomenon. "Wari" as a cultural concept was fractured across regions, villages, and perhaps even families. It is clear that most people in Peru knew about Wari and chose to engage with the Wari ideas and material culture. Those who did not were either too isolated to take advantage of new networks, chose to embrace other ideas that were in circulation, or intentionally turned to local traditions in a reaction to foreign ideas.

Even those locations without an apparent Wari footprint benefited in some way by the flows of goods, ideas, and people that were moving around at that time. Terraced agriculture was introduced into many parts of the sierra, for example, and new varieties of crops were introduced in different regions (e.g., Kellner and Schoeninger 2008: 239; Valdez 2000: 23; Williams 2002: 364, 368). The quipu, an accounting device made out of knotted strings, became more common in the Middle Horizon as well. These innovations, although probably not invented in Huari or necessarily considered "Wari" technologies, were spread thanks to the interactions spurred by the city.

Wari global culture paradoxically peaked in intensity in the later half of the Middle Horizon when there were indications that the officials at Huari were beginning to disengage with outlying regions.

Huari colonial outposts were by then increasingly isolated from Huari and interacting more and more with regional economies in order to survive. Subsistence concerns in the city had meanwhile led to a push to politically and economically integrate the valleys surrounding Huari in order to ensure that these products reached the city. As in our previous case studies, Huari was a victim of its own success. Peripheral regions that had initially depended on the city for imports, for example, were now also obtaining exotic goods from other groups. More exotic ideas were also coming to them from different places, and new people were coming up the road. Huari's growth had spurred the creation of a complex, dense network of interactions across the central Andes, but it was a network over which the people of Huari had little control.

Huari began a century-long decline around A.D. 900. This decline seems to have spurred efforts by city officials to revitalize Huari by recreating its core area for a third time. Many buildings in the monumental core of the city were abandoned, dismantled, and covered over with a layer of sand. A huge pile of building stones was then brought into the area and used as a raised causeway for workers constructing new compounds. The new compounds did not follow the orthogonal cellular design that was used during the city's second rebuilding but, instead, were made up of larger, trapezoidal buildings. The architectural revitalization project was never finished. Huari, along with most of the other major population centers in the Ayacucho Basin, was abandoned by around A.D. 1000 (Isbell 1997a: 208–9; 2001b: 160–2; 2009: 215; but see Finucane et al. 2007).

Huari's collapse had widespread implications. The decline of the city was contemporaneous, for instance, with the widespread abandonment of sites in the Nasca drainage (Conlee i.p.) and the rise of the powerful ritual center of Sicán on the far North Coast of Peru (Shimada 2000: 51–61). Yet, in many ways Wari global culture outlasted Huari itself. Some Wari centers, like Pikillacta (Glowacki 2005: 117) and Cerro Baúl (Williams and Nash 2002: 257), were occupied until around A.D. 1100, and Wari stylistic influence also remained strong in some areas in the decades following the abandonment of Huari (Jennings i.p.; Lau 2005). This seeming cultural unity masked deeper economic and political fragmentations that were occurring in the wake of the collapsing Huari-centered networks. Unable to sustain the broader interaction of the Middle Horizon without Huari involvement, most people in the Late Intermediate Period

(A.D. 1000–1470) focused instead on building up smaller regional exchange relationships (Conlee et al. 2004).

RECONCEPTUALIZING THE MIDDLE HORIZON

Scholars have struggled with the Wari phenomenon ever since the first scientific excavations in Peru at the end of the nineteenth century. To explain the existence of Wari material at site after site, archaeologists have thrown out many descriptors calling Wari a "state," "cult," "culture," "empire," "tradition," and "civilization." With the exception of "empire," the reason for choosing one descriptor over another has remained largely unexplained. Over the last fifty years, there has been a concerted effort to demonstrate the existence of a Wari Empire, and scholars have amassed a considerable amount of data to support their argument.

A closer examination of these data, however, suggests that the spread of Wari artifacts, architecture, and ideas is poorly explained through an imperial model. The story of Wari that emerges from the current data is *not* a story of empire but rather the story of the unintended consequences of a city struggling to survive. There were only a handful of isolated Huari colonial outposts outside of Ayacucho, and the city does not seem to have exercised significant control in other peripheral areas. Understanding Wari in terms of the early globalization model outlined in Chapter 3 is perhaps a better way of understanding the Wari phenomenon.

For food, for raw materials, for booty, and likely for the glory of god, Huari soldiers, traders, priests, and colonists fanned out across large parts of Peru soon after the city developed. The construction of sites of like Pikillacta, Viracochapampa, and Cerro Baúl hints at imperial ambitions at some point early in the Middle Horizon, but this dream quickly faded in the face of the logistical challenges of the Andes' unforgiving geography (e.g., Stein 1999: 62–4). Yet, the failed empire managed both to spread the tenets of Wari religion throughout the central Andes and create new trading connections between Huari and distant locations.

These interactions spurred new interactions between other groups as people took advantage of the burgeoning interregional relationships to do such things as find marriage partners, gain prestige, obtain new kinds of seeds, and find markets for their local products. Wari ideas became the dominant cultural capital of the era – a social glue that helped many people from disparate groups relate to each other, but it was far from the only game in town. This swirl of ideas, products, and people led to greater homogeneity and heterogeneity (another vegetable stew). Embraced, modified, and even reviled, Wari global culture spread far beyond the limits of Huari control, was transformed in new settings, and lasted a century or more after the demise of the city.

7

But Were They Really Global Cultures?

The existence of the widespread interactions described over the last few chapters will not come as a surprise to most readers. I remember as a boy curling up on the sofa to read about Genghis Khan's army sweeping across Eurasia, and I was fascinated with Hannibal's elephants, Hadrian's Wall, and the depictions of foreign diplomats laying gifts at Pharaoh's feet. We have learned since grade school about some of these earlier long-distance connections, and we know that these connections occasionally caused widespread cultural change. But I never read about ancient Egypt to learn more about my own world – I read to escape it (fighting evil forces on my way to Osiris was more fun than weeding the driveway). One of the great pleasures of reading about the past will always be in exploring different ways of life. Yet by treating the past as a qualitatively different world, we reify the Great Wall separating antiquity and modernity and diminish our ability to find patterns that connect the present to earlier eras.

For most scholars and general readers, ancient interactions are at best prologues to modern globalization – the expansion of Islam or the Inca Empire is seen as foreshadowing the radical changes that subsequently gripped the world. This book argues, however, that there were earlier periods of intense interactions that should be considered globalization eras in their own right. How do we determine if past globalizations occurred? As I argued earlier in this book, we just need to decide if an era meets the definitional criteria for globalization. Globalization for many scholars can be defined as (a) a surge in long-distance connections that (b) creates a global culture. If an earlier period meets these two criteria, then these eras should be considered as periods of globalization.

The idea that Uruk, Mississippian, and Wari expansion caused surges in interaction is hopefully easy for you to accept after reading the last three chapters. One might question the details of my descriptions, but the people described in these case studies would likely fit easily alongside the other early traders, preachers, adventurers, and warriors that many of us envision as crisscrossing parts of the world prior to modern globalization (e.g., Chanda 2007). You might still hesitate, however, before using the word "globalization" to describe these earlier eras since a surge in long-distance interactions in and of itself is not the same as globalization. Our definition of globalization also requires that a global culture is created through these relationships. Many changes occurred because of the Uruk, Mississippian, and Wari expansions, but were global cultures *really* created?

Those who study modern globalization argue vociferously about how to characterize the global culture that has emerged as a result of increasing long-distance interaction. Jargon abounds, and, as in most debates, people spend a good portion of their time talking past each other. Nonetheless, one can find at least eight general trends that scholars broadly recognize as indicative of today's global culture. Briefly introduced in Chapter 2, these trends are the *hallmarks* of globalization and thus the means through which we can determine if globalizations have previously occurred. We have to adjust our eyes to earlier eras – there were no Starbucks or supercomputers a thousand years ago – but I argue that all of these trends can be found in our three case studies. In the pages that follow, I discuss the eight closely related hallmarks of globalization, provide examples of these hallmarks in our world today, and then explain how they also occurred as a consequence of the Uruk, Mississippian, and Wari expansions. If all of these hallmarks are found in the past, then the answer to last paragraph's question is yes: there *really* were ancient global cultures.

Global cultures are complex, overlapping, dynamic, and often contradictory. Surging interregional interactions force people to adjust to new realities, and these adjustments are often radically different from one person to the next. Two of the hallmarks of globalization, for example, are increasing homogeneity *and* heterogeneity. Although seemingly mutually exclusive, both trends occur as groups decide to embrace, reject, or transform new ideas and products. The eight hallmarks of global cultures should all be widely discernable during a period of globalization, but this does not mean that each hallmark will be pervasive in all areas. We should expect that past global cultures were as inherently fractured, messy, and contingent as the one we live in today.

THE EIGHT HALLMARKS OF GLOBAL CULTURE

Hallmark 1 – time–space compression

The first general trend in globalization, *time–space compression*, refers to how the speeding up of economic and social processes shrinks one's experience of space and time. Coined by David Harvey (1989), the idea is that the political, economic, and technological changes that occur with globalization created a situation where, "the certainty of absolute space and place gave way to the insecurities of a shifting relative space, in which events in one place could have immediate and ramifying effects in several other places" (261). Since this feature of globalization creates the impression of a smaller world, time–space compression often leads to cultural strains as people redefine their relationships with other groups.

One example of this feature can be found in Rampura, the isolated south Indian village that we discussed in Chapter 2. In 1948, the village had few long-distance connections because interregional roads were in a "wretched state" (Srinivas 1976: 236). Streets were often impassable during the rainy season, and most people traveled in open carts drawn by bullocks. In the 1950s, roads improved dramatically, and bigger, newer buses began to bring villagers into more frequent contact with cities. Time and space were compressed relative to the past experiences of these villagers – they found themselves closer to the rest of the world with each of these changes. The divide between "local" and "outside" events became more and more blurred as the personal ramifications of something happening many kilometers away sometimes became more important than what was happening at a neighbor's house.

The Internet provides perhaps the most vivid example of time–space compression. When I first went to Peru's Cotahuasi Valley in 1997 to begin archaeological fieldwork, there was no Internet and no regular mail service; most people interacted with friends and family outside the valley through packages delivered via the bus lines and the occasional rushed call on one of the few expensive public phones. The introduction of the Internet to the valley in 1999 by a development agency did little to change the valley's isolation. The agency's two computers were connected via an excruciatingly slow modem – it took me ten minutes to send a sentence-long e-mail, and the phone line would short out whenever it rained. Six years later, however, there were three Internet kiosks in the major village. Each was reasonably fast (even by my standards) and was often full of people from the village writing e-mails, chatting electronically with friends, playing videogames, or just surfing the Web. Cotahuasi's extensive social networks, stretching from the valley to all parts of Peru and into many cities in the United States and Europe, seemed to contract in those six years because the scope and speed of Internet interactions made everyone seem closer together.

Nothing in the ancient world, of course, comes close to the Internet's ability to compress time and space. Yet there were processes afoot during the Uruk, Mississippian, and Wari expansions that led to significant time–space compression. One of the clearest examples comes from the introduction of the donkey in Mesopotamia during the fourth millennium B.C. The donkey opened up new possibilities of interregional exchange because these "beasts of burden enabled families with their goods, craft workers with their tools, and traders with their wares to move throughout Southwest Asia much more easily than before" (Wright 2001: 127). Donkeys, when combined with the continued improvement of watercraft and canal infrastructure, made it possible for people to travel across longer distances while carrying more goods during the Uruk Period (Algaze 2008: 141–2). As silly as this might sound, asses were an essential part of the worldwide web of ancient Mesopotamia in the sense that these beasts of burden helped to create the impression of a shrinking world.

The Mississippian and Wari expansions would have resulted in similar feelings for people in the Americas. Regular movement over longer distances leads to faster, more reliable connections when routes become more familiar, trails are improved, technologies tweaked, and the people along the way get used to seeing unfamiliar faces. The Wari expansion, for example, may have led to the creation of an extensive road network that greatly facilitated the movement of goods through the harsh Andean landscape (Schreiber 1991). Although travel times and efficiencies almost certainly decreased in all three case studies, the greatest time–space compression would have been psychological. Whether it was seeing a llama caravan coming down the trail, watching a trio of canoes glide by on the Mississippi, or becoming familiar with a wider variety of cylinder seal impressions, a farmer would have felt closer to the outside world and part of new relations that stretched off past the horizon. Just as in today's world, perceived distance from one place to another would have shrunk in the ancient world when one regularly shared ideas, exchanged goods, and sometimes even married outsiders.

Hallmark 2 – deterritorialization

The second general trend seen after the creation of a global culture is *deterritorialization*, a process related to time–space compression through which culture becomes increasingly abstracted from a local, geographically fixed, context (Appadurai 1990; Giddens 1990). Globalization causes deterritorialization because the flow of goods, finances, ideas, and people through localities results in cultures infused with a wide variety of foreign influences. Although deterritorialization does not lead to a complete unmooring of culture from local affairs (Inda and Rosaldo 2008: 14), the ties to a single location are weakened as a result of the myriad of long-distance interactions that connect that place to other regions. Much of what makes Paris, *Paris*, today, for example, has nothing to do with its location along the Seine River. Instead, Paris is known at least in part as an international center of fashion, culture, and cuisine with connections to places like New York, Tokyo, and Milan that are in many cases stronger than those the city has with the French countryside.

Changes that occurred in Rampura offer another example of deterritorialization. The sporadic use of bulldozers and tractors for farming in the village during the 1950s led to new concerns about the price of gasoline and the availability of spare parts. In the 1960s, youths coming back from college brought back transistors radios that delivered news broadcasts and new types of music to the village (Srinivas 1976: 238). Through these and other flows, the local became more global in the sense that socialization was stretched across many regions (e.g., Tomlinson 1999: 107). Not only did people have access to a wider range of products and ideas, but they increasingly had closer social relationships with people in distant regions (e.g., Giddens 1990: 18). A Rampura villager today might have a friendly relationship with a mechanic in the city and have grown up listening to the nightly opinion program of a journalist that they have neither met nor even seen. The mechanic, journalist, and villager all play a part in Rampura's culture.

Deterritorialization does not only occur through the stretching of social networks. It also occurs when foreign people, products, and ideas are incorporated into a place. Regardless of why the changes occur, introductions into the local setting are incorporated into one's life simply through daily, often unconscious, practices (Bourdieu 1977). The global became local as new products, ideas, and people began to feel more natural rather than unusual within the local environment. One of my favorite restaurants in Toronto is the Boulevard Café. When the Peruvian restaurant opened its door more than twenty years ago, it was one of the first ethnic restaurants in the area. The owner at the time was afraid that no one would come to eat at a place that did not offer Canadian food. Today the Boulevard Café is one of dozens of restaurants on its street that offers food from around the world. Toronto is now one of the most ethnically diverse cities in the world and the boundary between "local" and "global" in the city has blurred so much that restaurants advertising Canadian food are rarer than those offering Thai, Vietnamese, and Polish fare.

The clearest examples of deterritorialization during the Uruk, Mississippian, and Wari expansions might be found in the variation in pottery assemblages (e.g., Blackman 2003; Montoyo et al. 2001; Steponaitis et al. 1996). In my fieldwork in Cotahuasi, we conducted neutron activation analysis and thin section analysis on more than 100 ceramic Middle Horizon fragments to trace the source of the clay used to make the pots. None of the Wari-style pots came from the city of Huari. Instead, almost all of our Wari pots were made in the valley by local potters who created either very Wari-looking pots (i.e., almost identical to ceramics produced in and around Huari), Warish pots that blended a number of styles, or local Middle Horizon style pots. All of these styles are found mixed together in our excavations, and it is likely that they were used regularly by a wide spectrum of Cotahuasi society. Over the years, the customary use of these pots by villagers would have blurred the distinctions between the "global" and the "local" as these various styles were used in daily activities.

Deterritorialization can also be seen in the shift in burial practices that occurred in all three case studies. In contrast to both earlier and later periods, most people during the Middle and Late Uruk periods were disposed of in a way that left no trace in the archaeological record (Charvát 2002: 152). Status differences appeared for the first time in Mississippian era burials, and many groups switched from extended to flexed burial in Middle Horizon Peru (Isbell 1997b; Trubitt 2000). Although these changes were often a sharp break from local funerary traditions, evidence suggests that descent groups remained very important in all three civilizations. Local connections that had been important would have therefore remained important (who your aunt or father was still mattered), but changes in how the dead were treated also sent a clear signal of the livings' changing relationship to broader social currents (you bury your dead in a way that is similar to how burials are done elsewhere because of shared beliefs). Once again, the division between "local" and "global" blurred.

Hallmark 3 – standardization

The third hallmark of global cultures is *standardization*. When globalization occurs, people become enmeshed in new relationships that cross geographic and cultural boundaries. If ways of looking at the world are too alien to each other, then the parties can only view each other from the vantage point of their own particular standards. A common idiom is therefore needed in order to facilitate interaction and make each group's action comprehensible to the other (e.g., Anderson 1991; Wilk 1995). Some of the more obvious examples of standardization today are the adoption of universal or near universal standards, such as Greenwich Standard Time, English as a language for business, and the metric system for measurement. Standardization, however, is often a more subtle process that is perhaps best captured by Richard Wilk's concept of systems of "common difference" (1995).

Wilk uses the example of beauty and beauty pageants to illustrate how a system of common difference works. There is no cross-culturally held definition of beauty – it can be a "spiritual concept, not a visual one, or it may be a quality of old age and experience rather than youth, or of fierceness and power" (Wilk 2004: 91). Choosing a winner of the Miss World (let alone the rather expansively named Miss Universe pageant) should therefore be impossible since there would be no common ground that international judges could agree upon. Yet winners are chosen each year because the contestants, judges, and viewers have informally worked out a shared concept of beauty. This does not mean that people share the exact same ideas about the best body proportions and facial features, but it does mean that everyone must agree that a broad set of physical attributes and skills are "beautiful." Although there is no overtly expressed international standard of beauty, contests like the Miss World pageant have helped create an idea of beauty that is now commonly accepted by many groups around the globe. This idea of what beauty is anchors a system of common difference.

An even more subtle example of standardization can be seen in the changes that have occurred over the last fifty years in the Brazilian fishing village of Arembepe (Kottak 2006). The village was relatively isolated from the rest of Brazil in 1962 when the anthropologist Conrad Phillip Kottak began working there. By the 1980s, the village had become a popular tourist destination connected to the growing city of Salvadore by a paved road. The tourists brought with them the idea of a weekend, and this schedule was supported by programming on the first radios and televisions that came into the village during this period. The weekend became the major organizing trope of Arembepe life as the five-day work week replaced the lunar cycle followed by fishermen. Villagers adopted the weekend pattern favored by tourists of drinking beers while looking out on the beach. Those who reacted against drinking usually did not also reject the idea of a weekend and its other associated leisure activities. The weekend itself had become a standardized part of the week that was naturalized within the community over the space of a single generation.

Groups do not have an equal say in how standardization unfolds. The voice of the Filipinos are not as loud as the Americans in defining beauty, for example, and to win the Miss World contest Miss Philippines needs to engage on terms (and sometimes turf) that are tilted more toward American ideals. The weekend is also a product of unions and industrialization that does not jibe well with the rhythms of agricultural communities. Standardization, therefore, can often be quite disruptive when it is introduced since a new practice in one aspect of society often necessitates changes in many other areas.

One example of standardization from our case studies is the adoption of wall trenching in the Mississippian world. The pre-Mississippian method of wall construction was to dig each posthole individually, but in wall trenching an entire wall was prefabricated, placed into a trench, and then raised up into place (Pauketat 2004b: 80). This seemingly innocuous transformation had considerable implications when one realizes that setting posts and building homes were "important coordinated practices that involved familial and communal groups" (Pauketat and Alt 2005: 223). Changing how a wall was built changed how many people were needed to construct a house and when those people were needed in the process. Just as an Amish barn raising is much different than a father and son digging holes in the yard, the Mississippian way of building homes required new ways of coordinating labor.

As villages across the American mid-continent were brought into the expanding networks of the Mississippian era, they were confronted with this new, expedient manner of building homes. Many embraced the idea, but others were hesitant about altering long-held building practices (Alt 2001). Those who finally accepted wall trenching would have also tacitly accepted a changed social structure that fit more closely with Mississippian norms. A wall-trenched house became the standard way of building houses in many communities, even if the homes were built by those who rejected some of the more ostentatious elements of Mississippian civilization.

Standardization can also be seen in our other two case studies. Recent linguistic studies suggest that the Quechua and Aymara were related languages from the central highlands of Peru that likely spread across the central Andes around the time of the Middle Horizon (Heggarty 2007). Since large-scale population displacements have been largely ruled out genetically for the period (Lewis 2009; Lewis et al. 2007), it is likely that one or both of the languages acted as a lingua franca that facilitated relationships with local groups that were newly joined through trade, marriage, religion, or other mechanisms (Heggarty 2007: 48). In Uruk Mesopotamia, tokens, seals, and, by the end of the period, writing also would have worked to link disparate groups through a shared means of organizing and displaying information (Algaze 2008: 135–9; Schmandt-Besserat 1996). Similar to today, surging interaction in these civilizations brought with them massive communication problems as previously unconnected groups struggled to maintain connections. Standardization allowed for people from disparate groups to better understand each other.

Hallmark 4 – unevenness

The fourth characteristic of global cultures is *unevenness*. There is a "power geometry" in the world today that structures interregional relationships (Inda and Rosaldo 2008: 15). The unevenness that underlies today's interconnections is the result of the changes over the last few centuries that began soon after the European Voyages of Discovery. As interregional interactions expanded, new regions were usually brought into exchange networks at a distinct disadvantage (Harvey 1989; Wallerstein 1979; Wolf 1982). Western powers tended to dominate the political, economic, cultural, and technological apparatuses that organized these interactions. The world's power geometry has changed over this time – the decline and now meteoric rise of China is one example – but change tends to be limited because of the structural disadvantages faced by many nations.

Globalization's power geometry limits the ability of many people to benefit from the increased interactions that occur in an era of globalization. Large parts of Africa today, for example, lack the commodities (be they economic, political, or cultural) to attract outside interest or investment (Allen and Hamnett 1995). Without sufficient transport and communication technology, people in these regions find themselves isolated from the global flows that bind together other regions of the world. Being connected, however, is also fraught with problems. In many places, people feel far too connected to the outside world (Ferguson 2002). They might find their markets flooded with cheap imports or feel inundated with Western media without either access to the perceived benefits of Westernization or a global voice. The unevenness in global cultures is neither confined to the developing world nor defined by national borders. As many laid-off steel and auto workers in the United States know far too well, shifting relationships can shutter factories and end high-paying jobs (Ferguson 2002: 140).

Unevenness in globalization goes beyond military strength and the factory floor. Cultural hegemony is a process through which everyday practices and shared beliefs can provide the foundation for domination by outside groups (Gramsci 1971). In global cultures, certain places are seen as being important centers, and these locations often shape the views of those living in other places. A good example of cultural hegemony today comes from the world art market (Plattner 1996). New York City is widely regarded as one of the major centers of innovation in painting. With its critical mass of wealthy collectors, noted artists, well-connected dealers, and world-renowned museums, the city is able to define "good" art, and this taste is affirmed by the aspiring dealers, buyers, and artists who flock to New York. More importantly, people in the art world who live away from New York tend to accept this city's standard of art and judge their work as inherently inferior because it is not being produced or shown in this location. The power of a peripheral artist to rebel against New York's hegemony is limited because other people in the art world would still think that New York is *the* place to acquire paintings (for example, the collector buying the art or the dealer deciding who to take on as a client). People don't care that much about the good work being done in St. Louis or Manila because they reason if the work is that good, why aren't they in New York?

Unevenness in the ancient world has been repeatedly demonstrated by world systems theorists (e.g., Chase-Dunn and Anderson 2005). Uruk-Warka, Cahokia, and Huari held a considerable advantage over other settlements at one point or another during the histories of these cities. Unevenness is clearly seen in the cultural hegemony of the three centers. The roots of the Southeastern Ceremonial Complex, for example, can be traced back to Cahokia (Brown and Kelly 2000); and Uruk-Warka developed the first system of writing (Nissen 1986). Political and economic unevenness can also be demonstrated by each city's founding of colonies to pull together desired resources and send these goods to the city. Although the logistical difficulties of maintaining regular connections with these distant colonies ultimately made it impossible for these settlements to dominate local political economies (Stein 1999: 55–64), the mere *establishment* of these colonies by these cities suggests that a power differential existed since other sites were not able to extend their reach in this manner.

Unevenness can also be found if one takes a closer look at the geographic spread of Uruk-, Wari-, and Mississippian-related material. If I told you to use shades of red to color in today's "globalized" regions on a world map, you would undoubtedly hesitate on your shading selections – making every country red would be a gross oversimplification and deciding what exact shade of pink you would use in Pakistan versus Bangladesh would make your head spin. Just like today's map, the geographic spread of the earlier global cultures would appear as a similar blurry, ever-changing mosaic. This is just what you see in our three case studies (e.g., Frangipane 2001: 342; Pauketat 2007; Schreiber 1992: 9–10). The reasons for these ancient mosaics go beyond power geometry, but the many blank spots (and light pink spots if we continue the coloring analogy) are blank because of the simple geopolitical reality that then and now many of these places were geographically isolated regions with limited resources and small, scattered populations. With little to offer outside groups, people in these regions were largely overlooked and had no voice on the global stage.

Hallmark 5 – cultural homogenization

The fifth characteristic of globalization, *cultural homogenization*, is perhaps the most widely discussed hallmark of global culture (Thompson 1995; Tomlinson 1999). Homogenization goes beyond the widespread dissemination of foreign objects or people. Instead, cultural homogenization entails the diffusion of a way of being, "from musical forms, architecture, and modes of dress to eating habits, languages, philosophical ideas, and cultural values and dispositions" (Inda and Rosaldo 2008: 16–17). Since ways of being tend to be shaped by those cultures that have more wealth and power than other groups, the process of homogenization is sometimes referred to as McDonaldization. This term is derived from the title of a book by George Ritzer (1993) that describes the pervasive reach of McDonald's and how the fast food giant has changed the way that the world eats. Ritzer's book discusses the culinary aspects of the chain in his book, but he also looks at how the restaurant's business principles, from its focus on standardized restaurant layout to its streamlined cooking systems, have changed global culture in ways far removed from its menu (also see Ritzer 2006 and Schlosser 2001).

In theory, homogenization could result in the breakdown of cultural barriers and the global assimilation of a single culture. The degree of cultural homogenization of the world today, however, is often overstated by the popular media. Even though the global reach of many brands is undeniable, their presence alone needs not signal a deep-seated cultural shift (Hannerz 2002: 42) – eating a Big Mac does not turn you into an American. Moreover, flows between cultures always involve "interpretation, translation, mutation, adaptation, and 'indigenization' as the receiving culture brings its own cultural resources to bear, in dialectical fashion, upon 'cultural imports'" (Tomlinson 1999: 84). Homogenization, therefore, is not so much about the spread of a single way of life as it is about how people come into contact with widely shared ideas and products and make them their own.

To revisit McDonald's, the restaurant chain opened its first out-
let in Moscow in 1990. The response to the restaurant that year was
amazing – while 3.2 million people visited Lenin's Tomb that year,
almost 10 million visited Moscow's lone McDonald's restaurant
(Caldwell 2008: 250). The restaurant's initial appeal was its exoticness
and novelty. Since 1990, however, McDonald's has become a place
associated with local comfort food for many Muscovites, a social
space where friends gather, linger over their food, and even feel free
to bring their own lunch. Even though the menu is largely identical to the one found in the United States, Muscovites have reshaped
the social experience of eating at McDonald's over time (Caldwell
2008). This modification of the McDonald's experience is an example of what Marshall Sahlins calls the "indigenization of modernity"
(1994), the process by which the incorporation of modern objects and
practices into preexisting cultures modifies both the receiving cultures and the products that are received.

The best example of cultural homogenization in our three
ancient case studies might be the bevel-rim bowls of Uruk Period
Mesopotamia. With perhaps a few exceptions, the bowls were
locally mass-produced by the thousands in holes in the ground
that served as molds (Nicholas 1987: 62). The exact function of these
bowls remains under debate, but most archaeologists believe that
they were used to provide rations for people working for an elite
or central authority (Nissen 1988: 84–5). The gross similarity in the
size, form, and method of construction of the bevel-rim bowls across
Mesopotamia can be used to mark the extent of interregional interactions during the period. In most cases, the spread of ration bowls
reflects significant changes in labor organization and shows the
depth of Uruk's penetration at many sites (Algaze 2008: 131). At the
same time, some bevel rims are found at sites in context to suggest
that they were not always being used as ration bowls. The ubiquity
of the bowls does not mean that everyone was doing the same thing,
but it does suggest that they were likely aware of the radical social
changes that were occurring in some places.

On a broader scale, cultural homogenization can be seen in
our three case studies just in the fact that archaeologists have long
acknowledged the existence of what are sometimes called "cultural
horizons" (e.g., Rice 1993b). The bread and butter of archaeology is
defining culture areas based on stylistic similarities between artifacts. The spread of four corner hats, bronze weapons, Ramsey pots,

and all of the other artifacts that were used to define the spread of Mississippian, Uruk, and Wari are indicators of widespread cultural homogenization. Shifts in funerary practices, building techniques, and social structures also illustrate this trend. Everyone, of course, wasn't wearing the same thing or being buried in the same way. Ideas were being reworked/repurposed/resymbolized in local contexts, but people were all wrestling with the same ideas. Although we might argue about the existence of a Wari empire, Mississippian cult, and Uruk world systems, these debates are premised on the fact that people across a broad region were joined together in a cultural horizon marked by the spread of a shared material culture.

Hallmark 6 – cultural heterogeneity

Cultural heterogeneity is the sixth hallmark of global culture. When global cultures emerge, cultural variation actually increases in some ways. These seemingly contradictory effects are frequently commented upon by scholars and are the central points found within such popular books as *Jihad vs. McWorld* (Barber 1995) and *The Lexus and the Olive Tree* (Friedman 1999). Cultural heterogeneity occurs because globalization today is not synonymous with Americanization or Westernization (Inda and Rosaldo 2008: 24–5). Instead, a global culture is created through a mixture of ideas, products, and practices from areas throughout the system so that foreign elements, to one degree or another, are introduced into each culture. A global culture, therefore, is a mélange of elements – the cultural boundaries of *all* cultures are blurred through these exchanges (Gupta and Ferguson 2002).

An example of the cultural heterogeneity caused by globalization is the store Pier 1 Imports. With its tasteful accents derived from cultures around the world, the store provides millions of North American shoppers with items to decorate their homes. A red ceramic Buddha, bronze sculpture of a dancing Vishnu, and African wooden mask are bought as home décor. The consumer likely knows little or nothing about Buddhism or the role of sorcery in Africa since the original context of this material is often less important than its aesthetic appeal. Freed from their previous cultural meanings, the fusion of non-Western material in a Western home creates a totally new kind of interior decoration that signals the homeowner's worldliness and sophistication. This hybrid space, the idealized Pier 1 home, is a product of surging interregional interaction.

Heterogeneity is also seen in the way that global flows are significantly different from one region to another. Immigration into a country can be dominated by only a few ethnic groups, and certain television shows are vastly more popular in some countries than they are in others (Inda and Rosaldo 2008: 25). One example of the heterogeneity in global flows is found in the popularity of Indian cinema in Nigeria (Larkin 2008). Bollywood films far eclipse Hollywood films in popularity in this region, and the lives and fashion choices of Indian stars have been followed closely by Nigerians for over forty years. This does not mean, of course, that Bollywood movies map cleanly onto Nigeria's fractured cultural landscape. The films are especially enjoyed by the Hausa, a group whose Islamic values dictate sexual segregation. The need to separate the sexes puts local filmmakers who wish to emulate Bollywood's style in a bind since they can't do the song and dance routines fundamental to Indian love stories. To solve this dilemma, the cinematographers find ways to creatively insinuate the relationship between two people without actually showing them together romantically on screen (Larkin 2008: 335). The importance of Bollywood films in Nigeria runs counter to simplistic notions of Westernization and highlights the heterogeneity of global cultures.

Cultural heterogeneity in our three ancient case studies might best be seen in the stylist differences between the artifact assemblages of the Mississippian chiefdoms. The Mississippian social landscape can be broken down into a patchwork of regional and local artifact styles that relate to the rise and fall of chiefdoms throughout the American mid-continent (e.g., Smith 1978, 1990). Each of these chiefdoms developed a unique material culture because each of the chiefdoms acquired a unique set of interaction networks. Those who lived at the site of Spiro, for example, adopted a hybrid identity that blurred local traditions with Mississippian and other foreign traits that were acquired through their long-distance connections (Pauketat 2007: 111). The people of Fort Ancient meanwhile largely ignored their neighbors and adopted a limited set of Mississippian artifacts based on their close relationship to the major mound center of Etowah. Although some archaeologists have used this heterogeneity to argue against a shared culture, one would expect increasing local variation if a global culture emerged from "the tension inherent in practicing simultaneous strategies of detachment and attachment to the Mississippian world" (Cobb and Butler 2006: 343).

Similar degrees of cultural heterogeneity can be seen after the Uruk and Wari expansions, but the archaeologists in these regions have tended to emphasize cultural homogeneity over heterogeneity. Nonetheless, a significant degree of cultural heterogeneity is one of the reasons that there are a number of competing chronologies for the Uruk period in ancient Mesopotamia (Rothman 2001c: 8). Considerable temporal and stylistic variability occurs across this broad region during this period (e.g., Postgate 2002). Nineveh's ceramic chronology does not quite fit with Uruk-Warka; Uruk-Warka's chronology does not quite align with Tell Brak. This variability should be expected because Uruk ideas and artifacts spread out via different networks (instead of uniformly like a wine stain on a white tablecloth).

Differences in ceramic styles can also be used to underline the cultural heterogeneity that followed the Wari expansion. Although there are only about six major Wari styles, there are dozens of local ones that are variably called regional Wari styles, local Wari-influenced styles, or just local Middle Horizon styles that happen to look a bit Wari. Even the major Wari styles are often quite variable from one region of Peru to another. What I call the Viñaque style in Cotahuasi where I work is not quite the same as the Viñaque my friends find elsewhere. This stylistic heterogeneity is in part a reflection of differences between the classification schemes of archaeologists, but it is also a product of variation within the assemblages.

Hallmark 7 – re-embedding of local culture

Cultural heterogeneity is closely related to the *re-embedding of local culture*, the seventh hallmark of global culture. Increasing interregional interaction throws one's life into sharper relief. Talking about "local" lifeways only makes sense when one can compare them to other ways of living, and you don't go about protecting your culture until there is something that is perceived as threatening to it. There is often a tension in globalization between reaching toward the outside world and shrinking from it. As Thomas Ericksen notes, "Globalization is *centripetal* in that it connects people worldwide; and it is *centrifugal* in that it inspires a heightened awareness of, and indeed (re)construction of local uniqueness" (2007: 142, emphasis in original). The drive to protect this local uniqueness often leads to the re-embedding of local culture.

The attitudes of today's Maya youth exemplify this ambivalent attitude to globalization's promise and its potential erasure of the local (Green 2002). More and more of these youths are being drawn into the world economy through work in rural factories that assemble apparel for export. These youths are torn in conflicting directions between "being Indian" as defined by their families and "being modern" as defined by a popular culture that values Western ideas of consumerism and individualism (Green 2002: 116). "Being Indian" for these youths was not something that they thought about until they were confronted with another way of living. The re-embedding of culture occurs in these contexts when attempts are made to strengthen, re-create, and even invent a local culture that is used as a counterweight to the centripetal tendencies of globalization.

The re-embedding of culture can be seen also in the reaction of the Yup'ik Eskimos of western Alaska to recent changes in their way of life. Over the last few decades, the introduction of snowmobiles, availability of imported canned goods, access to cable television, and many other factors have led to significant cultural change among the Yup'ik (Feinup-Riordan 1990). These changes have fueled nostalgia for the older way of life when people were more fit, generous, and disciplined, and when the world in general was quieter, more stable, and without boundary markers. According to Ann Feinup-Riordan, these stories of the past are a "rhetorical attempt by the Yup'ik to publish themselves in opposition to the noisy, nasty non-native world" (1990: 223).

This past is an invented one that is shaped by the Yup'ik's current situation in a world that is in many ways beyond their control. Negative aspects of Yup'ik history like conflict, malnutrition, and isolation are wiped out of their history as an idealized past is created that represents an 'authentic' Yup'ik culture that is placed in opposition to life in the modern world. The invention of tradition is a common reaction to globalization and is one of the primary ways that local cultures become re-embedded in reaction to rapid culture change (Hobsbawm and Ranger 1983).

The re-embedding of local culture is harder to demonstrate archaeologically because it is often difficult to tell if outside influences were rare or absent in a location because they were rejected by a group or because these outside influences were minimal. In some cases, however, it is clear that people were repeatedly exposed to global currents and made a deliberate choice to turn inward. The best example of shunning new ideas from our case studies comes from the work at Tepe Gawra in Mesopotamia. Located along a major trade route, the village was well within the Uruk cultural sphere and close to the Uruk-influenced site of Nineveh.

The villagers at Tepe Gawra were fully enmeshed within the wide-ranging networks of the Middle Uruk period – they adopted new Uruk administrative techniques, and many goods passing through the village were undoubtedly coming and going from southern Mesopotamian sites – but they chose to reject most foreign influences. Uruk-style pottery is rare in the village and instead local potters decided to go back to making designs that were popular long before the Uruk expansion (Rothman 2002b: 60). Those living in Tepe Gawra also ignored new Uruk funerary trends and continued instead to bury their dead in tombs containing gold, turquoise, and other prestige goods (Rothman 2001b: 391). When Uruk influence intensified in the region during the Late Uruk Period, the people at Tepe Gawra abandoned the site.

This deep ambivalence of participation in a global culture can be seen in our other two case studies as well. The village of Ak'awillay in the highlands of Peru reacted to Wari global culture in a way that was roughly analogous to Tepe Gawra's reaction to Uruk. The village also sat along a major route near the impressive Wari center of Pikillacta. The people of Ak'awillay benefited immensely from the widening networks of the period, but seemed quite leery of involvements in most aspects of the Wari cultural package (Bélisle and Covey i.p.).

Larger sites also, of course, resisted full incorporation into these global cultures, and one of these sites in the Mississippian world was Toltec. The people at the site initially ignored the rapid changes swirling around them and continued to build houses and mounds in the ways that they had for generations (Nassaney 2001: 170). Finally, they decided to walk away from the mound and disperse into smaller communities rather than follow their neighbors in adopting the hierarchical political structures at the heart of Mississippian life (Nassaney 2001: 169).

Although often only hinted at in the archaeological record, the re-embedding of local culture was likely a widespread phenomenon in all three case studies as people attempted to find the best way to navigate through the cultural turmoil caused by rapidly expanding networks. Most people adopted some aspects of the array of new products and ideas circulating during this period. Yet, they also chose at the same time to strengthen (or invent) some local traditions in order to anchor themselves against a rapidly changing world.

Hallmark 8 – vulnerability

The final hallmark of a global culture is *vulnerability*. Increased vulnerability occurs when the interconnections forged by globalization make places increasingly dependent on actions that are occurring in other places around the world. One example of this vulnerability can be seen in the outsourcing of jobs from the United States to India in order to lower a firm's bottom line. American corporations have sought to capitalize on cheap overseas labor over the last one hundred years, but the pace of this outsourcing has increased rapidly over the last few decades because of technological advances.

While the debate rages on whether the overall impact of outsourcing is negative or positive on the American economy (Friedman 2006), it is clear that the ability of firms to outsource positions has made more American jobs vulnerable to cutbacks or elimination. Indeed, outsourcing is just one of a host of new forms of labor that have been created as companies decentralize in order to better target ever-changing niche markets. Employment for Americans, as well as those who hold the outsourced jobs in India, is increasingly tied to the vagaries of a volatile global market.

Vulnerability is also a state of mind. The interconnections of globalization, combined with the related erosion of the local, leaves people in times of need less secure about who they are, what they should do, and who they can trust (Eriksen 2007: 123). This insecurity leads to a heightened awareness of possible risks and to a fixation on these risks and how to avert them (Beck 1992). One example of both the real and perceived vulnerability that is created by globalization can be found in the global traffic of human organs (Scheper-Hughes 2000, 2004).

When Nancy Scheper-Hughes worked in a Brazilian shantytown in the 1980s, she heard rumors of children being kidnapped in order to harvest their organs for transplants in the United States and Japan. The residents of the shantytown residents reported:

> combi-vans scouring poor neighborhoods in search of stray youngsters. The children would be nabbed and shoved into the

trunk of the van, and their discarded and eviscerated bodies – minus heart, lungs, liver, kidneys, and eyes – would turn up later by the roadside, between rows of sugarcane, or in hospital dumpsters. (2000: 201)

Although there is a growing illicit global market of human organs and tissue removed from the poor and disempowered, the rumor in the shantytown was not grounded in actual kidnappings. Instead, the rumor was a reflection of people's feeling of increasing impotence. They felt unable to protect their children and were growing more and more uneasy about their marginalization in a globalized world.

Structural vulnerability is relatively easy to demonstrate in our three early case studies because we can document how exchange networks collapsed in relation to changes that occurred at Uruk-Warka, Cahokia, and Huari. In the case of Cahokia, the city's almost complete desertion in the thirteenth century led to a wave of population dispersals, colonial abandonments, and trade network realignments. Huari's two major rebuilding efforts (the first around A.D. 800 and the second occurring sometime around A.D. 950 just before the city collapsed) correlate with a similar suite of changes across Peru, and Uruk-Warka's shift toward consolidation of its hinterland led to the collapse of many of the networks that linked northern and southern Mesopotamia.

Although most interactions during these periods of widespread connections did not run through these cities, the sites were nonetheless critical nodes for network maintenance. When the cities collapsed, structural adjustments occurred that led to increased regionalization (in all three cases) and the eventual loss of a widely shared set of ideas (though in all three cases the ideas forged in these cities would long out-last their demise).

Without the benefit of written records it is harder to get at the *feelings* of vulnerability that may have occurred during these case studies. Yet, many of the situations that people found themselves in during these periods would have likely created feelings of uncertainty and confusion. The colonial outpost of Cerro Baúl, for example, was established during the initial wave of Huari colonization at the beginning of the Middle Horizon. The settlers virtually ignored the local population when they settled in the region, set up their sites according to Huari conventions, and began a series of massive public works projects to irrigate the arid valley (Moseley et al. 2005; Nash 2002; Williams 1997, 2001).

Less than two hundred years later, however, their utopia was flagging. The Wari colonists abandoned some sites, reorganized the primary settlement at Cerro Baúl, and reached out to neighboring groups. This transition must have been filled with uncertainty as the people of Cerro Baúl realized that many of the connections with Huari that they had relied on for generations were eroding. A similar sense of vulnerability would have likely pervaded the colonies of Cahokia and Uruk-Warka when they were reconfigured or abandoned. Moreover, it would not be difficult to imagine that people living close to these colonies (and elsewhere) were also concerned about the future as their personal networks shifted over time.

GLOBAL CULTURES IN AN ANCIENT WORLD

When archaeology was taking its first tentative steps toward becoming an academic discipline at the turn of the nineteenth century, a Danish antiquarian despaired that the past was "wrapped in a thick fog" that seemed impossible to penetrate (cited in Trigger 1989: 71). Even two hundred years later, the study of the past remains a tough slog especially for those interested in eras with little or no written records. Most sites don't give you a moment frozen in time like Pompeii and instead provide only a confusing, incomplete jumble of the stuff left behind by multiple generations. The slick scientific solutions to research problems – like ancient DNA, phytoliths, and soil chemistry – are incredibly helpful, but they often create more questions than answers. Ham-handed by coarse chronologies, shoestring budgets, and an ever-dwindling material record, archaeologists and other scholars can still only offer rough, tentative, sketches of past lifeways.

Despite all of these difficulties, considerable progress has been made. We can now peer thousands (indeed millions) of years back in time, and our vision of the past gets clearer every day. A growing array of tools allows scholars to obtain a wealth of data on past cultures, and these data allow us to continually check and redefine our interpretations (Brumfiel 1996). The information gleaned from the artifacts, ruins, and landscapes that have been left behind in the world allows us to tentatively compare the past to the present. In terms of our interests for this book, the accumulated scholarship shows unequivocally that there were earlier eras of intense interregional interaction that caused sweeping cultural changes.

The changes that occurred after urbanization in our three case studies were the same kinds of changes that are associated with the emergence of our modern global culture. From time–space compression to increasing vulnerability, all of the hallmarks of a global culture can be found in the Uruk, Mississippian, and Wari civilizations. These civilizations should therefore be considered as global cultures even though there remains much to be learned about these periods. Two thousand years from now, the detritus of our own global culture will only provide a partial, imperfect glimpse, into our world today (e.g., Macaulay 1979). Our ability to *see* the hallmarks of global culture in the ancient world, even as the details of these eras remain hazy, suggests that the reach of these earlier global cultures were deep, long, and transformative.

The existence of Uruk, Mississippian, and Wari global cultures means that our twin criteria for identifying a period of globalization have been met: during each of these eras there were (a) surges in long-distance connections that (b) created global cultures. The many scholars that use definitions similar to the one espoused in this book should therefore recognize that globalization, *not globalization-lite or something like globalization*, has occurred at least three times in human history prior to modern globalization. These earlier eras of globalization were, of course, very different – they were all smaller in geographic extent, for example, and brought together groups of less diverse backgrounds – but they have enough similarities to suggest that we might learn a few things by tacking back and forth between globalizations past, present, and future.

8

Learning from Past Globalizations

Echoing one of Mark Twain's old sayings, the anthropologist Clifford Geertz argued that even though history might not repeat itself, it does rhyme (2005: 10). The easiest of these rhythms to notice are those that occur in our own lifetimes. Your children make many of the mistakes that you did as a kid, many "innovations" are just more of the same, and another freedom fighter turns into a dictator when he comes into power. There are, of course, other rhythms in history that are more difficult to grasp because they unfold beyond living memory. Geertz's comment, for example, was part of a personal reflection on his struggles to understand the roots of Indonesian culture as the region went through drastic changes in the 1950s and 1960s. The world would "not stand still" for his pen, and he found that the unrelenting chatter of daily life kept on engulfing the deeper rhythms of history that he sought to explore (2005: 10).

Despite these challenges, uncovering long-term patterns is important because these processes help to structure current events and ultimately have a significant impact on how history unfolds (e.g., Braudel 1979). One of the most important long-standing rhythms in world history may be the peaks and valleys in long-distance connectivity that have typified interactions in different parts of the world over the last few millennia (Chase-Dunn and Anderson 2005; Frank 1993; Marcus 1998). Although archaeologists, world historians, and world system theorists have worked tirelessly to better understand these interactions, the earlier cycles of connectivity are often of only passing interest to most people. We like quoting George Santayana's famous aphorism, "Those who cannot remember the past are condemned to repeat it," but we don't tend to look to *ancient* cultures for lessons on tomorrow.

In lives that are both hectic and mundane, it is easier to think of antiquity as important only in that it provides us with stories that offer a momentary respite from reality. We take a few moments to read about the size of Ramses II sons' tomb in New Kingdom Egypt and marvel at how archaeologists can trace the route that the Uluburun ship took before it sunk to the bottom of the Mediterranean in the fourteenth century B.C. (Fagan 1995; Weeks 1999). But then we reluctantly wrest our mind back to the *modern* world in order to check our Blackberry for the price of gas, the latest celebrity gossip, and a quick update on the recent flare-up in the Middle East. The implication of seeing the past as a pleasant diversion is that the ancient world is somehow fake or at best inconsequential. The deep past doesn't really belong to the real world and has little bearing on our lives today.

Why do we think this way? Like many cultures around the world, Westerners tend to break up history into distinct time periods, and for almost a thousand years we have separated modernity from antiquity. Year after year, brick after brick, we have subconsciously built a Great Wall between these two eras. We might not have an exact date in mind for the beginning of modernity, but we have a sense that things irrevocably changed at some hazy point in recent human history. This barrier has been so deeply internalized that it has become visceral. Although our reasons are often difficult to articulate, it just doesn't *feel right* to compare a Maya stela to a billboard in Times Square (see Figure 1.1). By severing links to earlier eras, the Great Wall cuts across the rhythms of history and bolsters our sense that modernity is radically different from everything that came before it.

This book attempts to take on this Great Wall by explicitly comparing the spread of ancient civilization to modern globalization. Pairing the terms "globalization" and "ancient civilizations" also likely didn't *feel right* when you started reading this book, but this time your visceral reaction was supported by books that offered a litany of good reasons why the two terms do not go together. After all, there were no worldwide connections in antiquity, the interactions were slower, and fewer people were involved in previous networks. These and other significant differences clearly exist between past interactions and today, but I hope that I have shown that much of this variation is of degree and not of kind. Globalization is widely defined as (a) the consequence of a surge in long-distance connections that (b) caused an array of cultural changes that are associated with the creation of a global culture (i.e., Ritzer 2007: 1). If we use this definition, then the evidence outlined in this book demonstrates that globalization has occurred numerous times in the past.

The rapid urbanization of Uruk-Warka, Cahokia, and Huari created new flows of goods, ideas, and people across broad regions. These flows caused many outlying groups to forge new relationships with other partners who, in turn, caused more flows by expanding their own interaction networks. Some of these new relationships were with city dwellers, but many of them were not. The cascade of reactions to urbanization led to the creation of far-flung networks that achieved a surge of connectivity that appears to have been sufficient enough to breach the globalization threshold. I argue that global cultures emerged when this threshold was crossed, and that these cultures were as tumultuous and fractured as the one that we live in today. The existence of all the social changes commonly associated with the creation of a global culture, demonstrated point by point in the last chapter, shows that the Uruk, Mississippian, and Wari civilizations should be considered true examples of earlier globalizations.

So where does a recognition of multiple globalizations leave us? The linking of past globalizations to our modern one might seem largely academic until you realize that by accepting globalization as a repeated phenomenon in human history you make it possible to compare globalizing eras across space and time. Uruk, Mississippian, and Wari (and likely other civilizations) can be placed side by side to our modern global culture. Following the lead of world systems theorists (e.g., Chase-Dunn and Hall 1997), we could compare globalizations past and present to separate out the general characteristics of globalization from those characteristics unique to a particular historical, cultural, and environmental setting. With the help of such wide-ranging studies, we might be able to better understand the catalysts for globalization, how interregional interaction networks remain stable or change, and how the decline of these interregional networks can be more effectively managed.

An exhaustive comparative study of globalizations must wait for another book. Yet, I want to use this final chapter to briefly explore three tentative ideas that can show us what a pluralized globalization could tell us about our past and, perhaps more importantly, our future.

GLOBALIZATIONS AND A MORE COMPLICATED PAST

One takeaway from a pluralized globalizations is a better understanding of the past. A pluralized globalization would make us reconsider many of our models of how people interacted in the past. With little to no written records for most of human history, our view of the past is largely based on the few scraps left behind by earlier groups. Up until the middle of the twentieth century, the challenges of reconstructing the past led archaeologists and other scholars to define the boundaries of ancient cultures by lumping together those sites that shared the same basic kinds of pots, stone tools, or textiles. These archaeological cultures were often named after the most well-known of the various sites where this material was found, and it was thought that these cultures spread outward from an origin area through a mixture of migrations, conquest, and cultural diffusion (Trigger 1989: 148–206).

The models that have developed in the last half century for the spread of civilizations have all generally maintained the idea that outlying cultures changed through direct contact with more developed core areas. Although the nature of this relationship was questioned – Edward Schortman and Patricia Urban for example distinguished between egalitarian, coevolving, and hierarchical interactions (1998) – the relationship between core and periphery was at least implicitly considered the most important one (Jennings 2006a). The only major exception to this focus were peer-polity models that suggested that a shared culture could emerge between independent groups through imitation, warfare, and the exchange of goods and information (Renfrew and Cherry 1986). Peer-polities, however, were often considered a regional stage in the development of chiefdoms and city-states rather than a mechanism through which a culture could spread over a vast area.

If we recognize that the spread of some early civilizations was the result of earlier globalization eras, then we will need to replace our overly simplistic visions of the past with more complex, dynamic models that are explicitly linked to recent globalization research. Many of the counterparts to interaction models currently applied in archaeology today have been soundly criticized for years by scholars dealing with modern globalization. For example, leading scholar Arjun Appadurai suggested almost twenty years ago that

> The new global cultural economy has to be understood as a complex, overlapping, disjunctive order, which cannot any longer be understood in terms of existing center-periphery models (even those that might account for multiple centers and peripheries). Nor is it susceptible to simple models of push and pull (in terms of migration theory) or of surpluses or deficits (as in traditional models of balance of trade), or of consumers and producers (as in most neo-Marxist theories of development). (1990: 296)

Appadurai went on to introduce his own globalization model that involved five different kinds of global cultural flow: ethnoscapes (people), technoscapes (technology), finanscapes (global capital), mediascapes (media), ideoscapes (ideologies) (1990: 296–300).

Appadurai's critical point was that global flows today often occur independently of each other, at cross-purposes, and could change course rapidly and without warning (1990: 301). Although his model ignores the real structural advantages that certain nations hold in the modern global economy, it does highlight the deficiencies of archaeological models that too often collapse interregional interaction into neat, simple models that privilege the political sphere. A greater engagement with Appadurai's model, as well as the myriad of other globalization models that have been developed over the last twenty years, would bring a more nuanced, accurate understanding to one of the more critical dynamics underlying human history.

Chapter 3 was my attempt to use aspects of globalization theory to create a model for the spread of early civilization. The model is undoubtedly flawed – it places perhaps too much emphasis on the role of the city, largely ignores examples where civilizations emerged through the competition of multiple cities, and likely underemphasizes the roles of non-elites in many interactions. I argue nonetheless that this model provides a better explanation than many of the existing models for the data emerging from our three case studies. Migration, warfare, cultural diffusion, core-periphery, and peer-polity relationships all capture some of what was going on during the spread of early civilizations, but we are finding it increasingly difficult to shoehorn what we know about these periods into most models that privilege one or two of these relationships over others (e.g., Chase-Dunn and Babones 2006; Chase-Dunn and Hall 1997;

Gills and Thompson 2006). Just like modern globalization, these earlier eras are complex, overlapping, and disjunctive and we need to bring new tools to the table in order to better understand them.

THE FUTURE AND THE END OF A GLOBALIZATION CYCLE

The second idea that we can take away from a pluralized globalization is more specific: a knowledge that our current era of globalization will end. Our lives might seem far removed from those of Mesopotamian herders and Mississippian farmers, but modern globalization has followed a similar arc thus far from colonial expansion to the creation of a global culture. The general model that I offered in Chapter 3, derived from a cross-cultural survey of early cities and their broad geographic impact, fits what is happening today.

The model describes how a city's growth spurs an initial colonial expansion and the circulation of goods, people, and ideas across a broad region. These flows then encourage more and more interactions until a global culture that lasts for a few hundred years emerges. In the model, mounting conflict leads to the demise of the global culture and a subsequent period of balkanization. This general model is supported by the details of the rise and fall of Uruk, Mississippian, and Wari civilizations, and fits well with our current globalization cycle thus far.

Instead of asking *if* modern globalization will end, a better question is to ask would be *when*. Uruk globalization lasted for about 700 years, Mississippian globalization about 500 years, and Wari about 400 years. These lengths of time are not anomalies in world history. In her study of interaction networks from five different parts of the planet, Joyce Marcus (1998) found that ancient peaks of integration only lasted a few centuries even in those cases where imperial forces sought to foster these interactions. If our present globalization era began with the European Voyages of Discover starting in the second half of the fifteenth century, then historical precedence suggests that we should be coming close to its end.

The clearest sign that we are entering the end of a globalization cycle might paradoxically be the fluorescence of interregional interaction after World War II (e.g., Friedman and Chase-Dunn 2005). In all three of our case studies, the greatest degree of interaction occurred after their founding cities began to lose control over the colonial networks that they established. People opportunistically rushed in to create more and more informal interaction networks, and the variety of social changes associated with global cultures accelerated. Eventually the costs of maintaining that culture became too high – in terms of such thing as the loss of local traditions and the increased costs of long-distance exchange – and these networks broke apart and were replaced by more regional networks.

The increasing wariness of worldwide interactions in many quarters, when combined with the recent uptick in interregional interaction and the waning influence of the United States on the global stage, suggests that the recent fluorescence of interregional interaction might now be giving way to a post-globalization period of increased balkanization. Since a degree of regionalism is an inherent reaction to homogeneity in any global culture, we should be cautious in reading for signs of collapsing global networks. Yet, the rumblings are getting stronger.

Venezuela president's Hugo Chavez, for example, spearheaded efforts in 2008 to create a Union of South American Nations that would act in part to shield the member nations from the vagaries of the global economy. In the spring of 2009, Premier Wen Jiabao started to publically express his anxiety about China's trillion dollar U.S. investment as many of his countrymen called for more internal investment. More women are wearing veils in long-secular Turkey, while millions of North Americans are pledging to eat more local foods. Boisterous rallies protesting the ills of globalization have taken place in countries as diverse as Bolivia, France, Thailand, and South Africa in the last ten years. These and many other examples point to rising discontent with globalization's impacts, and likely herald changes to come in interregional interaction.

Although I am arguing that we will see greater and greater balkanization in the next few decades, I want to make it clear that I am *not* suggesting that you will wake up one day soon without the ability to check your e-mail or invest in international mutual funds (though I might recommend for your health that you spend at least a few days doing neither). A postglobalization landscape is not the same as a postapocalyptic landscape in a Mad Max movie. A look at the cycles of integration and regionalization in the past suggest that we never quite go back down to the previous low levels of interaction after a globalization cycle (see Figure 2.1). I suspect that most global connections will remain, and in some areas, such as communication technology, we will likely be even more globally integrated in the years to come.

Nonetheless, the end of our current globalization era would mean that some of the global networks that we now rely on would be curtailed or replaced by interaction networks that are more regional or local in scale. More and more people, for example, would turn toward local traditions – albeit often invented or modified – for guidance, and the connections between rural farmers and urban consumers would be strengthened. Regional political and economic pacts, like the European Union, would become more important. This lower level of global integration would persist until some constellation of forces creates a new surge in interaction that would once again bring people together into a global culture.

DEALING WITH A SMALLER WORLD

In his recent book *Why Your World Is about to Get a Whole Lot Smaller* (2009), the economist Jeff Rubin argues that the earth's dwindling oil supply will dramatically increase transportation costs and lead to a host of changes. Since you will need to eat local, for instance, you might have to forgo your morning coffee and forget about those bananas shipped in from Costa Rica. We'll also need to reopen mothballed factories closer to home, diversify the local economy, invest heavily in mass transportation, and increase urban densities. For Rubin, the era of globalization is coming to an end and we will soon "face the wrenching choice between adapting to the realities of a new, smaller world or clinging to the artifacts of an old world we can no longer have" (2009: 265).

Whether or not we can find a technological fix for the impending oil crisis (or whether or not there is an oil crisis at all), the long-term patterns of globalization outlined in this book suggest that our world is about to get smaller. As Rubin suggests, how we deal with this smaller world will be a choice that we need to make, and we should begin planning now for the "turbulent ride" ahead (2009: 248). Globalizations have occurred repeatedly in human history. Some societies have weathered these cycles with aplomb, while others have shattered. If we want to prepare ourselves for increasing regionalization, then it would be prudent to look toward earlier eras of globalization for lessons that we can learn. A better understanding of how to deal with increasing balkanization is the third idea that we can take away from a pluralized globalization.

There are subwaves of integration within the larger cycle of globalization, and the valleys in these subwaves are often marked by crises that demand structural transformation in political economies (Arrighi 1994; Chase-Dunn et al. 2000). In other words, things sometimes go bad in the midst of a globalization cycle, and people often demand costly solutions to these problems. Some societies weather these mini-storms better than others. In all three of our case studies, we see shifts in the organization of Uruk-Warka, Cahokia, and Huari that likely correspond to attempts to adjust to these mini-cycles.

The people living in these sites showed varying abilities to adjust city life to changing social conditions. Cahokia's leaders seem to have been the least successful in managing changing conditions – the city was in steep decline after only a few generations. Huari appears to have survived at least one structural adjustment in interregional interaction and managed to prosper for over four hundred years. In the end, however, the city could not survive the increasing regionalization that typifies the end of a globalization cycle. Huari was abandoned as planners attempted to reinvent the city's organization.

Only Uruk-Warka managed to survive both the crises of the mini-cycles and the dramatic balkanization at the end of the globalization cycle that we have yet to face in our modern era. With its colonies failing and its northern trade networks collapsing, the city actually expanded in size, and it would remain an important city in Mesopotamia for the next thousand years. When Uruk-Warka's world got a whole lot smaller, the people in the city prospered. Why did Uruk-Warka succeed where others had failed?

In the last centuries of the fourth millennium B.C., Uruk-Warka was facing increased competition from rival towns that was leading to both increased violence and jeopardized long-distance exchange networks. The city's first reaction to these problems appears to have been to try to resolidify its access to resource zones by further colonization of Upper Mesopotamia. Projecting power over distances, however, is quite costly (e.g., Stein 1999), and there is some evidence for violent confrontations at places like Hamoukar (Lawler 2006, 2007). As time went on, leaders at Uruk-Warka seem to have refocused their energies toward creating a more regionally based political economy that would rely much less on production taking place hundreds of kilometers away.

By the end of the Late Uruk period (around 3100 B.C.), the results of this shift in economic focus are clear. More products were being made in the city by an increasingly specialized work force. One of the biggest industries was woolen textiles. Instead of bringing in finished textiles from the north, herds were now pastured locally, and cloth was created in the city and its environs (Algaze 2008: 84). As weavers made shirts, knappers worked flint, and blacksmiths forged tools, the cacophonous beat of urban life was put into order by scribes who were part of a new array of bureaucratic innovations that allowed for far more efficient information storage, retrieval, and dispersal (Englund 2004). Although the city would always depend to some degree on imports, Uruk-Warka's diverse industries made it less vulnerable to the vagaries of interregional trade.

Making more things at Uruk-Warka required more people, and the city would continue to grow. Bringing more people into the city was made possible by squeezing more out of the surrounding countryside. Clear buffer zones between rival towns were emerging (Algaze 2008: 114), and settlement pattern and early texts suggest that Uruk-Warka was extracting more goods from its hinterland (Pollock 2001: 218). Much of the city's success likely derives by the extension of its canal system. With more and better-connected waterways, barges laden with wool, grains, pigs, and other products could efficiently meet the needs of city dwellers (Algaze 2008: 58–71). In the subsequent Jemdet Nasr Period, Uruk-Warka had made the transition with the rest of the southern alluvium to an economy based largely on local resource extraction and urban production (Matthews 1992).

What lessons can we take from Uruk-Warka's successful navigation through the end of a globalization cycle? The leaders of the city were prescient in recognizing the need to shift to a more intensive economy, and scholars like Jeffery Rubin are certainly right in advocating that countries should start taking steps now to make local communities stronger, more diverse, and more efficient (2009). The intensity of the social changes required by Uruk-Warka's population, however, makes it clear that we will need to do more than just take the subway and eat in season to weather the coming storm. We'll have to radically transform the way that we live. Human history is littered with cultures that failed to quickly adapt to changing conditions. Facing concerns similar to those in Uruk-Warka, the people of Huari and Cahokia were unable or unwilling to take the necessary steps to save their cities. How will we fare when our world gets a whole lot smaller?

LEARNING FROM THE PAST

We have gotten used to emphasizing all of the undeniable, critical differences between our lives and that of people living ten, or even two, generations ago. A litany of inventions from antiseptics to airplanes, oral contraceptives, cell phones, and bar codes separates us from the deep past, and this feeling of disjuncture is strengthened by the wide array of tectonic economic, political, and cultural shifts that have taken place over the last few decades. We have become so fixated on change that we need a reminder that our similarities to earlier generations outweigh these differences.

A wealth of human universals links us together across space and time (Brown 1991). People smile when they are happy, cry when they are sad, and share food with loved ones. This shared humanity reaches deep into the past. We can often empathize with people living thousands of years ago once we understand their particular social, environmental, and historical context. We can easily understand Sophocles' concern about family, Gilgamesh's search for immortality, and Scheherazade's fear of death as she tells tale after tale in *A Thousand and One Nights*. Our reactions to life's ups and downs are likely not that much different from those of our ancestors. The essence of globalization is not in the speed that an object travels or the number of people on the move. Instead, it is in how a sudden, significant increase in interregional interaction destabilizes local conditions. More than anything else, globalization is the social product of the multigenerational struggle to come to terms with a flood of new relationships.

Globalization has played out in broadly related ways in the past because people in antiquity reacted to influxes of new ideas, goods, and people in ways that were similar to the ways that people do today. Confronted with a new god, the invention of writing, or the personal computer, we have long asked the same basic questions like: What is this? How can it help me? Am I sure that I really want it? Although the scale, speed, and depth of connections today are unique in human history, earlier surges in interregional interaction were also quite traumatic. The vectors that connected people together in the world's first civilizations were not the same as those today – there was no Internet, automobile, or stock market – but globalization cannot be tied directly to a particular technology, mode of production, or ideology. Any mechanism that can quickly bring more and more people together, be it Facebook, Twitter, horse stirrups, sails, or wheels, can act as catalysts for globalization. Understanding how we have experienced these cycles in the past can help us better navigate our future.

Our ability to relate to past generations should make us leery of those who suggest that we have irrevocably broken from our past. If we can hang an "s" on globalization, then we should also question the uniqueness of other quintessentially "modern" phenomena. Global warming, for example, has occurred repeatedly in human history (Fagan 2004, 2008; Redman et al. 2004), and ever since we settled down in villages, we have been trying to figure out the best place to put our trash (Sabloff 2008; Smith 2009). There are, of course, many aspects of our climate and waste disposal problems that are unique to the present, but don't you think that we might learn a thing or two from studying how these things have played out in the past? Far more than just a pleasant diversion, ancient history's long record of humanity's failures and successes can help guide us into the future.

References Cited

Abu-Lughod, Janet L. 1989 *Before European Hegemony: The World System AD 1250–1350*. New York: Oxford University Press.

1991 Writing against Culture. In *Recapturing Anthropology*, edited by Richard Fox. Pp. 137–62. Santa Fe: School of American Research.

Adams, Robert McC. 1981 *Heartland of Cities*. Chicago: University of Chicago Press.

2004 Reflections on the Early Southern Mesopotamian Economy. In *Archaeological Perspectives on Political Economies*, edited by Gary M. Feinman and Linda M. Nicholas. Pp. 41–56. Salt Lake City: University of Utah Press.

Adams, Robert McC., and Hans J. Nissen 1972 *The Uruk Countryside: The Natural Setting of Urban Societies*. Chicago: University of Chicago Press.

Adovasio, J. M., and David Pedler 2005 The Peopling of North America. In *North American Archaeology*, edited by Timothy R. Pauketat and Diana DiPaolo Loren. Pp. 30–55. Malden: Blackwell.

Alden Smith, Eric, Monique Borgerhoff Mulder, Samuel Bowles, Michael Gurven, Tom Hertz, and Mary K. Shenk 2010 Production Systems, Inheritance, and Inequality in Premodern Societies. *Current Anthropology* 51(1): 85–94.

Algaze, Guillermo 1989 The Uruk Expansion: Cross-Cultural Exchange in Early Mesopotamian Civilization. *Current Anthropology* 30(5): 571–608.

1993a *The Uruk World System: The Dynamics of Expansion of Early Mesopotamian Civilization*. Chicago: University of Chicago Press.

1993b The Expansionary Dynamics of Some Early Pristine States. *American Anthropologist* 95: 303–33.

2001a The Prehistory of Imperialism: The Case of Uruk Period Mesopotamia. In *Uruk Mesopotamia and Its Neighbors: Cross-Cultural Interactions in the Era of State Formation*, edited by Mitchell S. Rothman. Pp. 27–83. Santa Fe: School of American Research Press.

2001b Initial Social Complexity in Southwestern Asia: The Mesopotamian Advantage. *Current Anthropology* 42: 199–233.

2005 *The Uruk World System: The Dynamics of Expansion of Early Mesopotamian Civilization*, Second Edition. Chicago: University of Chicago Press.

2007 The Sumerian Takeoff. In *Settlement and Society: Essays Dedicated to Robert McCormick Adams*, edited by Elizabeth C. Stone. Pp. 343–68. Los Angeles: Cotsen Institute of Archaeology.

2008 *Ancient Mesopotamia and the Dawn of Civilization: The Evolution of an Urban Landscape*. Chicago: University of Chicago Press.

Allen, John, and Christ Hamnett 1995 Introduction. In *A Shrinking World? Global Unevenness and Inequality*, edited by John Allen and Chris Hamnett. Pp. 1–10. New York: Oxford University Press.

Alt, Susan M. 1999 Spindle Whorls and Fiber Production at Early Cahokian Settlements. *Southeastern Archaeology* 18: 124–33.

2001 Cahokian Change and the Authority of Tradition. In *The Archaeology of Tradition: Agency and History Before and After Columbus*, edited by Timothy R. Pauketat. Pp. 141–56. Gainesville: University Press of Florida.

Ambrose, Stanley H., Jane Buikstra, and Harold W. Krueger 2003 Status and Gender Differences in Diet at Mound 72, Cahokia, Revealed by Isotopic Analysis of Bone. *Journal of Anthropological Archaeology* 22: 217–26.

Anders, Martha B. 1991 Structure and Function at the Planned Site of Azangaro: Cautionary Notes for the Model of Huari as a Centralized Secular State. In *Huari Administrative Structures*, edited by William Isbell and Gordon McEwan. Pp. 165–98. Washington: Dumbarton Oaks.

Anderson, Atholl 2002 Faunal Collapse, Landscape Change and Settlement History in Remote Oceania. *World Archaeology* 33(3): 375–90.

Anderson, Benedict R. 1991 *Imagined Communities: Reflection of the Origin and Spread of Nationalism*, Second Edition. New York: Verso.

Anderson, David G. 1994 *The Savannah River Chiefdoms: Political Change in the Late Prehistoric Southeast*. Tuscaloosa: University of Alabama Press.

1996 Fluctuations between Simple and Complex Chiefdoms: Cycling in the Late Prehispanic Southeast. In *Political Structure and Change in the Prehistoric Southeastern United States*, edited by John F. Scarry. Pp. 231–52. Gainesville: University Press of Florida.

1997 The Role of Cahokia in the Evolution of Southeastern Mississippian Society. In *Cahokia: Domination and Ideology in the Mississippian World*, edited by Timothy R. Pauketat and Thomas E. Emerson. Pp. 248–68. Lincoln: University of Nebraska Press.

Anderson, Karen 2009 Tiwanaku Influence on Local Drinking Patterns in Cochabamba, Bolivia. In *Drink, Power, and Society in the Andes*, edited by Justin Jennings and Brenda J. Bowser. Pp. 167–99. Gainesville: University Press of Florida.

Andrews, Anthony P. 1983 *Maya Salt Production and Trade*. Tucson: University of Arizona Press.

Appadurai, Arjun 1990 Disjuncture and Difference in the Global Cultural Economy. *Theory, Culture, and Society* 7: 295–310.

1996 *Modernity at Large*. Minneapolis: University of Minnesota Press.

Arnold, Dean E. 1993 *Ecology and Ceramic Production in an Andean Community*. New York: Cambridge University Press.

Arnold, Denise Y., and Christine A. Hastorf 2008 *Heads of State: Icons, Power, and Politics in the Ancient and Modern Andes*. Walnut Creek: Left Coast Press.

Arrighi, Giovanni 1994 *The Long Twentieth Century: Money, Power, and the Origins of Our Times*. New York: Verso.

Bafna, Sonit, and Sudha Shah 2007 The Evolution of Orthogonality in Built Space: An Argument from Space Syntax. *Proceedings, 6th International Space Syntax Symposium, Istanbul 2007*. Paper 054: 1–14.

Bakker, Jan Albert, Janusz Kruk, Albert E. Lanning, and Sarunas Milisaukas 1999 The Earliest Evidence of Wheeled Vehicles in Europe and the Near East. *Antiquity* 73: 778–90.

Bandy, Matthew S. 2004 Fissioning, Scalar Stress, and Social Evolution in Early Village Societies. *American Anthropologist* 106(2): 322–33.

2005 Energetic Efficiency and Political Expediency in Titicaca Basin Raised Field Agriculture. *Journal of Anthropological Archaeology* 24(3): 271–96.

Banning, E. B. 2003 Housing Neolithic Farmers. *Near Eastern Archaeology* 66: 4–21.

Barber, Benjamin R. 1996 *Jihad vs. McWorld: How Globalism and Tribalism are Reshaping the World*. New York: Ballantine Books.

Barker, Alex W., Craig E. Skinner, M. Steven Shackley, Michael D. Glascock, and J. Daniel Rogers 2002 Mesoamerican Origin for an Obsidian Scrapper from the Precolumbian Southeastern United States. *American Antiquity* 67(1): 103–8.

Bauer, Brian S. 2004 *Ancient Cuzco: Heartland of the Inca*. Austin: University of Texas Press.

Bawden, Garth 1996 *The Moche*. Malden: Blackwell.

Beck Jr., Robin A. 2003 Consolidation and Hierarchy: Chiefdom Variability in the Mississippian Southeast. *American Antiquity* 68(4): 641–61.

2006 Persuasive Politics and Domination at Cahokia and Moundville. In *Leadership and Polity in Mississippian Society*, edited by Brian M. Butler and Paul D. Welch. Pp. 19–42. Carbondale: Center for Archaeological Investigations.

Beck, Ulricke 1992 *Risk Society: Towards a New Modernity*. London: Sage.

Bélisle, Véronique, and R. Alan Covey i.p. Local Settlement Continuity and Wari Impact in Middle Horizon Cusco. In *Beyond Wari Walls: Exploring the Nature of Middle Horizon Peru Away from Wari Centers*, edited by Justin Jennings. Albuquerque: University of New Mexico Press.

Benavides C., Mario 1991 Cheqo Wasi, Huari. In *Huari Administrative Structures: Prehistoric Monumental Architecture and State Government*, edited by William H. Isbell and Gordon F. McEwan. Pp. 55–69. Washington, DC: Dumbarton Oaks.

1999 Tejidos Wari/Wari Textiles. In *Tejidos Milenarios del Peru/Ancient Peruvian Textiles*, edited by Jose Antonio de Lavalle and Rosario de Lavalle Cardenas. Pp. 353–411. Lima: AFP Integra.

Bennett, Gwen P. 2007 Context and Meaning in Late Neolithic Lithic Production in China: The Lonshan Period in Southeastern Shandong Province. In *Rethinking Craft Specialization in Complex Societies: Archaeological Analyses of the Social Meaning of Production*, edited by Zachary X. Hruby and Rowan K. Flad. Pp. 52–67. *Archaeological Papers of the American Anthropological Association*, vol. 17. Arlington: American Anthropological Association.

Benson, Larry V., Timothy R. Pauketat, and Edward R. Cook 2009 Cahokia's Boom and Bust in the Context of Climate Change. *American Antiquity* 74(3): 467–83.

Bernardini, Wesley 2004 Hopewell Geometric Earthworks: A Case Study in the Referential and Experiential Meaning of Monuments. *Journal of Anthropological Archaeology* 23: 331–56.

Bernstein, William J. 2008 *A Splendid Exchange: How Trade Shaped the World*. New York: Atlantic Monthly Press.

Birmingham, Robert A., and Lynne G. Goldstein 2005 *Aztalan: Mysteries of an Ancient Indian Town*. Madison: Wisconsin Historical Society Press.

Blackman, M. James 2003 Chemical Characterizations of Clay Sealing from Arslantepe. In *Patterns and Process: A Festschrift in honor of Dr. Edward V. Sayre*, edited by Lambertus van Zelst. Pp. 173–84. Smithsonian Center for Materials Research and Education, Suitland.

Blanton, Richard, and Gary Feinman 1984 The Mesoamerican World System. *American Anthropologist* 86: 673–82.

Blanton, Richard, Stephen A. Kowalewski, Gary M. Feinman, and Laura M. Finsten 1993 *Ancient Mesoamerica: A Comparison of Three Regions*, Second Edition. New York: Cambridge University Press.

Blitz, John H. 1993 Big Pots for Big Shots: Feasting and Storage in a Mississippian Community. *American Antiquity* 58(1): 80–96.

1999 Mississippian Chiefdoms and the Fission-Fusion Process. *American Antiquity* 64(4): 577–92.

Blitz, John H., and Karl G. Lorenz 2006 *The Chattahoochee Chiefdoms*. Tuscaloosa: University of Alabama Press.

Boas, Franz 1989 *A Franz Boas Reader: The Shaping of American Anthropology, 1883–1911*, edited by George W. Stocking, Jr. Chicago: University of Chicago Press.

Boehmer, Rainer Michael 1991 Uruk 1980–1990: A Progress Report. *Antiquity* 65: 465–78.

Boone, Elizabeth Hill 1994 Introduction: Writing and Recording Knowledge. In *Writing without Words: Alternative Literacies in the Mesoamerica and the Andes*, edited by Elizabeth Hill Boone and Walter D. Mignolo. Pp. 3–26. Durham: Duke University Press.

Bourdieu, Pierre 1977 *Outline of a Theory of Practice*. Cambridge: Cambridge University Press.

Bowser, Brenda J. 2000 From Pottery to Politics: An Ethnoarchaeological Study of Political Factionalism, Ethnicity, and Domestic Pottery Style in the Ecuadorian Amazon. *Journal of Archaeological Method and Theory* 7(3): 219–48.

Boytner, Ran 2006 Class, Control, and Power: The Anthropology of Textile Dyes at Pacatnamu. In *Andean Textile Traditions: Papers from the 2001 Mayer Center Symposium at the Denver Art Museum*, edited by Margaret Young-Sánchez and Fronia W. Simpson. Pp. 43–74. Denver: Denver Art Museum.

Brackenridge, Herny Marie 1814 [1962] *Views of Louisiana Together with a Journal of a Voyage up the Missouri River, in 1811*. Chicago: Quadrangle Books Edition.

Bragayrac D., Enrique 1991 Archaeological Investigations in the Vegachayoc Moqo Sector of Huari. In *Huari Administrative Structures: Prehistoric*

Monumental Architecture and State Government, edited by William H. Isbell and Gordon F. McEwan. Pp. 71–80. Washington: Dumbarton Oaks.

Braudel, Fernand 1979 *Civilization and Capitalism: 15th–18th Century*, 3 vols., translated by Siân Reynolds. New York: Harper & Row.

Browman, David L. 1997 Political Institutional Factors Contributing to the Integration of the Tiwanaku State. In *Emergence and Change in Early Urban Societies*, edited by Linda Manzanilla. Pp. 229–43. New York: Plenum Press.

1999 Wari Impact on the Upper Mantaro Basin. Paper presented at the 64th annual meeting of the Society for American Archaeology, Chicago.

Brown, Don 1991 *Human Universals*. New York: McGraw-Hill.

Brown, James A. 1996 *The Spiro Ceremonial Center: The Archaeology of the Arkansas Valley Caddoan Culture in Eastern Oklahoma*. Ann Arbor: University of Michigan Press.

2005 The Cahokian Experience: Creating Court and Cult. In *Hero, Hawk, and Open Hand: American Indian Art of the Ancient Midwest and South*, edited by Richard F. Townsend. Pp. 105–23. New Haven: Yale University Press and the Art Institute of Chicago.

2007 Chronological Implications of the Bellow-Shaped Apron. In *Southeastern Ceremonial Complex: Chronology, Content, Context*, edited by Adam King. Pp. 38–56. Tuscaloosa: University of Alabama Press.

Brown, James A., and John E. Kelly 2000 Cahokia and the Southeastern Ceremonial Complex. In *Mounds, Modoc, and Mesoamerica: Papers in Honor of Melvin L. Fowler*, edited by Steven R. Ahler. Pp. 469–510. *Illinois State Museum Scientific Papers Series*, vol. XXVIII. Springfield: Illinois State Museum.

Brown, James A., Richard A. Kerber, and Howard D. Winters 1990 Trade and the Evolution of Exchange Relations at the Beginning of the Mississippian Period. In *The Mississippian Emergence*, edited by Bruce D. Smith. Pp. 251–80. Washington, DC: Smithsonian Institution Press.

Brown, Kenneth L. 1984 Hallucinogenic Mushrooms, Jade, Obsidian, and the Guatemalan Highlands: What Did the Olmecs Really Want? In *Trade and Exchange in Early Mesoamerica*, edited by Kenneth G. Hirth. Pp. 215–33. Albuquerque: University of New Mexico Press.

Brumfiel, Elizabeth 1994 The Economic Anthropology of the State: An Introduction. In *The Economic Anthropology of the State*, edited by Elizabeth Brumfiel. Pp. 1–12. Lanham: University Press of America.

1996 The Quality of Tribute Cloth: The Place of Evidence in Archaeological Argument. *American Antiquity* 61(3): 453–62.

Brumfiel, Elizabeth, and Timothy Earle 1987 Specialization, Exchange, and Complex Societies: An introduction. In *Specialization, Exchange, and Complex Societies*, edited by Elizabeth Brumfiel and Timothy Earle. Pp. 1–9. New York: Cambridge University Press.

Buckler IV, Edward S., Deborah M. Pearsall, and Timothy P. Holtsford 1998 Climate, Plant Ecology, and Central Mexican Archaic Subsistence. *Current Anthropology* 39(1): 152–64.

Buikstra, Jane E., and George R. Milner 1991 Isotopic and Archaeological Interpretations of Diet in the Central Mississippi Valley. *Journal of Archaeological Science* 18: 319–29.

Burger, Richard L. 1992 *Chavín and the Origins of Andean Civilization*. New York: Thames and Hudson.

Burger, Richard L., Karen L. Mohr Chávez, and Sergio J. Chávez 2000 Through the Glass Darkly: Prehispanic Obsidian Procurement and Exchange in Southern Peru and Northern Bolivia. *Journal of World Prehistory* 14: 267–362.

Burger, Richard L., and Ramiro Matos Mendieta 2002 Atlla: A Center on the Periphery of the Chavín Horizon. *Latin American Antiquity* 13(2): 153–77.

Butler, Brian M., and Paul D. Welch (eds.) 2006 *Leadership and Polity in Mississippian Society*. Carbondale: Center for Archaeological Investigations.

Byrd, Brian F. 2005 Reassessing the Emergence of Village Life in the Near East. *Journal of Archaeological Research* 13(3): 231–90.

Cabera Romero, Martha 1996 Unidades habitacionales, iconografía, y rituales en un poblado rural de la época Huari. Unpublished thesis presented for the license of archaeology to the Univerdidad Nacional de San Critobal de Huamanga, Ayacucho.

Caldwell, Melissa 2008 Domesticating the French Fry: McDonald's and Consumerism in Moscow. In *The Anthropology of Globalization: A Reader*, Second Edition, edited by Jonathan Xavier Inda and Renato Rosaldo. Pp. 237–53. Malden: Blackwell.

Calinescu, Matei 1987 *Five Faces of Modernity: Modernism, Avant-Garde, Decadence, Kitsch, Postmodernism*. Durham: Duke University Press.

Carr, Christopher 2006 Rethinking Interregional Hopewellian "Interaction." In *Gathering Hopewell: Society, Ritual, and Ritual Interaction*, edited by Christopher Carr and D. Troy Case. Pp. 575–623. New York: Springer.

Carter, Robert 2006 Boat Remains and Maritime Trade in the Persian Gulf during the Sixth and Fifth Millennia BC. *Antiquity* 80: 52–63.

Castells, Manuel 1996 *The Rise of Network Society: The Information Age: Economy, Society and Culture 1*. Oxford: Blackwell.

1997 *The Power of Identity: The Information Age: Economy, Society and Culture 2*. Oxford: Blackwell.

1998 *The End of the Millennium: The Information Age: Economy, Society and Culture 3*. Oxford: Blackwell.

2006 Nothing New Under the Sun? In *Connections in Antiquity: Globalization as Long-Term Historical Process*, edited by Øystein S. Bianca and Sandra Arnold Scham. Pp. 158–67. London: Equinox Publishing.

Castillo, Luis Jaime 2001 La presencia de Wari en San José de Moro. In *Huari y Tiwanaku: Modelos y Evidencias, Primera Parte*, edited by Peter Kaulicke and William Isbell. Pp. 143–79. *Boletín de Arqueología PUCP* no. 4. Lima: Fondo Editorial de la Pontificia Universidad Católica del Perú.

Catherwood, Frederick 1844 *Views of Ancient Monuments in Central America, Chiapas, and Yucatan*. London: Frederick Catherwood.

Chanda, Nayan 2007 *Bound Together: How Traders, Preachers, Adventurers, and Warriors Shaped Globalization*. New Haven: Yale University Press.

Chapdelaine, Claude 2009 Domestic Life in and around the Urban Sector of the Huacas of Moche Site, Northern Peru. In *Domestic Life in Prehispanic Capitals: A Study of Specialization, Hierarchy, and Ethnicity*, edited by Linda R. Manzanilla and Claude Chapdelaine. Pp. 181–96. Memoirs of the Museum of Anthropology, University of Michigan, Number 46. Ann Arbor: Museum of Anthropology.

i.p. Moche and Wari during the Middle Horizon on the North Coast of Peru. In *Beyond Wari Walls: Exploring the Nature of Middle Horizon Peru Away from Wari Centers*, edited by Justin Jennings. Albuquerque: University of New Mexico Press.

Charvát, Petr 2002 *Mesopotamia before History*. London: Routledge.

Chase-Dunn, Christopher 2006 Globalization: A World Systems Perspective. In *Global Social Change: Historical and Comparative Perspectives*, edited by Christopher Chase-Dunn and Salvatore J. Babones. Pp. 79–105. Baltimore: John Hopkins University Press.

Chase-Dunn, Christopher, and E. N. Anderson (eds.) 2005 *The Historical Evolution of World-Systems*. New York: Palgrave Macmillan.

Chase-Dunn, Christopher, and Salvatore Babones (eds.) 2006 *Global Social Change: Comparative and Historical Perspectives*. Baltimore: Johns Hopkins University Press.

Chase-Dunn, Christopher, and Thomas D. Hall 1991 *Core/Periphery Relations in Precapitalist Worlds*. Boulder: Westview Press.

1997 *Rise and Demise: Comparing World-Systems*. Boulder: Westview Press.

Chase-Dunn, Christopher, Yukio Kawano, and Benjamin Brewer 2000 Trade Globalization since 1795: Waves of Integration in the World-System. *American Sociological Review* 65: 77–95.

Chazan, Michael, and Mark Lehner 1990 An Ancient Analogy: Pot Baked Bread in Ancient Egypt and Mesopotamia. *Paléorient* 16(2): 21–34.

Childe, V. Gordon 1950 The Urban Revolution. *Town Planning Review* 21(1): 3–17.

1951 [1936] *Man Makes Himself*. New York: New American Library.

Chilton, Elizabeth 2005 Farming and Social Complexity in the Northeast. In *North American Archaeology*, edited by Timothy R. Pauketat and Diana DiPaolo Loren. Pp. 138–60. Malden: Blackwell.

Clark, John E., and Mary E. Pye 2006 The Pacific Coast and the Olmec Question. In *Olmec Art and Archaeology in Mesoamerica*, edited by John E. Clark and Mary E. Pye. Pp. 217–51. Washington, DC: National Gallery of Art.

Clark, Robert P. 1997 *The Global Imperative: An Interpretive History of the Spread of Human Kind*. Boulder: Westview Press.

Cobb, Charles R. 2003 Mississippian Chiefdoms: How Complex? *Annual Review of Anthropology* 32: 63–84.

2005 Archaeology and the "Savage Slot": Displacement and Emplacement in the Premodern World. *American Anthropologist* 107(4): 563–74.

Cobb, Charles R., and Brian M. Butler 2006 Mississippian Migration and Emplacement in the Lower Ohio Valley. In *Leadership and Polity in Mississippian Society*, edited by Brian M. Butler and Paul D. Welch. Pp. 328–47. Carbondale: Center for Archaeological Investigations.

Cobb, Charles R., and Adam King 2005 Re-inventing Mississippian Tradition at Etowah Georgia. *Journal of Archaeological Method and Theory* 12(3): 167–93.

Collins, Paul 2000 *The Uruk Phenomenon: The Role of Social Ideology in the Expansion of the Uruk Culture during the Fourth Millennium BC*. BAR International Series 900. Oxford: British Archaeological Reports.

Conlee, Christina A. i.p. Nasca and Wari: Local Opportunism and Colonial Ties during the Middle Horizon. In *Beyond Wari Walls: Exploring the Nature of Middle Horizon Peru Away from Wari Centers*, edited by Justin Jennings. Albuquerque: University of New Mexico Press.

Conlee, Christina A., Jalh Dulanto, Carol J. Mackey, and Charles Stanish 2004 Late Prehispanic Social Complexity. In *Andean Archaeology*, edited by Helaine Silverman. Pp. 209–36. Malden: Blackwell.

Conlee, Christina A., and Katharina J. Schreiber 2006 The Role of Intermediate Elites in the Balkanization and Reformation of Post-Wari Society in Nasca, Peru. *Intermediate Elites in Precolumbian States and Empires*, edited by Christina M. Elson and Alan R. Covey. Pp. 94–111. Tucson: University of Arizona Press.

Conrad, Lawrence A. 1991 The Middle Mississippian Cultures of the Central Illinois Valley. In *Cahokia and Its Hinterland*, edited by Thomas E. Emerson and R. Barry Lewis. Pp. 119–56. Urbana: University of Illinois Press.

Cook, Anita G. 2001 Huari D-Shaped Structures, Sacrificial Offerings, and Divine Rulership. In *Ritual Sacrifice in Ancient Peru*, edited by Elizabeth P. Benson and Anita G. Cook. Pp. 137–63. Austin: University of Texas Press.

Cook, Anita G., and Mary Glowacki 2003 Pots, Politics, and Power: Huari Ceramic Assemblages and Imperial Administration. In *The Archaeology and Politics of Food and Feasting in Early States and Empires*, edited by Tamara L. Bray. Pp. 173–202. New York: Kluwer Academic/Plenum.

Cook, Robert A., and Mark R. Schurr 2009 Eating between the Lines: Mississippian Migration and Stable Carbon Isotope Variation in Fort Ancient Populations. *American Anthropologist* 111(3): 344–59.

Cordy-Collins, Alana 1977 Chavín Art: Its Shamanic/Hallucinogenic Origins. In *Pre-Columbian Art History*, edited by Alana Cordy-Collins and Jean Stern. Pp. 353–62. Palo Alto: Peek Publications.

Cowgill, George L. 2003 Teotihuacan: Cosmic Glories and Mundane Needs. In *The Social Construction of Ancient Cities*, edited by Monica L. Smith. Pp. 37–55. Washington, DC: Smithsonian Institution.

2004 Origins and Development of Urbanism: Archaeological Perspectives. *Annual Review of Anthropology* 33: 525–49.

Cusik, James G. (ed.) 1998 *Studies in Culture Contact: Interaction, Culture Change, and Archaeology*. Carbondale: Center for Archaeological Investigations.

Dalan, Rinita A. 1997 The Construction of Mississippian Cahokia. In *Cahokia: Domination and Ideology in the Mississippian World*, edited by Timothy R. Pauketat and Thomas E. Emerson. Pp. 89–102. Lincoln: University of Nebraska Press.

Dalan, Rinita A., George R. Holley, William I. Wood, Harold W. Watters, Jr., and John A. Koepke 2003 *Envisioning Cahokia: A Landscape Perspective*. DeKalb: Northern Illinois University Press.

D'Altroy, Terence, and Timothy Earle 1985 Staple Finance, Wealth Finance, and Storage in the Inka Political Economy. *Current Anthropology* 26(2): 187–206.

Dancey, William S. 2005 The Enigmatic Hopewell of the Eastern Woodlands. In *North American Archaeology*, edited by Timothy R. Pauketat and Diana DiPaolo Loren. Pp. 108–37. Malden: Blackwell.

D'Andrade, Roy 2000 The Sad Story of Anthropology 1950–1999. *Cross-Cultural Research* 34(3): 219–32.

DeMarrais, Elizabeth, Timothy Earle, and Luis Jaime Castillo 1996 Ideology, Materialization, and Power Strategies. *Current Anthropology* 37(1): 15–31.

Denemark, Robert A., Jonathan Friedman, Barry K. Gills, and George Modelski. 2000 An Introduction to World-System History: Towards a Social Science of Long-Term Change. In *World System History: The Social Science of Long-Term Change*, edited by Robert A. Denemark, Jonathan Friedman, Barry K. Gills, and George Modelski. Pp. xv–xxii. New York: Routledge.

Dillehay, Thomas D., Duccio Bonavia, and Peter Kaulicke 2004a The First Settlers. In *Andean Archaeology*, edited by Helaine Silverman. Pp. 16–34. Malden: Blackwell.

Dillehay, Thomas D., Alan L. Kolata, and Mario Pino Q. 2004b Pre-Industrial Human and Environment Interactions in Northern Peru during the Late Holocene. *The Holocene* 14(2): 272–81.

Drooker, Penelope B. 1999 Exotic Ceramics at Madisonville: Implications for Interaction. In *Taming the Taxonomy: Toward a New Understanding of Great Lakes Archaeology*, edited by Ron F. Williamson and Christopher M. Watts. Pp. 71–82. Toronto: Eastendbooks.

Druc, Isabelle C. 1998 *Ceramic Production and Distribution in the Chavín Sphere of Influence*. New York: Oxford University Press.

Durkheim, Emile 1984 [1893] *The Division of Labor in Society*. New York: Free Press.

Earle, Timothy 2002 *Bronze Age Economics: The Beginnings of Political Economies*. Boulder: Westview Press.

Earle, Timothy, and Terrence D'Altroy 1989 Political Economy of the Inka Empire: The Archaeology of Power and Finance. In *Archaeological Thought in America*, edited by C. C. Lamberg-Karlovsky. Pp. 183–204. New York: Cambridge University Press.

Ekholm, Kasja, and Jonathan Friedman 1979 "Capital" Imperialism and Exploitation in Ancient World Systems. In *Power and Propaganda*, edited by Mogens T. Larsen. Pp. 41–58. Copenhagen: Akademish.

    1985 Towards a Global Anthropology. *Critique of Anthropology* 5(1): 97–119.

el-Ojeili, Chamsy, and Patrick Hayden 2006 *Critical Theories of Globalization*. New York: Palgrave Macmillan.

Emberling, Geoff, Jack Cheng, Torben E. Larsen, Holly Pittman, Tim B. B. Skuldboel, Jill Weber, and Henry T. Wright 1999 Excavations at Tell Brak 1998: Preliminary Report. *Iraq* LXI: 1–41.

Emberling, Geoff, and Helen McDonald 2002 Recent Finds from the Northern Mesopotamian City of Tell Brak. *Antiquity* 76: 949–50.

    2003 Excavations at Tell Brak 2001–2002: Preliminary Report. *Iraq* LXV: 1–75.

Emerson, Thomas E. 1997 *Cahokia and the Archaeology of Power*. Tuscaloosa: University of Alabama Press.

Emerson, Thomas E., and Randall E. Hughes 2000 Figurines, Flint Clay Sourcing, the Ozark Highlands, and Cahokian Acquisition. *American Antiquity* 65(1): 79–101.

Emerson, Thomas E., Randall E. Hughes, Mary R. Hynes, and Sarah U. Wisseman 2003 The Sourcing and Interpretation of Cahokia-Style Figurines in the Trans-Mississippi South and Southeast. *American Antiquity* 68(2): 297–313.

Englund, Robert K. 2004 Proto-Cuneiform Account-Books and Journals. In *Creating Economic Order: Record-Keeping, Standardization, and the Development of Accounting in the Ancient Near East*, edited by Michael Hudson and Cornelia Wunsch. Pp. 23–46. Bethesda: CDL Press.

Eriksen, Thomas Hylland 2007 *Globalization*. New York: Berg.

Esin, Ufuk 1985 Some Small Finds from the Chalcolithic Occupation at Degirmentepe (Malatya) in Eastern Turkey. In *Studi di Paletnologia in Onore de Salvatore M. Puglisi*, edited by Mario Liverani, Alba Palmieri, and Renato Peroni. Pp. 253–63. Rome: Università de Roma "La Sapienza."

Fagan, Brian 1995 *Time Detectives: How Archaeologists Use Technology to Recapture the Past*. New York: Simon & Schuster.

2004 *The Long Summer: How Climate Changed Civilization*. New York: Basic Books.

2008 *The Great Warming: Climate Change and the Rise and Fall of Civilizations*. New York: Bloomsbury.

Featherstone, Mike (ed.) 1990 *Global Culture: Nationalism, Globalization, and Modernity*. New York: Sage Books.

Feinman, Gary, Richard Blanton, and Stephen Kowalewski 1984 Market System Development in the Prehispanic Valley of Oaxaca, Mexico. In *Trade and Exchange in Early Mesoamerica*, edited by Kenneth G. Hirth. Pp. 157–78. Albuquerque: University of New Mexico Press.

Ferguson, James 2002 Global Disconnect: Abjection in the Aftermath of Globalization. In *The Anthropology of Globalization: A Reader*, edited by Jonathan Xavier Inda and Renato Rosaldo. Pp. 136–53. Malden: Blackwell.

Fienup-Riordan, Ann 1990 *Eskimo Essays: Yup'ik Lives and How We See Them*. New Brunswick: Rutgers University Press.

Finkbeiner, Uwe 1991 *Uruk: Kampagne 35–37, 1982–1984. Die archäologishe Oberflächenuntersuchung* (Survey). Baghdad: Deutches Archäologisches Institut Abteilung Baghdad.

Finucane, Brian Clifton, J. Ernesto Valdez, Ismael Pérez Calderon, Cirio Vivanco Pomacanchari, Lidio M. Valdez, and Tamsin O'Connell 2007 The End of Empire: New Radiocarbon Dates from the Ayacucho Valley, Peru, and Their Implications for the Collapse of the Wari State. *Radiocarbon* 49(2): 579–92.

Fishel, Richard L. 1997 Medicine Birds and Mill Creek-Middle Mississippian Interaction: The Contents of Feature 8 at the Phipps Site (13CK21). *American Antiquity* 62(3): 538–53.

Flad, Rowan K. 2007 Rethinking the Context of Production through an Archaeological Study of Ancient Salt Production in the Sichuan Basin, China. In *Rethinking Craft Specialization in Complex Societies: Archaeological Analyses of the Social Meaning of Production*, edited by Zachary X. Hruby and Rowan K. Flad. Pp. 108–28. Archaeological Papers of the American Anthropological Association, vol. 17. Arlington: American Anthropological Association.

Fletcher, Roland 1995 *The Limits of Settlement Growth: A Theoretical Outline.* New York: Cambridge University Press.

Florida, Richard 2005 The World Is Spiky: Globalization Has Changed the Economic Playing Field, but Hasn't Leveled It. *Atlantic*, October, 50–1.

Fortier, Andrew C. 2001 A Tradition of Discontinuity: American Bottom Early and Middle Woodland Culture History Reexamined. In *The Archaeology of Tradition: Agency and History Before and After Columbus*, edited by Timothy R. Pauketat. Pp. 174–94. Gainesville: University Press of Florida.

Fowler, Melvin L., Jerome Rose, Barbara Vander Leest, and Steven A. Ahler 1999 *The Mound 72 Area: Dedicated and Sacred Space in Early Cahokia.* Illinois State Museum, Reports of Investigation 54. Springfield: Illinois State Museum.

Frangipane, Marcella 2001 Centralization Processes in Greater Mesopotamia: Uruk "Expansion" as the Climax of Systematic Interactions among Areas of the Greater Mesopotamian Region. In *Uruk Mesopotamia and its Neighbors: Cross-Cultural Interactions in the Era of State Formation*, edited by Mitchell S. Rothman. Pp. 307–47. Santa Fe: School of American Research Press.

2002 'Non-Uruk' Developments and Uruk-Linked Features on the Northern Borders of Greater Mesopotamia. In *Artefacts of Complexity: Tracking the Uruk in the Near East*, edited by J. N. Postgate. Pp. 123–48. British Archaeological School in Iraq, Iraq Archaeological Reports 5. Wiltshire: Aris and Phillips.

Frangipane, Marcella, Gian Maria Di Nocera, Andreas Hauptman, Paola Morbidelli, Alberto M. Palmieri, Laura Sadori, Michael Schultz, and Tyede Schmidt-Schultz 2001 New Symbols of a New Power in a "Royal" Tomb from 3000 bc, Arslantepe, Malatya (Turkey). *Paléorient* 27(2): 105–39.

Frank, André Gunder 1966 The Development of Underdevelopment. *Monthly Review* 18: 17–31.

1967 *Capitalism and Underdevelopment in Latin America: Historical Studies of Chile and Brazil.* New York: Monthly Review Press.

1993 *The World System: Five Hundred Years or Five Thousand?* London: Routledge.

1998 *ReORIENT: Global Economy in the Asian Age.* Berkeley: University of California Press.

Frank, André Gunder, and Barry K. Gills 2000 The Five Thousand Year World System in Theory and Praxis. In *World System History: The Social Science of Long-Term Change*, edited by Robert A. Denemark, Jonathan Friedman, Barry K. Gills, and George Modelski. Pp. 3–23. New York: Routledge.

Friedman, Jonathan 1992 General Historical and Culturally Specific Properties of Global Systems. *Review* 15(3): 335–72.

2005 Plus Ça Change? On Not Learning from History. In *Hegemonic Decline: Present and Past*, edited by Jonathan Friedman and Christopher Chase-Dunn. Pp. 89–114. Boulder: Paradigm Publishers.

Friedman, Jonathan, and Christopher Chase-Dunn 2005 *Hegemonic Decline: Present and Past.* Boulder: Paradigm Publishers.

Friedman, Thomas 1999 *The Lexus and the Olive Tree: Understanding Globalization*. New York: Farrar, Strauss and Giroux.

2005 *The World Is Flat: A Brief History of the Twenty-First Century*. New York: Farrar Straus & Giroux.

2006 *The World Is Flat: A Brief History of the Twenty-First Century*, Updated and Expanded. New York: Farrar Straus & Giroux.

Friesen, T. Max 1999 Resource Structure, Scalar Stress, and the Development of Inuit Social Organization. *World Archaeology* 31(1): 21–37.

Geertz, Clifford 1980 *Negara: The Theatre State in 19th Century Bali*. Princeton: Princeton University Press.

2005 Shifting Aims, Moving Targets: On the Anthropology of Religion. *Journal of the Royal Anthropological Institute* 11: 1–15.

Gensheimer, Thomas R. 1984 The Role of Shell in Mesopotamia: Evidence for Trade Exchange with Oman and the Indus Valley. *Paléorient* 10(1): 65–73.

Gibson, McGuire, Amr al-Azm, Clemens Reichel, Salam Quntar, Judith A. Franke, Lamya Khalidi, Carrie Hritz, Mark Altaweel, Collen Coyle, Carlo Colantoni, Jonathan Tenney, Ghassan Abdul Aziz, and Tobin Hartnell 2002 Hamoukar: A Summary of Three Seasons of Excavations. *Akkadia* 123: 11–34.

Gibson, Shimon, and Yorke M. Rowan 2006 The Chalcolithic in the Central Highlands of Palestine: A Reassessment Based on a New Examination of Khirbet es-Sauma'a. *Levant* 38: 85–108.

Giddens, Anthony 1979 *Central Problems in Social Theory: Action, Structure, and Contradictions in Social Analysis*. Los Angeles: University of California Press.

1990 *The Consequences of Modernity*. Stanford: Stanford University Press.

1999 *Runaway World: How Globalization Is Reshaping Our Lives*. London: Profile Books.

Gills, Barry K., and William R. Thompson (eds.) 2006 *Globalization and Global History*. London: Routledge.

Glowacki, Mary 2002 The Huaro Archaeological Site Complex: Rethinking the Huari Occupation of Cuzco. In *Andean Archaeology I: Variations of Sociopolitical Organization*, edited by W. H. Isbell and H. Silverman. Pp. 267–85. New York: Kluwer Academic.

2005 Dating Pikillacta. In *Pikillacta: The Wari Empire in Cuzco*, edited by Gordon F. McEwan. Pp. 115–24. Iowa City: University of Iowa Press.

Glowacki, Mary, and Gordon F. McEwan 2001 Pikillacta, Huaro y la gran región del Cuzco: Nuevas interpretaciones de la ocupación Wari en la sierra sur. In *Huari y Tiwanaku: Modelos vs. Evidencias*, edited by Peter Kaulicke and William H. Isbell. Pp. 31–49. Boletín de Arqueología PUCP no. 5. Lima: Fondo Editorial de la Pontificia Universidad Católica del Perú.

Goff, Claire 1971 Luristan before the Iron Age. *Iran* IX: 131–52.

Goldstein, Lynn 2000 Mississippian Ritual as Viewed through the Practice of Secondary Disposal of the Dead. In *Mounds, Modoc, and Mesoamerica: Papers in Honor of Melvin L. Fowler*. Pp. 193–205. Illinois State Museum Scientific Papers Series, vol. XXVIII. Springfield: Illinois State Museum.

Goldstein, Paul S. 2003 From Stew-Eaters to Maize-Drinkers: The Chicha Economy and the Tiwanaku Expansion. In *The Archaeology and Politics of Food and Feasting in Early States and Empires*, edited by Tamara L. Bray. Pp. 143–72. New York: Kluwer Academic/Plenum.

2004 *Andean Diaspora: The Tiwanaku Colonies and Origins of South American Empire*. Tallahassee: University Press of Florida.

González Carré, Enrique 1981 La Antigua Ciudad de Wari en Ayacucho. *Boletín de Lima* 16–18: 83–97.

González Carré, Enrique, Enrique Bragayrac Dávila, Cirilo Vivanco Pomacanchari, Vera Tiesler Blos, and Máximo López Quispe 1996 *El Templo Mayor en la Ciudad de Wari: estudios arqueologicos en Vegachayoq Moqo-Ayacucho*. Ayacucho: Facultad de Ciencias Sociales, Universidad Nacional de San Cristobal de Huamanga.

Goody, Jack 2006 *The Theft of History*. New York: Cambridge University Press.

Gordon, Robert J. 1992 *The Bushman Myth: The Making of a Namibian Underclass*. Boulder: Westview Press.

Gramsci, Antonio 1971 *Selections from the Prison Notebooks*. New York: International Publishers.

Green, Linda 2002 Notes on Mayan Youth and Rural Industrialization in Guatemala. In *The Anthropology of Globalization: A Reader*, edited by Jonathan Xavier Inda and Renato Rosaldo. Pp. 101–20. Malden: Blackwell.

Green, Margaret W. 1980 Animal Husbandry at Uruk in the Archaic Period. *Journal of Near Eastern Studies* 39: 1–35.

Griffin, James B. 1967 Eastern North American Archaeology: A Summary. *Science* New Series 156 (3772): 175–91.

1992 Fort Ancient Has No Class: The Absence of an Elite Group in Mississippian Societies in the Central Ohio Valley. In *Lords of the Southeast: Social Inequality and the Native Elites of Southeastern North America*, edited by Alex W. Barker and Timothy R. Pauketat. Pp. 53–9. Archaeological Papers of the American Anthropological Association, vol. 3. Arlington: American Anthropological Association.

Gugler, Josef (ed.) 1997 *Cities in the Developing World: Issues, Theory, and Policy*. New York: Oxford University Press.

Gupta, Akhil, and James Ferguson 2002 Beyond "Culture": Space, Identity, and the Politics of Difference. In *The Anthropology of Globalization: A Reader*, edited by Jonathan Xavier Inda and Renato Rosaldo. Pp. 65–80. Malden: Blackwell.

Gut, Renate V. 2002 The Significance of the Uruk Sequence in Ninevah. In *Artefacts of Complexity: Tracking the Uruk in the Near East*, edited by J. N. Postgate. Pp. 17–48. British Archaeological School in Iraq, Iraq Archaeological Reports 5. Wiltshire: Aris and Phillips.

Haas, Jonathan, and Winifred Creamer 2004 Cultural Transformations in the Central Andean Late Archaic. In *Andean Archaeology*, edited by Helaine Silverman. Pp. 35–50. Malden: Blackwell.

Haeberli, Joerg 2006 When and Where Did the Nasca Proliferous Style Emerge. In *Andean Archaeology III: North and South*, edited by William H. Isbell and Helaine Silverman. Pp. 401–34. New York: Springer.

Hall, Thomas D., and Christopher Chase-Dunn 2006 Global Social Change in the Long Run. In *Global Social Change: Historical and Comparative Perspectives*, edited by Christopher Chase-Dunn and Salvatore J. Babones. Pp. 33–58. Baltimore: John Hopkins University Press.

Hannerz, Ulf 2002 Notes of the Global Ecumene. In *The Anthropology of Globalization: A Reader*, edited by Jonathan Xavier Inda and Renato Rosaldo. Pp. 37–45. Malden: Blackwell.

Hard, Robert J., and William L. Merril 1992 Mobile Agriculturalists and the Emergence of Sedentism: Perspectives from Northern Mexico. *American Anthropologist* 94(3): 601–20.

Hart, John P. 1990 Modeling Oneota Agricultural Production: A Cross-Cultural Evaluation. *Current Anthropology* 31(5): 569–77.

Hartley, Leslie Poles 1953 *The Go-Between*. London: Hamish Hamilton.

Harvey, David 1989 *The Condition of Postmodernity*. Cambridge: Blackwell.

Hastorf, Christine 1993 *Agriculture and the Onset of Political Inequality before the Inka*. Cambridge: Cambridge University Press.

    1999 *Early Settlement at Chiripa, Bolivia: Research of the Taraco Archaeological Project*. Berkeley: Archaeological Research Facility.

Hayden, Brian 1994 Village Approaches to Cultural Complexity. In *Archaeological Views from the Countryside: Village Communities in Early Complex Societies*, edited by Glenn M. Schwartz and Steven E. Falconer. Pp. 198–206. Washington: Smithsonian Institution.

Heggarty, Paul 2007 Linguistics for Archaeologists: Principles, Methods and the Case of the Incas. *Cambridge Archaeological Journal* 17(3): 311–40.

    2008 Linguistics for Archaeologists: A Case-Study in the Andes. *Cambridge Archaeological Journal* 18(1): 35–56.

Held, David, and Anthony McGrew 2000 The Great Globalization Debate: An Introduction. In *The Global Transformations Reader: An Introduction to the Globalization Debate*, edited by David Held and Anthony McGrew. Pp. 1–45. Malden: Polity Press.

Helms, Mary 1988 *Ulysses' Sail: An Ethnographic Odyssey of Power, Knowledge, and Geographical Distance*. Princeton: Princeton University Press.

Henrickson, Elizabeth F. 1994 The Outer Limits: Settlement and Economic Strategies in the Central Zagros Highlands during the Uruk Era. In *Chiefdoms and Early States in the Near East: The Organizational Dynamics of Complexity*, edited by Gil Stein and Mitchell S. Rothman. Pp. 85–102. Monographs in World Archaeology no. 18. Madison: Prehistory Press.

Hester, Thomas R., and Harry J. Shafer 1994 The Ancient Maya Craft Community at Colha, Belize, and Its External Relationships In *Archaeological Views from the Countryside: Village Communities in Early Complex Societies*, edited by Glenn M. Schwartz and Steven E. Falconer. Pp. 48–63. Washington, DC: Smithsonian Institution.

Hirth, Kenneth G. 1984 The Analysis of Prehistoric Economic Systems: A Look to the Future. In *Trade and Exchange in Early Mesoamerica*, edited by Kenneth G. Hirth. Pp. 281–302. Albuquerque: University of New Mexico Press.

Hitchner, R. Bruce 2008 Globalization Avant la Letre: Globalization and the History of the Roman Empire. *New Global Studies* 2(2): 1–12.

Hobsbawm, Eric, and Terrence Ranger (eds.) 1983 *The Invention of Tradition*. Cambridge: Cambridge University Press.

Hodder, Ian 2007 Çatalhöyük in the Context of the Middle Eastern Neolithic. *Annual Review of Anthropology* 36: 105–20.

Hole, Frank 1988 Patterns of Burial in the Fifth Millennium. In *Upon These Foundations: The 'Ubaid Reconsidered*, edited by Elizabeth F. Henrickson and Ingolf Thuesen. Pp. 149–80. Copenhagen: Museum Tusculanum Press.

1999 Economic Implications of Possible Storage Structures at Tell Ziyadeh, NE Syria. *Journal of Field Archaeology* 26: 267–83.

Holt, Julie Zimmermann 2009 Rethinking the Ramey State: Was Cahokia the Center of a Theatre State? *American Antiquity* 74(2): 231–54.

Hopkins, Anthony G. 2002 *Globalization in World History*, edited by Anthony G. Hopkins. London: Pimlico.

2006 *Global History: Interactions between the Universal and the Local*. Houndsmills: Palgrave Macmillan.

Hunt, Robert C. 1991 The Role of Bureaucracy in Provisioning of Cities: A Framework of Analysis. In *The Organization of Power: Aspects of Bureaucracy in the Ancient Near East*, edited by McGuire Gibson and Robert D. Biggs. Pp. 141–68. Chicago: The Oriental Institute of the University of Chicago.

Hyslop, John 1984 *The Inka Road System*. New York: Academic Press.

Inda, Jonathan Xavier, and Renato Rosaldo 2008 Tracking Global Flows. In *The Anthropology of Globalization: A Reader*, Second Edition, edited by Jonathan Xavier Inda and Renato Rosaldo. Pp. 3–46. Malden: Blackwell.

Inomata, Takeshi 2006 Plazas, Performers, and Spectators: Political Theaters of the Classic Maya. *Current Anthropology* 47(5): 805–42.

Isbell, William H. 1977 *The Rural Foundations of Urbanism*. Illinois Studies in Anthropology 10. Chicago: University of Illinois.

1985 El origen del estado en el valle de Ayacucho. *Revista Andina* 3(1): 57–106.

1987 State origins in the Ayacucho Valley, Central Highlands, Peru. In *The Origins and Development of the State in the Andes*, edited by Jonathon Hass, Sheila Pozorski, and Thomas Pozorski. Pp. 83–90. Cambridge: Cambridge University Press.

1988 City and State in Middle Horizon Wari. In *Peruvian Prehistory*, edited by Richard W. Keatings. Pp. 164–89. Cambridge: Cambridge University Press.

1989 Honcopampa: Was It a Huari Administrative Center? In *The Nature of Wari*, edited by R. M. Czwarno, F. M. Meddens, and A. Morgan. Pp. 98–114. BAR International Series 525. Oxford: B.A.R. Publications.

1991a Huari Administration and the Orthogonal Cellular Architecture Horizon. In *Huari Administrative Structures*, edited by William Isbell and Gordon McEwan. Pp. 293–316. Washington, DC: Dumbarton Oaks.

1991b Honocopampa: Monumental Ruins in Peru's North Highlands. *Expedition* 33(3): 27–36.

1997a Reconstructing Huari: A Cultural Chronology for the Capital City. In *Emergence and Change in Early Urban Societies*, edited by Linda Manzanilla. Pp. 181–227. New York: Plenum Press.

1997b *Mummies and Mortuary Monuments: A Postprocessual History of Central Andean Social Organization*. Austin: University of Texas Press.

2001a Repensando el Horizonte Medio: El caso the Conchapata, Ayacucho, Peru. In *Huari y Tiwanaku: Modelos y Evidencias. Primera Parte*, edited by Peter Kaulicke and William Isbell. Pp. 6–68. *Boletín de Arqueología PUCP* no. 4. Lima: Fondo Editorial de la Pontificia Universidad Católica del Perú.

2001b Huari: Crecimiento y desarrollo de la capital imperial. In *Wari: Arte Precolombino Peruano*, edited by Luis Millones. Pp. 99–172. Seville: Fundacíon el Monte.

2008 Wari and Tiwanaku: International Identities in the Central Andean Middle Horizon. In *Handbook of South American Archaeology*, edited by Helaine Silverman and William H. Isbell. Pp. 731–59. New York: Springer.

2009 Huari: A New Direction in Central Andean Urban Evolution. In *Domestic Life in Prehispanic Capitals: A Study of Specialization, Hierarchy, and Ethnicity*, edited by Linda R. Manzanilla and Claude Chapdelaine. Pp. 197–219. Memoirs of the Museum of Anthropology, University of Michigan, no. 46. Ann Arbor: Museum of Anthropology.

i.p. Agency, Identity, and Control: Understanding Wari Space and Power. In *Beyond Wari Walls: Exploring the Nature of Middle Horizon Peru Away from Wari Centers*, edited by Justin Jennings. Albuquerque: University of New Mexico Press.

Isbell, William H., Christine Brewster-Wray, and Lynda E. Spickard 1991 Architecture and Spatial Organization at Huari. In *Huari Administrative Structures*, edited by William Isbell and Gordon McEwan. Pp. 19–54. Washington, DC: Dumbarton Oaks.

Isbell, William H., and Patricia J. Knobloch 2006 Missing Links, Imaginary Links: Staff God Imagery in the South Andean Past. In *Andean Archaeology III: North and South*, edited by William H. Isbell and Helaine Silverman. Pp. 307–51. New York: Springer.

Isbell, William H., and Gordon F. McEwan 1991 A History of Huari Studies and Introduction to Current Interpretations. In *Huari Administrative Structures*, edited by William Isbell and Gordon McEwan. Pp. 1–17. Washington, DC: Dumbarton Oaks.

Isbell, William H., and Katharina J. Schreiber 1978 Was Huari a State? *American Antiquity* 43(3): 372–89.

Isla, Elizabeth, and Daniel Guerrero 1987 Socos: Un sitio Wari en el valle de Chillón. *Gaceta Arqueológica Andina* 4(41): 23–8.

Janusek, John Wayne 2002 Out of Many, One: Style and Social Boundaries in Tiwanaku. *Latin American Antiquity* 13(1): 35–61.

2008 *Ancient Tiwanku*. New York: Cambridge University Press.

Janusek, John Wayne, and Deborah E. Blom 2006 Identifying Tiwanaku Urban Populations: Style, Identity, and Ceremony in Andean Cities. In *Urbanism in the Preindustrial World: Cross-Cultural Approaches*, edited by Glen R. Storey. Pp. 233–51. Tuscaloosa: University of Alabama Press.

Jasim, Sabah Abboud 1988 Structure and Function in an 'Ubaid Village. In *Upon These Foundations: The 'Ubaid Reconsidered*, edited by Elizabeth F. Herickson and Ingolf Thuesen. Pp. 79–90. Copenhagen: Museum Tusculanum Press.

Jennings, Justin 2002 Prehistoric Imperialism and Cultural Development in the Cotahuasi Valley, Peru. Unpublished Ph.D. dissertation, University of California, Santa Barbara.

2006a Core, Peripheries, and Regional Realities in Middle Horizon Peru. *Journal of Anthropological Archaeology* 25: 346–70.

2006b Understanding Middle Horizon Peru: Hermeneutic Spirals, Interpretative Traditions, and Wari Administrative Centers. *Latin American Antiquity* 16: 265–86.

2008 Catastrophe, Revitalization, and Religious Change on the Prehispanic North Coast of Peru. *Cambridge Archaeological Journal* 18(2): 177–94.

i.p. Becoming Wari: Globalization and the Role of the Wari State in the Cotahuasi Valley of Southern Peru. In *Beyond Wari Walls: Exploring the Nature of Middle Horizon Peru Away from Wari Centers*, edited by Justin Jennings. Albuquerque: University of New Mexico Press.

Jennings, Justin, and Nathan Craig 2001 Politywide Analysis and Imperial Political Economy: The Relationship between Valley Political Complexity and Administrative Centers in the Wari Empire of the Central Andes. *Journal of Anthropological Archaeology* 20: 479–502.

Joffe, Alexander H. 2000 Egypt and Syro-Mesopotamia in the 4th Millennium: Implications of the New Chronology. *Current Anthropology* 41(1): 113–23.

Johnson, Allen W., and Timothy Earle 1987 *The Evolution of Complex Societies*. Stanford: Stanford University Press.

Johnson, Gregory A. 1973 *Local Exchange and Early State Development in Southwestern Iran*. Ann Arbor: The University of Michigan Museum of Anthropology.

1975 Locational Analysis and the Investigation of Uruk Local Exchange Systems. In *Ancient Civilization and Trade*, edited by Jeremy A. Sabloff and C. C. Lamberg-Karlovsky. Pp. 341–68. Albuquerque: University of New Mexico Press.

1978 Information Sources and the Development of Decision-Making Organizations. In *Social Archaeology: Beyond Subsistence and Dating*, edited by Charles Redman. Pp. 87–112. New York: Academic Press.

1980 Spatial Organization of Early Uruk Settlement Systems. In *L'Archéologie de L'Iraq du Début de L'Époque Néolithique a 333 avant notre Ère*. Pp. 233–63. Paris: Éditions du Centre National de la Recherche Scientifique.

1982 Organizational Structure and Scalar Stress. In *Theory and Explanation in Archaeology*, edited by Colin Renfrew, Michael Rowlands, and Brian Seagraves. Pp. 389–421. New York: Academic Press.

1989 Late Uruk in Greater Mesopotamia: Expansion or Collapse? *Origini* 14: 595–613.

Joyce, Arthur A. 2000 Founding of Monte Albán: Sacred Propositions and Social Practices. In *Agency in Archaeology*, edited by Marcia-Ann Dobres and John E. Robb. Pp. 71–91. New York: Routledge.

2004 Sacred space and social relations in the Valley of Oaxaca. In *Mesoamerican Archaeology*, edited by Julie Hendon and Rosemary Joyce. Pp. 192–216. Oxford: Blackwell.

Julien, Daniel 1988 Ancient Cuismancu: Settlement and Cultural Dynamics in the Cajamarca Region of the North Highlands of Peru, 200 B.C.–A.D. 1532. Unpublished Ph.D. dissertation, University of Texas, Austin.

Kaplan, David 2000 The Darker Side of the "Original Affluent Society." *Journal of Anthropological Research* 56(3): 301–24.

Kardulias, P. Nick 1999 *World Systems Theory in Practice: Leadership, Production, and Exchange*, edited by P. Nick Kardulias. Lanham: Rowman & Littlefield.

2007 Negotiation and Incorporation on the Margins of World-Systems: Examples from Cyprus and North America. *Journal of World-Systems Research* XIII(1): 55–82.

Kardulias, P. Nick, and Thomas D. Hall 2008 Archaeology and World-Systems Analysis. *World Archaeology* 40: 572–83.

Kaulicke, Peter 1997 *Contextos Funerarios de Ancón: Esbozo de una síntesis analítica*. Lima: Fondo Editorial de la Pontifica Universidad Católica del Perú.

2001 La sombra de Pachacamac: Huari en la costa central. In *Huari y Tiwanaku: Modelos y Evidencias, Primera Parte*, edited by Peter Kaulicke and William Isbell. Pp. 313–58. *Boletín de Arqueología PUCP* no. 4. Lima: Fondo Editorial de la Pontificia Universidad Católica del Perú.

Kellner, Corina M., and Margaret J. Schoeninger 2008 Wari's Imperial Influence on Local Nasca Diet: The Stable Isotope Evidence. *Journal of Anthropological Archaeology* 27: 226–43.

Kelly, John E. 1990a The Emergence of Mississippian Culture in the American Bottom Region. In *The Mississippian Emergence*, edited by Bruce D. Smith. Pp. 113–52. Washington, DC: Smithsonian Institution Press.

1990b Range Site Community Patterns and the Mississippian Emergence. In *The Mississippian Emergence*, edited by Bruce D. Smith. Pp. 67–112. Washington, DC: Smithsonian Institution Press.

1991a Cahokia and Its Role as a Gateway Center in Interregional Exchange. In *Cahokia and Hinterlands: Middle Mississippian Cultures of the Midwest*, edited by Thomas E. Emerson and R. Barry Lewis. Pp. 61–80. Urbana: University of Illinois Press.

1991b The Evidence for Prehistoric Exchange and Its Implications for the Development of Cahokia. *New Perspectives on Cahokia: Views from the Periphery*, edited by John B. Stoltman. Pp. 65–92. Madison: Prehistory Press.

2006 The Ritualization of Cahokia: The Structure and Organization of Early Cahokia Crafts. In *Leadership and Polity in Mississippian Society*, edited by Brian M. Butler and Paul D. Welch. Pp. 73–90. Carbondale: Center for Archaeological Investigations.

Kembel, Silvia Rodriquez, and John W. Rick 2004 Building Authority at Chavín de Huantar: Models of Social Organization and Development in the Initial Period and Early Horizon. In *Andean Archaeology*, edited by Helaine Silverman. Pp. 51–76. Malden: Blackwell.

Kemp, Barry J. 1989 *Ancient Egypt: Anatomy of a Civilization*. London: Routlege.

King, Adam 2003 *Etowah: The Political History of a Chiefdom Capital*. Tuscaloosa: University of Alabama Press.

2006 Leadership Strategies and the Nature of Mississippian Chiefdoms in Northern Georgia. In *Leadership and Polity in Mississippian Society*, edited by Brian M. Butler and Paul D. Welch. Pp. 73–90. Carbondale: Center for Archaeological Investigations.

2007a The Southeastern Ceremonial Complex: From Cult to Complex. In *Southeastern Ceremonial Complex: Chronology, Content, Context*, edited by Adam King. Pp. 1–14. Tuscaloosa: University of Alabama Press.

2007b Whither SECC? In *Southeastern Ceremonial Complex: Chronology, Content, Context*, edited by Adam King. Pp. 251–8. Tuscaloosa: University of Alabama Press.

Knapp, A. Bernard 1990 Production, Location and Integration in Bronze Age Cyprus. *Current Anthropology* 31: 147–76.

Knappett, Carl, Tim Evans, and Ray Rivers 2008 Modelling Maritime Interaction in the Aegean Bronze Age. *Antiquity* 82(318): 1009–24.

Knight, Jr., Vernon James 1990 Social Organization and the Evolution of Hierarchy in Southeastern Chiefdoms. *Journal of Anthropological Research* 46(1): 1–23.

Knobloch, Patricia J. 1976 A Study of the Huarpa Ceramic style of the Andean Early Intermediate Period. Unpublished M.A. Thesis, Department of Anthropology, State University of New York, Binghamton.

1983 A Study of the Andean Huari Ceramics of the Middle Horizon 1. Unpublished Ph.D. dissertation, Department of Anthropology, State University of New York, Binghamton.

Knudson, Kelly J. 2008 Tiwanaku Influence in the South Central Andes: Strontium Isotope Analysis and Middle Horizon Migration. *Latin American Antiquity* 19(1): 3–23.

Knudson, Kelly J., and Christopher M. Stojanowski 2008 New Directions in Bioarchaeology: Recent Contributions to the Study of Human Social Identities. *Journal of Archaeological Research* 16(4): 240–76.

Kohl, Phillip 1978 The Balance of Trade in Southwest Asia in Mid-Third Millennium B.C. *Current Anthropology* 19: 463–92.

1987 The Use and Abuse of World Systems Theory: The Case of the "Pristine" West Asian State. *Advances in Archaeological Method and Theory* 11: 1–35.

2007 *The Making of Bronze Age Eurasia*. Cambridge: Cambridge University Press.

Kottak, Conrad Phillip 2006 *Assault on Paradise: The Globalization of a Little Community in Brazil*, Fourth Edition. New York: McGraw-Hill.

Kramer, Karen L., and James L. Boone 2002 Why Intensive Agriculturists Have Higher Fertility: A Household Energy Budget Approach. *Current Anthropology* 43(3): 511–17.

Kroeber, Alfred, and Clyde Kluckhohn 1952 *Culture, a Critical Review of Concepts and Definitions*. New York: Vintage.

Kudrle, Robert T. 2004 Globalization by the Numbers: Quantitative Indicators and the Role of Policy. *International Studies Perspectives* 5(4): 341–55.

Kuijt, Ian 2008 The Regeneration of Life: Neolithic Structures of Symbolic Remembering and Forgetting. *Current Anthropology* 49(2): 171–97.

LaBianca, Øystein S., and Sandra Arnold Scham (eds.) 2006 *Connectivity in Antiquity: Globalization as Long-Term Historical Process*. London: Equinox Publishing.

Larkin, Brian 2008 Itineraries of Indian Cinema: African Videos, Bollywood, and Global Media. In *The Anthropology of Globalization: A Reader*, Second

Edition, edited by Jonathan Xavier Inda and Renato Rosaldo. Pp. 334–51. Malden: Blackwell.

Larsen, Clark Spencer 2002 Bioarchaeology: The Lives and Lifestyles of Past People. *Journal of Anthropological Research* 10: 119–66.

Lau, George 2005 Core–Periphery Relations in the Recuay Hinterlands: Economic Interaction at Chinchawas, Peru. *Antiquity* 79: 78–99.

2006 Northern Exposures: Recuay-Cajamarca Boundaries and Interaction. In *Andean Archaeology III: North and South*, edited by William H. Isbell and Helaine Silverman. Pp. 143–70. New York: Springer Science.

Lawler, Andrew 2006 North Versus South, Mesopotamian Style. *Science* 312: 1458–63.

2007 Murder in Mesopotamia? *Science* 317: 1164–5.

Lechtman, Heather 1980 The Central Andes: Metallurgy without Iron. In *The Coming of the Age of Iron*, edited by Theodore A. Wertime and James D. Muhly. Pp. 267–334. New Haven: Yale University Press.

2003 Middle Horizon Bronze: Centers and Outliers. In *Patterns and Process: A Festschrift in Honor of Dr. Edward V. Sayre*, edited by Lambertus van Zelst. Pp. 248–68. Smithsonian Center for Materials Research and Education, Suitland.

2005 Arsenic Bronze at Pikillacta. In *Pikillacta: The Wari Empire in Cuzco*, edited by Gordon McEwan. Pp. 131–146. Iowa City: University of Iowa Press.

Lee, Richard B. 1984 *The Dobe !Kung*. New York: Harcourt Brace.

Leoni, Juan B. 2006 Ritual and Society in Early Intermediate Period Ayachucho: A View from the Site of Ñawinpukyo. In *Andean Archaeology III: North and South*, edited by William H. Isbell and Helaine Silverman. Pp. 279–306. New York: Springer.

Lesure, Richard E. 2004 Shared Art Styles and Long-Distance Contact in Early Mesoamerica. In *Mesoamerican Archaeology*, edited by Julie A Hendon and Rosemary A. Joyce. Pp. 73–96. Malden: Blackwell.

Lewis, R. Barry, and Charles Stout (eds.) 1998 *Mississippian Towns and Sacred Spaces: Searching for an Architectural Grammar*. Tuscaloosa: University of Alabama Press.

Lewis Jr., Cecil M. 2009 Difficulties in Rejecting a Local Ancestry with mtDNA Haplogroup Data in the South-Central Andes. *Latin American Antiquity* 20(1): 76–90.

Lewis Jr., Cecil M., Jane E. Buikstra, and Anne C. Stone 2007 Ancient DNA and Genetic Continuity in the South Central Andes. *Latin American Antiquity* 18(2): 145–60.

Lewis-Williams, David 2004 Constructing a Cosmos: Architecture, Power, and Domestication in Çatalhöyük. *Journal of Social Archaeology* 4(1): 28–59.

Liu, Li 2006 Urbanization in China: Erlitou and Its Hinterland. In *Urbanism in the Preindustrial World: Cross-Cultural Approaches*, edited by Glen R. Storey. Pp. 161–89. Tuscaloosa: University of Alabama Press.

Lumbreras, Luis 1974 *The Peoples and Cultures of Ancient Peru*. Washington, DC: Smithsonian Institution Press.

Macaulay, David 1979 *Motel of the Mysteries*. New York: Houghton-Mifflin.

MacGillivray, Alex 2006 *A Brief History of Globalization*. New York: Carroll & Graf.

Makowski, Krzystof 2008 Andean Urbanism. In *Handbook of South American Archaeology*, edited by Helaine Silverman and William H. Isbell. Pp. 633–57. New York: Springer.

Malville, Nancy J. 2001 Long Distance Transport of Bulk Goods in the Pre-Hispanic American Southwest. *Journal of Anthropological Archaeology* 20(2): 230–43.

Manzanilla, Linda 1997a Early Urban Societies: Challenges and Perspectives. In *Emergence and Change in Early Urban Societies*, edited by Linda Manzanilla. Pp. 3–39. New York: Plenum Press.

  1997b *Emergence and Change in Early Urban Societies*. New York: Plenum Press.

  1997c Teotihuacan: Urban Archetype, Cosmic Model. In *Emergence and Change in Early Urban Societies*, edited by Linda Manzanilla. Pp. 109–31. New York: Plenum Press.

Marcone, Giancarlo i.p. What Role Did Wari Play in the Lima Political Economy? The Peruvian Central Coast at the Beginning of the Middle Horizon. In *Beyond Wari Walls: Exploring the Nature of Middle Horizon Peru Away from Wari Centers*, edited by Justin Jennings. Albuquerque: University of New Mexico Press.

Marcus, Joyce 1998 The Peaks and Valleys of Ancient States: An Extension of the Dynamic Model. In *Archaic States*, edited by Gary M. Feinman and Joyce Marcus. Pp. 59–94. Santa Fe: School of American Research Press.

Masuda, Shozo, Izumi Shimada, and Craig Morris (eds.) 1985 *Andean Ecology and Civilization*. Tokyo: University of Tokyo Press.

Matthews, Roger J. 1992 Jemdet Nasr: The Site and the Period. *Biblical Archaeologist* 55(4): 196–203.

Matthews, Roger J., and Hassan Fazeli 2004 Copper and Complexity: Iran and Mesopotamia in the Fourth Millennium BC. *Iran* 42: 61–75.

McCorriston, Joy 1997 The Fiber Revolution: Textile Extensification, Alienation, and Social Stratification in Ancient Mesopotamia. *Current Anthropology* 38(4): 517–49.

McEwan, Gordon F. 1991 Investigations at the Pikillacta Site: A Provincial Huari Center in the Valley of Cuzco. In *Huari Administrative Structures*, edited by William Isbell and Gordon McEwan. Pp. 93–120. Washington, DC: Dumbarton Oaks.

  1996 Archaeological Investigations at Pikillacta, a Wari Site in Peru. *Journal of Field Archaeology* (23)2: 169–86.

  2005a *Pikillacta: The Wari Empire in Cuszco*, edited by Gordon F. McEwan. Iowa City: University of Iowa Press.

  2005b Excavations at Pikillacta. In *Pikillacta: The Wari Empire in Cuzco*, edited by Gordon F. McEwan. Pp. 29–62. Iowa City: University of Iowa Press.

  2005c Pikillacta Architecture and Construction Requirements. In *Pikillacta: The Wari Empire in Cuzco*, edited by Gordon F. McEwan. Pp. 147–64. Iowa City: University of Iowa Press.

  2005d Conclusion: The Function of Pikillacta. In *Pikillacta: The Wari Empire in Cuzco*, edited by Gordon F. McEwan. Pp. 147–64. Iowa City: University of Iowa Press.

McMahon, Augsta, and Joan Oates 2007 Excavations at Tell Brak 2006–2007. *Iraq* LXIX: 145–71.

McNeil, William H. 2008 Globalization: Long Term Process or New Era in Human Affairs. *New Global Studies* 2(1): 1–9.

Meddens, Frank 1991 A Provincial Perspective of Huari Organization Viewed from the Chicha/Soras Valley. In *Huari Administrative Structures*, edited by William Isbell and Gordon McEwan. Pp. 215–32. Washington, DC: Dumbarton Oaks.

Meddens, Frank, and Nicholas Branch i.p. The Wari State, Its Use of Ancestors, Rural Hinterland and Agricultural Infrastructure. In *Beyond Wari Walls: Exploring the Nature of Middle Horizon Peru Away from Wari Centers*, edited by Justin Jennings. Albuquerque: University of New Mexico Press.

Mehrer, Mark W. 1995 *Cahokia's Countryside: Household Archaeology, Settlement Patterns, and Social Power*. DeKalb: Northern Illinois University Press.

Mellink, Machteld J. 1989 Anatolian and Foreign Relations of Tarsus in the Early Bronze Age. In *Anatolia and the Ancient Near East: Studies in Honor of Tahsin Özgüç*, edited by Kutlu Emre, Barthel Hrouda, Machteld Mellink, and Nimet Özgüç. Pp. 319–31. Ankara: Türk Tarih Kurumu Basimevi.

Menzel, Dorothy 1964 Style and Time in the Middle Horizon. *Ñawpa Pacha* 2: 1–106.

1977 *The Archaeology of Ancient Peru and the Work of Max Uhle*. Berkeley: R. H. Lowie Museum of Anthropology, University of California.

Meyers, Maureen S. 2006 Leadership at the Edge. In *Leadership and Polity in Mississippian Society*, edited by Brian M. Butler and Paul D. Welch. Pp. 156–77. Carbondale: Center for Archaeological Investigations.

Millard, A. R. 1988 The Bevelled-Rim Bowls: Their Purpose and Significance. *Iraq* 50: 49–57.

Miller, Heather M.-L. 2007 Associations and Ideologies in the Locations of Urban Craft Production at Harappa, Pakistan (Indus Civilization). In *Rethinking Craft Specialization in Complex Societies: Archaeological Analyses of the Social Meaning of Production*, edited by Zachary X. Hruby and Rowan K. Flad. Pp. 37–51. Archaeological Papers of the American Anthropological Association, vol. 17. Arlington: American Anthropological Association.

Milner, George R. 1990 The Late Prehistoric Cahokia Cultural System of the Mississippi River Valley: Foundations, Florescence, and Fragmentation. *Journal of World Prehistory* 4(1): 1–43.

1998 *The Cahokia Chiefdom: The Archaeology of a Mississippian Society*. Washington, DC: Smithsonian Institution Press.

Minnegal, Monica, and Peter D. Dwyer 1998 Intensification and Social Complexity in the Interior Lowlands of Papau New Guinea: A Comparison of Bedamuni and Kubo. *Journal of Anthropological Archaeology* 17: 375–400.

Montoyo, Eduardo, Mary Glowacki, Julinho Zapata, and Pablo Mendoza 2001 Chemical Characterization of Archaeological Ceramics using k_o Based INAA: A Study in the Production and Distribution of Middle Horizon Pottery from Cuzco Peru. *Nuclear Analytical Techniques in*

Archaeological Investigations. Technical Reports Series, no. 416. Pp. 163–84. Vienna: International Atomic Energy Agency.

Morgan, Lewis Henry 1963 [1877] *Ancient Society, or Researches in the Lines of Human Progress from Savagery through Barbarism to Civilization.* New York: Meridian Books.

Morris, Ian 2006 The Growth of Greek Cities in the First Millennium BC. In *Urbanism in the Preindustrial World: Cross-Cultural Approaches,* edited by Glen R. Storey. Pp. 27–51. Tuscaloosa: University of Alabama Press.

Moseley, Michael E. 1999 Convergent Catastrophe: Past Patterns and Future Implications of Collateral Natural Disasters in the Andes. In *The Angry Earth: Disaster in Anthropological Perspective,* edited by Anthony Oliver-Smith and Susan M. Hoffman. Pp. 59–71. New York: Routledge.

2002 Modelling Protracted Drought, Collateral Natural Disaster, and Human Responses in the Andes. In *Catastrophe and Culture: The Anthropology of Disaster,* edited by Susan A. Hoffman and Anthony Oliver-Smith. Pp. 187–212. Santa Fe: School of American Research.

Moseley, Michael E., Donna J. Nash, Patrick Ryan Williams, Susan D. deFrance, Anna Miranda, and Mario Ruales 2005 Burning Down the Brewery: Establishing and Evacuating an Ancient Imperial Colony at Cerro Baúl, Peru. *Proceedings of the National Academy of Sciences* 102(48): 17264–71.

Muller, Jon 1997 *Mississippian Political Economy.* New York: Plenum Press.

Nash, Dapne 1987 Imperial Expansion under the Roman Republic. In *Centre and Periphery in the Ancient World,* edited by Michael Rowlands, Morgens Larsen, and Kristian Kristiansen. Pp. 87–103. New York: Cambridge University Press.

Nash, Donna J. 2002 The Archaeology of Space: Places of Power in the Wari Empire. Unpublished Ph.D. dissertation, Department of Anthropology, University of Florida, Gainesville.

Nash, Donna J., and Patrick Ryan Williams 2005 Architecture and Power on the Wari-Tiwanaku Frontier. In *Foundations of Power in the Prehispanic Andes,* edited by Kevin J. Vaughn, Dennis Ogburn, and Christina A. Conlee. Pp. 151–74. Archaeological Papers of the American Anthropological Association, vol. 14. Arlington: American Anthropological Association.

Nass, John P., and Richard W. Yerkes 1995 Social Differentiation in Mississippian and Fort Ancient Societies. In *Mississippian Communities and Households,* edited by J. Daniel Rogers and Bruce D. Smith. Pp. 58–80. Tuscaloosa: University of Alabama Press.

Nassaney, Michael S. 2001 The Historical-Processual Development of Late Woodland Societies. In *The Archaeology of Tradition: Agency and History Before and After Columbus,* edited by Timothy R. Pauketat. Pp. 157–73. Gainesville: University Press of Florida.

Naveh, Danny 2003 PPNA Jericho: a Socio-political Perspective. *Cambridge Archaeological Journal* 13: 83–96.

Neely, James A., and Henry T. Wright 1994 *Early Settlement and Irrigation on the Deh Luran Plain: Villages and Early State Societies in Southwestern Iran.* Ann Arbor: The University of Michigan Museum of Anthropology.

Nelson, Kit, Nathan Craig, and Manuel Perales i.p. Piecing Together the Middle: The Middle Horizon in the Norte Chico. In *Beyond Wari*

Walls: Exploring the Nature of Middle Horizon Peru Away from Wari Centers, edited by Justin Jennings. Albuquerque: University of New Mexico Press.

Nerderveen Pieterse, Jan 2004 *Globalization and Culture*. Malden: Rowman and Littlefield.

Nicholas, Ilene M. 1987 The Function of Bevelled-Rim Bowls: A Case Study at the Tuv Mound, Tal-E Malyan, Iran. *Paléorient* 13(2): 61–72.

Nissen, Hans J. 1986 The Archaic Texts from Uruk. *World Archaeology* 17(3): 317–34.

    1988 *The Early History of the Ancient Near East 9000–2000 BC*. Chicago: University of Chicago Press.

    2001 Cultural and Political Networks in the Ancient Near East during the Fourth and Fifth Millennium. In *Uruk Mesopotamia and its Neighbors: Cross-Cultural Interactions in the Era of State Formation*, edited by Mitchell S. Rothman. Pp. 149–79. Santa Fe: School of American Research Press.

    2002 Uruk: Key Site of the Period and Key Site of the Problem. In *Artefacts of Complexity: Tracking the Uruk in the Near East*, edited by J. N. Postgate. Pp. 1–16. British Archaeological School in Iraq, Iraq Archaeological Reports 5. Wiltshire: Aris and Phillips.

Oakland, Amy S. 1986 Tiwanaku Textile Style from the South Central Andes, Bolivia and North Chile. Unpublished Ph.D. thesis, Department of Anthropology, University of Texas, Austin.

Oates, Joan 1993 Trade and Power in the Fifth and Fourth Millennium bc: New Evidence from Northern Mesopotamia. *World Archaeology* 24(3): 403–22.

    2002 Tell Brak: The 4th Millennium Sequence and its Implications. In *Artefacts of Complexity: Tracking the Uruk in the Near East*, edited by J. N. Postgate. Pp. 111–22. British Archaeological School in Iraq, Iraq Archaeological Reports 5. Wiltshire: Aris and Phillips.

Oates, Joan, and David Oates 2004 The Role of Exchange Relations in the Origins of Mesopotamian Civilization. In *Explaining Social Change: Studies in Honor of Colin Renfrew*, edited by John Cherry, Chris Scarre, and Stephen Shennan. Pp. 177–92. Cambridge: McDonald Institute of Archaeology.

O'Brien, Patricia J. 1991 Early State Economics: Cahokia, Capital of the Ramsey State. In *Early State Economics*, edited by Henri J. M. Claessen and Pieter van de Velde. Pp. 143–75. London: Transaction Publishers.

Ochatoma Paravicino, José y Martha Cabrera Romero 2001a *Poblados rurales Huari: una visión desde Aqo Wayqo*. Lima: CANO.

    2001b Arquitectura y áreas de actividad en Conchopata. In *Huari y Tiwanaku: Modelos y Evidencias. Primera Parte*, edited by Peter Kaulicke and William Isbell. Pp. 449–88. *Boletín de Arqueología PUCP* no. 4. Lima: Fondo Editorial de la Pontificia Universidad Católica del Perú.

    2002 Religious Ideology and Military Organization in the Iconography of a D-Shaped Ceremonial Precinct at Conchopata. In *Andean Archaeology II: Art, Landscape and Society*, edited by Helaine Silverman and William H. Isbell. Pp. 225–48. New York: Kluwer Academic/Plenum.

Oka, Rahul, and Chapurukha M. Kusimba 2008 The Archaeology of Trading Systems, Part 1: Towards a New Trade Synthesis. *Journal of Archaeological Research* 16: 339–95.

Orwell, George 1996 [1946] *Animal Farm*. New York: Signet Classic.

Osterhammel, Jürgen, and Niels P. Petersson 2005 *Globalization: A Short History*. Princeton: Princeton University Press.

Owen, Bruce 2005 Distant Colonies and Explosive Collapse: The Two Stages of the Tiwanaku Diaspora in the Osmore Drainage. *Latin American Antiquity* 16(1): 45–80.

Paredes, Juan, Berenince Quintana, and Moisés Linares 2001 Tumbas de la época Wari en el Callejón de Huaylas, Ancash. In *Huari y Tiwanaku: Modelos y Evidencias, Primera Parte*, edited by Peter Kaulicke and William Isbell. Pp. 253–88. *Boletín de Arqueología PUCP* no. 4. Lima: Fondo Editorial de la Pontificia Universidad Católica del Perú.

Parkinson, William A., and Michael L. Galaty 2007 Secondary States in Perspective: An Integrated Approach to State Formation in the Prehistoric Aegean. *American Anthropologist* 109(1): 113–29.

Patterson, Thomas C. 1971 Chavín: An Interpretation of Its Spread and Influence. In *Dumbarton Oaks Conference on Chavín, October 26th and 27th, 1968*, edited by Elizabeth P. Benson. Pp. 29–48. Washington, DC: Dumbarton Oaks.

Pauketat, Timothy R. 1998 Refiguring the Archaeology of Greater Cahokia. *Journal of Archaeological Research* 6(1): 45–89.

2001 A New Tradition in Archaeology. In *The Archaeology of Traditions: Agency and History Before and After Columbus*, edited by Timothy R. Pauketat. Pp. 1–16. Gainesville: University Press of Florida.

2003 Resettled Farmers and the Making of a Mississippian Polity. *American Antiquity* 68(1): 39–66.

2004a The Economy of the Moment: Cultural Practices and Mississippian Chiefdoms. In *Archaeological Perspectives on Political Economies*, edited by Gary M. Feinman and Linda M. Nicholas. Pp. 25–39. Salt Lake City: University of Utah Press.

2004b *Ancient Cahokia and the Mississippians*. Cambridge: Cambridge University Press.

2005 The Forgotten History of the Mississippians. In *North American Archaeology*, edited by Timothy R. Pauketat and Diana DiPaolo Loren. Pp. 187–211. Malden: Blackwell.

2007 *Chiefdoms and Other Archaeological Delusions*. Lanham, MD: Altamira Press.

Pauketat, Timothy R., and Susan M. Alt 2003 Mounds, Memories, and Contested Mississippian History. In *Archaeologies of Memory*, edited by Ruth M. Van Dyke and Susan E. Alcock. Pp. 151–79. Malden: Blackwell.

2004 The Making and Meaning of a Mississippian Axe-Head Cache. *Antiquity* 78: 779–97.

2005 Archaeology in a Postmold? Physicality and the Archaeology of Culture Making. *Journal of Archeological Method and Theory* 12(3): 213–36.

Pauketat, Timothy R., and Thomas E. Emerson 1991 The Ideology of Authority and the Power of the Pot. *American Anthropologist* 93: 919–41.

Pauketat, Timothy R., Lucretia S. Kelly, Gayle J. Fritz, Neal H. Lopinot, Scott Elias, and Eve Hargrave 2002 The Residues of Feasting and Public Ritual at Early Cahokia. *American Antiquity* 67(2): 257–79.

Pauketat, Timothy R., and Neal H. Lopinot 1997 Cahokian Population Dynamics. In *Cahokia: Domination and Ideology in the Mississippian World*, edited by Timothy R. Pauketat and Thomas E. Emerson. Pp. 103–23. Lincoln: University of Nebraska Press.

Pauketat, Timothy R., and Diana D. Loren 2005 Alternative Histories and North American Archaeology. In *North American Archaeology*, edited by Timothy R. Pauketat and Diana D. Loren. Pp. 1–29. Oxford: Blackwell.

Payne, Claudine 2006 The Foundations of Leadership in Mississippian Chiefdoms: Perspectives from Lake Jackson and Upper Nodena. In *Leadership and Polity in Mississippian Society*, edited by Brian M. Butler and Paul D. Welch. Pp. 91–111. Carbondale: Center for Archaeological Investigations.

Peregrine, Peter N. 1992 *Mississippian Evolution: A World-System Perspective*. Madison: Prehistory Press.

    1996 Hyperopia or Hyberbole? The Mississippian World-System. In *Pre-Columbian World Systems*, edited by Peter N. Peregrine and Gary M. Feinman. Pp. 39–49. Madison: Prehistory Press.

Peregrine, Peter N., and Gary M. Feinman (eds.) 1996 *Pre-Columbian World Systems*. Madison: Prehistory Press.

Pérez Calderón, Ismael 1995 *Excavaciones de salvataje y propuesta sobre conservación de estructuras descubiertas, area museo de sitio en Wari*. Convenio Instituto Nacional de Cultura – Universidad Nacional San Cristóbal de Huamanga, Ayacucho.

Philander, S. George 1990 *El Niño, La Niña and the Southern Oscillation*. San Diego: Academic Press.

Philip, Graham 2002 Contacts between the 'Uruk' World and the Levant during the Fourth Millennium BC: Evidence and Interpretation. In *Artefacts of Complexity: Tracking the Uruk in the Near East*, edited by J. N. Postgate. Pp. 207–36. British Archaeological School in Iraq, Iraq Archaeological Reports 5. Wiltshire: Aris and Phillips.

Pittman, Holly 2001 Mesopotamian Intraregional Relations Reflected through Glyptic Evidence in the Late Chalcolithic Period 1–5 Periods. In *Uruk Mesopotamia and its Neighbors: Cross-Cultural Interactions in the Era of State Formation*, edited by Mitchell S. Rothman. Pp. 403–43. Santa Fe: School of American Research Press.

Pitts, Martin 2008 Globalizing the Local in Roman Britain: An Anthropological Approach to Social Change. *Journal of Anthropological Archaeology* 27: 493–506.

Plattner, Stuart 1996 *High Art Down Home*. Chicago: University of Chicago Press.

Plog, Fred, and Daniel G. Bates 1988 *Cultural Anthropology*, Second Edition. New York: Random House.

Pollack, David, and A. Gwynn Henderson 1992 Towards a Model of Fort Ancient Society. In *Fort Ancient Cultural Dynamics in the Middle Ohio River Valley*, edited by A. Gwynn Henderson. Pp. 281–94. Monographs in World Archaeology no. 8. Madison: Prehistory Press.

Pollock, Susan 1988 Power Politics in the Susa A Period. In *Upon These Foundations: The 'Ubaid Reconsidered*, edited by Elizabeth F. Herickson and Ingolf Thuesen. Pp. 281–92. Copenhagen: Museum Tusculanum Press.

    1999 *Ancient Mesopotamia: The Eden that Never Was*. New York: Cambridge University Press.

    2001 The Uruk Period in Southern Mesopotamia. In *Uruk Mesopotamia and Its Neighbors: Cross-Cultural Interactions in the Era of State Formation*, edited by Mitchell S. Rothman. Pp. 181–231. Santa Fe: School of American Research Press.

Ponte, Víctor 2001 Transformación social y política en el Callejón de Huaylas, Ancash. In *Huari y Tiwanaku: Modelos y Evidencias, Primera Parte*, edited by Peter Kaulicke and William Isbell. Pp. 219–51. *Boletín de Arqueología PUCP* no. 4. Lima: Fondo Editorial de la Pontificia Universidad Católica del Perú.

Pope, Melody, and Susan Pollock 1995 Trade, Tools, and Tasks: A Study of Uruk Chipped Stone Industries. *Research in Economic Anthropology* 16: 227–65.

Porubcan, Paula J. 2000 Human and Nonhuman Surplus Display at Mound 72, Cahokia. In *Mounds, Modoc, and Mesoamerica: Papers in Honor of Melvin L. Fowler*. Pp. 207–25. Illinois State Museum Scientific Papers Series, vol. XXVIII. Springfield: Illinois State Museum.

Postgate, J. N. 1994 *Early Mesopotamia: Society and Economy at the Dawn of History*. New York: Routledge.

    2002 *Artefacts of Complexity: Tracking the Uruk in the Near East*, edited by J. N. Postgate. British Archaeological School in Iraq, Iraq Archaeological Reports 5. Wiltshire: Aris and Phillips.

    2003 Learning the Lessons of the Future: Trade in Prehistory through a Historian's Lens. *Bibliotheca Orientalis* (1–2): 5–25.

Pournelle, Jennifer R. 2007 KLM to CORONA: A Bird's Eye View of Cultural Ecology and Early Mesopotamian Civilization. In *Settlement and Society: Essays Dedicated to Robert McCormick Adams*, edited by Elizabeth C. Stone. Pp. 29–62. Los Angeles: Cotsen Institute of Archaeology.

Price, T. Douglas, and Gary M. Feinman (eds.) 1995 *Foundations of Social Inequality*. New York: Springer.

Quilter, Jeffrey 1989 *Life and Death at La Paloma: Society and Mortuary Practices in a Preceramic Village*. Iowa City: University of Iowa Press.

Radcliffe-Brown, A. R. 1964 *The Andaman Islanders*. New York: The Free Press.

Rauch, Jonathan 2002 Seeing around Corners. *The Atlantic*, April, 35–48.

Raymond, J. Scott 1992 Highland Colonization of the Peruvian Montana in Relation to the Political Economy of the Huari Empire. *Journal of the Steward Anthropological Society* 20(1–2): 17–36.

Raymond, J. Scott, and William H. Isbell 1969 Cultural Remains in the Pampas River Valley, Peru. Paper presented at the 34th Annual Meeting of the Society for American Archaeology, Milwaukee.

Redman, Charles L., Steven R. James, Paul R. Fish, and J. Daniel Rogers (eds.) 2004 *The Archaeology of Global Change: The Impact of Humans on their Environment*. Washington, DC: Smithsonian Institution Press.

Reichel, Clemens 2002 Administrative Complexity in Syria during the 4th Millennium B.C.: The Seals and Sealings from Tell Hamoukar. *Akkadica* 123: 35–56.

Reiss, Wilhelm, and Alphons Stübel 1880–1887 *The Necropolis of Ancon in Peru*, translated by A. H. Keane. New York: A. Ascher and Company.

Renfrew, Colin, and John F. Cherry 1986 *Peer Polity Interaction and Socio-Political Change*. Cambridge: Cambridge University Press.

Restall, Matthew 2005 Foreword. In *The Post Classic to Spanish-Era Transition in Mesoamerica: Archaeological Perspectives,* edited by Susan Kepecs and Rani T. Alexander. Pp. xi–xii. Albuquerque: University of New Mexico Press.

Rice, Don S. (ed.) 1993a *Latin American Horizons: A Symposium at Dumbarton Oaks, 11th and 12th of October 1986*. Washington, DC: Dumbarton Oaks.

Rice, Don S. 1993b The Making of Latin American Horizons: An Introduction to the Volume. In *Latin American Horizons: A Symposium at Dumbarton Oaks, 11th and 12th of October 1986,* edited by Don Stephen Rice. Pp. 1–13. Washington, DC: Dumbarton Oaks.

  2006 Late Classic Maya Populations: Characteristics and Implications. In *Urbanism in the Preindustrial World: Cross-Cultural Approaches,* edited by Glen R. Storey. Pp. 1–23. Tuscaloosa: University of Alabama Press.

Rick, John 2005 The Evolution of Authority and Power at Chavín de Huántar, Peru. In *Foundations of Power in the Prehispanic Andes,* edited by Kevin J. Vaughn, Dennis Ogburn, and Christina A. Conlee. Pp. 71–89. Archaeological Papers of the American Anthropological Association, vol. 14. Arlington: American Anthropological Association.

Rindos, David 1980 Symbiosis, Instability, and the Origins and Spread of Agriculture: A New Model. *Current Anthropology* 21(6): 751–72.

Ritzer, George 1993 *The McDonaldization of Society: An Investigation into the Changing Character of Contemporary Social Life*. Thousand Oaks: Pine Forge Press.

  2006 *McDonaldization: The Reader*. Thousand Oaks: Pine Forge Press.

  2007 Introduction. In *The Blackwell Companion to Globalization,* edited by George Ritzer. Pp. 1–13. Malden: Blackwell.

Roaf, Michael 1988 'Ubaid Social Organization and Social Activities as seen from Tell Madhhur. In *Upon These Foundations: The 'Ubaid Reconsidered,* edited by Elizabeth F. Herickson and Ingolf Thuesen. Pp. 91–146. Copenhagen: Museum Tusculanum Press.

Robertson, Roland 1992 *Globalization: Social Theory and Global Culture*. London: Sage Publications.

Rogers, J. Daniel 1995 Dispersed Communities and Integrated Households: A Perspective from Spiro and the Arkansas Basin. In *Mississippian Communities and Households,* edited by J. Daniel Rogers and Bruce D. Smith. Pp. 81–98. Tuscaloosa: University of Alabama Press.

  1996 Markers of Social Integration: The Development of Centralized Authority in the Spiro Region. In *Political Structure and Change in the Prehistoric Southeastern United States,* edited by John F. Scarry. Pp. 53–68. Gainesville: University Press of Florida.

Rogers, J. Daniel, and Bruce D. Smith (eds.) 1995 *Mississippian Communities and Households*. Tuscaloosa: University of Alabama Press.

Rose, Jerome C. 1999 Mortuary Data and Analyis. In *The Mound 72 Area: Dedicated and Sacred Space in Early Cahokia*, edited by Melvin L. Fowler, Jerome Rose, Barbara Vander Leest, and Steven A. Ahler. Pp. 63–82. Illinois State Museum, Reports of Investigation 54. Springfield: Illinois State Museum.

Rosenberg, Michael 1998 Cheating at Musical Chairs: Territoriality and Sedentism in an Evolutionary Context. *Current Anthropology* 39(5): 653–81.

Rosenmüller, Christoph 2008 *Patrons, Partisans, and Palace Intrigues: The Court Society of Colonial Mexico, 1702–1710*. Calgary: University of Calgary Press.

Rossel, Stine, Fiona Marshall, Joris Peters, Tom Pilgram, Matthew D. Adams, and David O'Connor 2008 Domestication of the Donkey: Timing, Processes, and Indicators. *Proceedings of the National Academy of Sciences* 105(10): 3715–20.

Rothman, Mitchell S. 1994 Sealings as Control Mechanism in Prehistory: Tepe Gawra XI, X, and VIII. In *Chiefdoms and Early States in the Near East: The Organizational Dynamics of Complexity*, edited by Gill Stein and Mitchell S. Rothman. Pp. 103–20. Monographs in World Archaeology no. 18. Madison: Prehistory Press.

2001a *Uruk Mesopotamia and Its Neighbors: Cross-Cultural Interactions in the Era of State Formation*, edited by Mitchell S. Rothman. Santa Fe: School of American Research Press.

2001b The Tigris Piedmont, Eastern Jazira, and Highland Western Iran in the Fourth Millennium BC. In *Uruk Mesopotamia and its Neighbors: Cross-Cultural Interactions in the Era of State Formation*, edited by Mitchell S. Rothman. Pp. 349–401. Santa Fe: School of American Research Press.

2001c The Local and the Regional: An Introduction. In *Uruk Mesopotamia and Its Neighbors: Cross-Cultural Interactions in the Era of State Formation*, edited by Mitchell S. Rothman. Pp. 3–26. Santa Fe: School of American Research Press.

2002a *Tepe Gawra: The Evolution of a Small Prehispanic Center in Northern Iraq*. University Museum Monograph 112. Philadelphia: University of Pennsylvania.

2002b Tepe Gawra: Chronology and Socio-Economic Change in the Foothills of Northern Iraq. In *Artefacts of Complexity: Tracking the Uruk in the Near East*, edited by J. N. Postgate. Pp. 49–78. British Archaeological School in Iraq, Iraq Archaeological Reports 5. Wiltshire: Aris and Phillips.

2004 Studying the Development of Complex Society: Mesopotamia in the Late Fifth and Fourth Millennium BC. *Journal of Archaeological Research* 12(1): 75–119.

Rowlands, Michael, Mogens Larsen, and Kristian Kristiansen (eds.) 1987 *Centre and Periphery in the Ancient World*. Cambridge: Cambridge University Press.

Rubin, Jeff 2009 *Why Your World Is about to Get a Whole Lot Smaller: Oil and the End of Globalization*. Toronto: Random House.

Sabloff, Jeremy A. 2008 *Archaeology Matters: Action Archaeology in the Modern World*. Walnut Creek: Left Coast Press.

Sahlins, Marshall 1972 *Stone Age Economics*. Hawthorne: Aldine.

1981 *Historical Metaphors and Mythical Realities: Structure in the Early History of the Sandwich Islands.* Ann Arbor: University of Michigan Press.

1994 Goodbye to Tristes Tropes: Ethnography in the Context of Modern World History. In *Assessing Culture Anthropology*, edited by Robert Borofsky. Pp. 377–93. New York: McGraw-Hill.

1996 The Sadness of Sweetness: The Native Anthropology of Western Cosmology. *Current Anthropology* 37: 395–428.

Sallnow, Michael J. 1987 *Pilgrims of the Andes: Regional Cults in the Andes.* Washington: Smithsonian Institution.

Salzer, Robert J., and Grace Rajnovich 2000 *The Gottschall Rockshelter: An Archaeological Mystery.* St. Paul: Prairie Smoke Press.

Sassaman, Kenneth E. 2005 Structure and Practice in the Archaic Southeast. In *North American Archaeology*, edited by Timothy R. Pauketat and Diana DiPaolo Loren. Pp. 79–107. Malden: Blackwell.

Scarry, John F. 1996 *Political Structure and Change in the Prehistoric Southeastern United States*, edited by John F. Scarry. Gainesville: University Press of Florida.

2007 Connections between the Etowah and Lake Jackson Chiefdoms: Patterns in the Iconographic and Material Evidence. In *Southeastern Ceremonial Complex: Chronology, Content, Context*, edited by Adam King. Pp. 134–50. Tuscaloosa: University of Alabama Press.

Schäfer, Wolf 2007 Global History. In *Encyclopedia of Globalization*, 4 vols., edited by Jan Aart Scholte and Roland Robertson. Pp. 516–21. New York: Routledge.

Scheper-Hughes, Nancy 2000 The Global Traffic in Human Organs. *Current Anthropology* 41(2): 191–244.

2004 Parts Unknown: Undercover Ethnography of the Organs-Trafficking Underworld. *Ethnography* 5(1): 29–73.

Schlosser, Eric 2001 *Fast Food Nation: The Dark Side of the All-American Meal.* New York: Houghton-Mifflin.

Schmandt-Besserat, Denise 1996 *How Writing Came About.* Austin: University of Texas Press.

Schneider, Jane 1977 Was There a Pre-Capitalist World System? *Peasant Studies* 6: 20–9.

Scholte, Jan Aart 2000 *Globalization: A Critical Introduction.* New York: St. Martin's Press.

Schortman, Edward M., and Patricia A. Urban 1992 Current Trends in Interaction Research, In *Resources, Power, and Interregional Interaction*, edited by Edward M. Schortman and Patricia A. Urban. Pp. 235–55. New York: Plenum Press.

1994 Living on the Edge: Core/Periphery Relations in Ancient Southeastern Mesoamerica. *Current Anthropology* 35: 401–30.

1998 Culture Contact Structure and Process. In *Studies in Culture Contact: Interaction, Culture Change, and Archaeology*, edited by James G. Cusik. Pp. 102–25. Carbondale: Center for Archaeological Investigations.

Schreiber, Katharina J. 1991 The Association between Roads and Polities: Evidence for Wari Roads in Peru. In *Ancient Road Networks and Settlement Hierarchies in the New World*, edited by Charles D. Trombold. Pp. 243–52. Cambridge: Cambridge University Press.

1992 *Wari Imperialism in Middle Horizon Peru*. Ann Arbor: Museum of Anthropology, University of Michigan.

1999 Regional Approaches to the Study of Prehistoric Empires: Examples from Ayacucho and Nasca, Peru. In *Settlement Pattern Studies in the Americas: Fifty Years Since Viru*, edited by Brian Billman and Gary Feinman. Pp. 160–71. Washington, DC: Smithsonian Institution Press.

2001 The Wari Empire of Middle Horizon Peru: The Epistemological Challenge of Documenting an Empire without Documentary Evidence. In *Empires: Perspectives from Archaeology and History*, edited by Susan E. Alcock, Terrence N. D'Altroy, Kathleen D. Morrison, and Carla M. Sinopoli. Pp. 70–92. New York: Cambridge University Press.

2005 Old Issues, New Directions. *Cambridge Archaeological Journal* 15(2): 264–6.

Schroeder, Sissel 2004a Power and Place: Agency, Ecology, and History in the American Bottom, Illinois. *Antiquity* 78: 812–27.

2004b Current Research on Late Precontact Societies of the Midcontinental United States. *Journal of Anthropological Research* 12(4): 311–72.

Schurr, Mark R., and Margaret J. Schoeninger 1995 Associations between Agricultural Intensification and Social Complexity: An Example for the Prehistoric Ohio Valley. *Journal of Anthropological Archaeology* 14: 315–39.

Schwartz, Glenn M. 1994 Rural Economic Specialization and Early Urbanization in the Khabur Valley, Syria. In *Archaeological Views from the Countryside: Village Communities in Early Complex Societies*, edited by Glenn M. Schwartz and Steven E. Falconer. Pp. 19–36. Washington, DC: Smithsonian Institution.

2001 Syria and the Uruk Expansion. In *Uruk Mesopotamia and its Neighbors: Cross-Cultural Interactions in the Era of State Formation*, edited by Mitchell S. Rothman. Pp. 233–64. Santa Fe: School of American Research Press.

Schwartz, Glen M., and Steven E. Falconer 1994 Rural Approaches to Social Complexity. In *Archaeological Views from the Countryside: Village Communities in Early Complex Societies*, edited by Glenn M. Schwartz and Steven E. Falconer. Pp. 1–18. Washington, DC: Smithsonian Institution.

Sciscento, Margaret Mary 1989 Imperialism in the High Andes: Inka and Wari Involvement in the Chuquibamba Valley, Peru. Unpublished Ph.D. dissertation, Department of Anthropology, University of California, Santa Barbara.

Scott, James C. 1998 *Seeing Like a State: How Certain Schemes to Improve the Human Condition Have Failed*. New Haven: Yale University Press.

Segura Llanos, Rafael 2001 *Rito y economía en Cajamarquilla: Investigaciones arqueológicas en el Conjunto Arquitectónico Julio C. Tello*. Lima: Fondo Editorial de la Pontificia Universidad Católica del Perú.

Segura Llanos, Rafael, and Izumi Shimada i.p. The Wari Footprint on the Central Coast: A View from Cajamarquilla and Pachacamac. In *Beyond Wari Walls: Exploring the Nature of Middle Horizon Peru Away from Wari Centers*, edited by Justin Jennings. Albuquerque: University of New Mexico Press.

Shady Solís, Ruth 1982 La Cultura Nievería y la interacción social en el mundo andino en la epoca Huari. *Arqueológicas* 19: 15–108.

1988 Época Huari como interacción de las sociedades regionales. *Revista Andina* 6(1): 67–99.

2004 *Caral, la Ciudad del Fuego Sagrado.* Lima: SA Interbank.

2006 America's First City? The Case of Late Archaic Caral. In *Andean Archaeology III: North and South*, edited by William H. Isbell and Helaine Silverman. Pp. 28–66. New York: Springer.

Shady Solís, Ruth, Jonathan Haas, and Winifred Creamer 2001 Dating Caral, a Preceramic Site in the Supe Valley on the Central Coast of Peru. *Science* 292: 723–6.

Sheets, Payson 2000 Provisioning the Ceren Household: The Vertical Economy, Village Economy, and Household Economy in the Southeastern Maya Periphery. *Ancient Mesoamerica* 11: 217–30.

Shen, Chen 2003 Compromises and Conflict: Production and Commerce in the Royal Cities of Eastern Zhou, China. In *The Social Construction of Ancient Cities*, edited by Monica L. Smith. Pp. 290–310. Washington, DC: Smithsonian Institution.

Sherratt, Andrew 2004 Material Resources, Capital, and Power: The Coevolution of Society and Culture. In *Archaeological Perspectives on Political Economies*, edited by Gary M. Feinman and Linda M. Nicholas. Pp. 79–103. Salt Lake City: University of Utah Press.

Shimada, Izumi 1994 *Pampa Grande and the Mochica Culture.* Austin: University of Texas Press.

1995 *La Cultura Sicán: Dios, Riqueza, y Poder en la Costa Norte.* Lima: Banco Continental.

2000 The Late Prehispanic Coastal States, In *The Inca World: The Development of Pre-Columbian Peru, A.D. 1000–1534*, edited by Laura Laurencich-Minelli. Pp. 49–110. Norman: University of Oklahoma Press.

Shimada, Izumi, Crystal Barker Schaaf, Lonnie G. Thompson, and Ellen Mosley-Thompson 1991 Cultural Impacts of Severe Droughts in the Prehistoric Andes: Applications of a 1,500-Year Ice Core Precipitation Record. *World Archaeology* 22(3): 247–70.

Silva, Jorge 1992 Patrones de asentamiento en el Valle del Chillón. In *Estudios de arqueología peruana*, edited by Duccio Bonavia. Pp. 395–415. Lima: Fomciencias,.

Silverman, Helaine 1993 *Cahuachi in the Ancient Nasca World.* Iowa City: University of Iowa Press.

Sklair, Leslie 2002 *Globalization: Capitalism and Its Alternatives.* Oxford: Oxford University Press.

2006 Competing Conceptions of Globalization. In *Global Social Change: Historical and Comparative Perspectives*, edited by Christopher Chase-Dunn and Salvatore J. Babones. Pp. 59–78. Baltimore: John Hopkins University Press.

Slovak, Nicole 2007 Examining Imperial Influence on Peru's Central Coast: Isotopic and Cultural Analyses of Middle Horizon Burials at Ancón. Unpublished Ph.D. dissertation, Stanford University, Palo Alto.

Slovak, Nicole M., Adina Paytan, and Bettina A. Wiegand 2009 Reconstructing Middle Horizon Mobility Patterns on the Coast of Peru through Strontium Isotope Analysis. *Journal of Archaeological Science* 36: 157–65.

Smith, Adam T. 2003 *The Political Landscape: Constellations of Authority in Early Complex Polities*. Berkeley: University of California Press.

Smith, Bruce D. (ed.) 1978 *Mississippian Settlement Patterns*. New York: Academic Press.

(ed.) 1990 *The Mississippian Emergence*. Washington: Smithsonian Institution Press.

Smith, Carol 1976 Regional Economic Systems: Linking Geographical Models and Socioeconomic Problems. In *Regional Analysis*, vol. 1, edited by Carol Smith. Pp. 3–63. New York: Academic Press.

Smith, Michael E. 2009 Editorial – Just How Comparative Is Comparative Urban Geography? A Perspective from Archaeology. *Urban Geography* 30(2): 113–17.

Smith, Monica L. 2003a *The Social Construction of Ancient Cities*, edited by Monica L. Smith. Washington, DC: Smithsonian Institution.

2003b Introduction: The Social Construction of Cities. In *The Social Construction of Ancient Cities*, edited by Monica L. Smith. Pp. 1–36. Washington, DC: Smithsonian Institution.

Spickard, Linda 1983 The Development of Huari Administrative Architecture. In *Investigations of the Andean Past*, edited by Daniel H. Sandweiss. Pp. 136–60. Ithaca: Latin American Studies Program, Cornell University.

Srinivas, M. N. 1976 *The Remembered Village*. Los Angeles: University of California Press.

Stanish, Charles 2004 The Evolution of Chiefdoms: An Economic Anthropological Model. In *Archaeological Perspectives on Political Economies*, edited by Gary M. Feinman and Linda M. Nicholas. Pp. 7–24. Salt Lake City: University of Utah Press.

Steadman, Sharon R. 1996 Isolation of Interaction: Prehistoric Cilicia and the Fourth Millennium Uruk Expansion. *Journal of Mediterranean Archaeology* 9(2): 131–65.

Stein, Gil J. 1994 Economy, Ritual, and Power in 'Ubaid Mesopotamia. In *Chiefdoms and Early States in the Near East: The Organizational Dynamics of Complexity*, edited by Gil Stein and Mitchell S. Rothman. Pp. 35–46. Monographs in World Archaeology no. 18. Madison: Prehistory Press.

1999 *Rethinking World-Systems: Diasporas, Colonies, and Interaction in Uruk Mesopotamia*. Tucson: University of Arizona Press.

2001 Indigenous Social Complexity at Hacinebi (Turkey) and the Organization of Uruk Colonial Contact. In *Uruk Mesopotamia and Its Neighbors: Cross Cultural Interactions in the Era of State Formation*, edited by Mitchell S. Rothman. Pp. 265–306. Santa Fe: School of American Research.

2002 Colonies without Colonialism: A Trade Diaspora Model of Fourth Millennium BC Mesopotamian Enclaves in Anatolia. In *The Archaeology of Colonialism*, edited by Claire L. Lyons and John K. Papadopoulos. Pp. 27–64. Los Angeles: Getty Research Institute.

2004 Structural Parameters and Sociocultural Factors in the Economic Organization on North Mesopotamian Urbanism in the Third Millennium BC. In *Archaeological Perspectives on Political Economies*, edited by Gary M. Feinman and Linda M. Nicholas. Pp. 61–78. Salt Lake City: University of Utah Press.

2005a *The Archaeology of Colonial Encounters: Comparative Perspectives.* Santa Fe: School of American Research Press.

2005b The Political Economy of Mesopotamian Colonial Encounters. In *The Archaeology of Colonial Encounters: Comparative Perspectives,* edited by Gil J. Stein. Pp. 33–68. Santa Fe: School of American Research Press

Stein, Gil J., and Rana Özbal 2007 A Tale of Two Oikumenai: Variation in the Expansionary Dynamics of 'Ubaid and Uruk Mesopotamia. In *Settlement and Society: Essays Dedicated to Robert McCormick Adams,* edited by Elizabeth C. Stone. Pp. 329–42. Los Angeles: Cotsen Institute of Archaeology.

Steponaitis, Vincas P. 1986 Prehistoric Archaeology in the Southeastern United States, 1970–1985. *Annual Review of Anthropology* 15: 363–404.

Steponaitis, Vincas P., M. James Blackman, and Hector Neff 1996 Large-Scale Patterns in the Chemical Composition of Mississippian Pottery. *American Antiquity* 61(3): 555–72.

Stoltman, James B. 1991 Cahokia as Seen from the Peripheries. In *New Perspectives on Cahokia: Views from the Periphery,* edited by James B. Stoltman. Pp. 349–54. Madison: Prehistory Press.

Stoltman, James B., Danielle M. Berden, and Robert F. Boszhardt 2008 New Evidence in the Upper Mississippi Valley for Pre-Mississippian Cultural Interaction with the American Bottom. *American Antiquity* 73(2): 317–36.

Storey, Glenn R. 2006a Introduction: Urban Demography of the Past. In *Urbanism in the Preindustrial World: Cross-Cultural Approaches,* edited by Glen R. Storey. Pp. 1–23. Tuscaloosa: University of Alabama Press.

2006b *Urbanism in the Preindustrial World: Cross-Cultural Approaches,* edited by Glenn R. Storey. Tuscaloosa: University of Alabama Press.

Storey, Rebecca 1992 *Life and Death in the Ancient City of Teotihuacan: A Modern Paleodemographic Synthesis.* Tuscaloosa: University of Alabama Press.

Stout, Charles, and R. Barry Lewis 1998 Mississippian Towns in Kentucky. In *Mississippian Towns and Sacred Spaces: Searching for an Architectural Grammar,* edited by R. Barry Lewis and Charles Stout. Pp. 151–78. Tuscaloosa: University of Alabama Press.

Strommenger, Eva 1980 The Chronological Division of Archaic Levels of Uruk-Eanna VI to III/II: Past and Present. *American Journal of Archaeology* 84(4): 479–87.

Stübel, Alfons, and Max Uhle 1892 *Die Ruinenstaette von Tiahuanaco im Hochlande de Alten Perú: Eine Kulturgeschichtliche Studie Auf grund Selbstaendiger Aufnahmen.* Leipzig: Verlag von Karl W. Heirsemann.

Sürenhagen, Dietrich 1986 Archaische Keramik Aus Uruk-Warka. Erster Teil: Die Keramik der Schichten XVI–VI aus den Sondagen "Tiefschnitt" und "Sägegraben" in Eanna. *Baghdader Mitteilungen* 17: 7–96.

1987 Archaische Keramik Aus Uruk-Warka. Zweiter Teil: Die Keramik der V aus dem "Sägegraben"; Keramik der Schichten VII bis II in Eanna; Keramik aus den Sondagen O XI–XII und K–L XII–XIII; Keramic von der Anu-Zikkurrat in K XVIII. *Baghdader Mitteilungen* 18: 1–92.

Tello, Julio C. 1942 Origen y Desarrollo de las Civilizaciones Prehistóricas Andinas. In *Actas y Trabajos Científicos, 27th International Congress of Americanists* 1: 589–720.

1970 Las Ruinas de Huari. In *100 Años de arequeología en el Peru*, edited by Rogger Ravines. Pp. 519–25. Lima: Instituto de Estudios Peruanos.

Theler, James L., and Robert F. Boszhardt 2006 Collapse of Crucial Resources and Culture Change: A Model for the Woodland to Oneota Transformation in the Upper Midwest. *American Antiquity* 71(3): 433–72.

Thompson, John B. 1995 *The Media and Modernity: A Social Theory of the Media*. Cambridge: Polity Press.

Thompson, R. Campbell, and M. E. L. Mallowan 1933 The British Excavations at Ninevah, 1931–32. *Liverpool Annals of Archaeology and Anthropology* 20: 71–186.

Tilly, Charles 1995 *Popular Culture in Great Britain, 1758–1834*. Cambridge: Harvard University Press.

Tomlinson, John 1999 *Globalization and Culture*. Chicago: University of Chicago Press.

Topic, John R. 1991 Huari and Huamachuco. In *Huari Administrative Structure: Prehistoric Monumental Architecture and State Government*, edited by William H. Isbell and Gordon F. McEwan. Pp. 63–83. Washington, DC: Dumbarton Oaks.

Torrence, Robin 1986 *Production and Exchange of Stone Tools: Prehistoric Obsidian in the Aegean*. New York: Cambridge University Press.

Trigger, Bruce 1989 *A History of Archaeological Thought*. New York: Cambridge University Press.

Trubitt, Mary Beth D. 2000 Mound Building and Prestige Goods Exchange: Changing Strategies in the Cahokia Chiefdom. *American Antiquity* 65(4): 669–90.

Tung, Tiffany A. 2008 Dismembering Bodies for Display: A Bioarchaeological Study of Trophy Heads from the Wari Site of Conchopata, Peru. *American Journal of Physical Anthropology* 136: 294–308.

Ucko, Peter, Ruth Trigham, and G. W. Dimbleby (eds.) 1972 *Man, Settlement, and Urbanism*. Cambridge: Schenkman.

Underhill, Anne P., and Hui Fang 2004 Early State Economic Systems in China. In *Archaeological Perspectives on Political Economies*, edited by Gary M. Feinman and Linda M. Nicholas. Pp. 129–44. Salt Lake City: University of Utah Press.

Upham, Stanley 1986 Imperialists, Isolationists, World Systems, and Political Realities: Perspectives on Mesoamerican-Southwestern Interaction. In *Ripples in the Chichimec Sea*, edited by Frances J. Mathien and Randall H. McGuire. Pp. 205–19. Carbondale: Southern Illinois University Press.

Ur, Jason A. i.p. Cycles of Civilization in Northern Mesopotamia, 4400–2000 BC. *Journal of Archaeological Research*.

Ur, Jason A., Phillip Karsgaard, and Joan Oates 2007 Early Urban Development in the Near East. *Science* 317: 1188.

Valdez, Lidio M. 2000 La Arqueología del valle de Acarí, Arequipa. *Boletín del Museo de Arqueología y Antropología de la Universidad Nacional Mayor De San Marcos* 12: 19–25.

Valdez, Lidio M., and J. Ernesto Valdez 1998 Inkapyarqan: Un Canal de las Punas de Ayacucho. *Boletín del Museo de Arqueología y Antropología de la Universidad Nacional Mayor De San Marcos* 6: 4–9.

Valkenier, Lisa 1995 New Evidence for Chimu Capac and the Early Horizon Period in the Supe Valley, Peru. *Journal of the Steward Anthropological Society* 23(1/2): 269–86.

Van Gijseghem, Hendrik 2001 Household and Family at Moche Peru: An Analysis of Building and Residence Patterns in a Prehispanic Urban Center. *Latin American Antiquity* 12(3): 257–73.

2006 A Frontier Perspective in on Paracas Society and Nasca Ethnogenesis. *Latin American Antiquity* 17(4): 419–44.

Vivanco P., Cirilo, and Lidio M. Valdez C. 1993 Poblados Wari en la Cuenca del Pampas-Qaracha, Ayacucho. *Gaceta Arqueológica Andina* 23: 83–102.

Von Hagen, Adriana, and Craig Morris 1998 *The Cities of the Ancient Andes*. New York: Thames and Hudson.

Wallerstein, Immanuel 1974 *The Modern World System I*. San Diego: Academic Press.

1979 *The Capitalist World-Economy*. Cambridge: Cambridge University Press.

Watson, Robert J. 2000 Sacred Landscapes at Cahokia: Mound 72 and the Mound 72 Precinct. In *Mounds, Modoc, and Mesoamerica: Papers in Honor of Melvin L. Fowler*. Pp. 227–43. Illinois State Museum Scientific Papers Series, vol. XXVIII. Springfield: Illinois State Museum.

Wattenmaker, Patricia 1994 State Formation and the Organization of Domestic Craft Production at Third-Millennium B.C. Kurban Höyük, Southeast Turkey. In *Archaeological Views from the Countryside: Village Communities in Early Complex Societies*, edited by Glenn M. Schwartz and Steven E. Falconer. Pp. 109–20. Washington, DC: Smithsonian Institution Press.

Webb, R. Esmée, and David J. Rindos 1997 The Mode and Temp of the Initial Colonisation of Empty Landmasses: Sahul and the Americas Compared. In *Rediscovering Darwin: Evolutionary Theory and Archaeological Explanation*, edited by C. Michael Barton and Geoffrey Clark. Pp. 233–50. Archaeological Papers of the American Anthropological Association, vol. 7. Arlington: American Anthropological Association.

Weeks, Kent R. 1999 *The Lost Tomb*. New York: Harper Perennial.

Weiss, Harvey, and T. Cuyler Young, Jr. 1975 The Merchants of Susa: Godin V and Plateau-Lowland Relations in the Late Fourth Millennium. *Iran* 13: 1–17.

Wells, Peter S. 1999 *The Barbarian Speaks: How the Conquered Peoples Shaped Roman Europe*. Princeton: Princeton University Press.

Wengrow, David 2008 Prehistories of Commodity Branding. *Current Anthropology* 49(1): 7–34.

Wenke, Robert J., and Deborah I. Olszewski 2006 *Patterns in Prehistory: Humankind's First Three Million Years*. New York: Oxford University Press.

Weyland, Petra 1993 *Inside the Third World Village*. New York: Routledge.

White, Christine W., Fred J. Longstaffe, and Kimberly R. Law 2001 Revisiting the Teotihuacan Connection at Altun Ha: Oxygen-Isotope Analysis of Tomb f-8/1. *Ancient Mesoamerica* 12: 65–72.

White, Christine W., Fred J. Longstaffe, Hillary Stuart-Williams, and Kimberly R. Law 2002 Geographic Identities of the Sacrificial Victims at the Temple of Quetzalcoatl: Implications for the Nature of State Power. *Latin American Antiquity* 13: 217–36.

White, Christine W., Michael Spence, and Fred J. Longstaffe 2004 Demography and Ethnic Continuity in the Tlailotlacan Enclave of Teotihuacan: The Evidence from Stable Oxygen Isotopes. *Journal of Anthropological Archaeology* 23(4): 385–403.

Wiessner, Polly 1996 Leveling the Hunter: Constraints on the Status Quest in Foraging Societies. In *Food and the Status Quest*, edited by Polly Wiessner and Wulf Schiefenhovel. Pp. 171–91. Oxford: Berghahn.

Wilk, Richard 1995 Learning to Be Local in Belize: Global Systems of Common Difference. In *Worlds Apart: Modernity through the Prism of the Local*, edited by Daniel Miller. Pp. 110–33. New York: Routledge.

2004 Miss Universe, the Olmec and the Valley of Oaxaca. *Journal of Social Archaeology* 4(1): 81–98.

Wilkinson, Toby A. H. 2002 Uruk into Egypt: Imports and Imitations. In *Artefacts of Complexity: Tracking the Uruk in the Near East*, edited by J. N. Postgate. Pp. 237–48. British Archaeological School in Iraq, Iraq Archaeological Reports 5. Wiltshire: Aris and Phillips.

Wilkinson, Tony J. 1990 Town and Countryside in Southeastern Anatolia, vol. 1. Settlement and Land Use at Kurban Höyük and Other Sites in the Lower Karababa Basin. University of Chicago Oriental Institute Publications, vol. 109. Chicago: Oriental Institute of the University of Chicago.

2003 *Archaeological Landscapes of the Near East*. Tucson: University of Arizona Press.

Williams, Carlos, and Jose Pineda 1985 Desde Ayacucho hasta Cajamarca: Formas arquitectónicas con filiación Wari, unidad del espacio andino. *Boletín de Lima* 7(40): 55–61.

Williams, Patrick Ryan 1997 The Role of Disaster in the Development of Agriculture and the Evolution of Social Complexity in the South-Central Andes. Unpublished Ph.D. dissertation, Department of Anthropology, University of Florida, Gainesville.

2001 Cerro Baúl: A Wari Center on the Tiwanaku Frontier. *Latin American Antiquity* 12(1): 67–83.

2002 Rethinking Disaster-Induced Collapse in the Demise of the Andean Highland States: Wari and Tiwanaku. *World Archaeology* 33(3): 361–74.

Williams, Patrick Ryan, and Johny Isla 2002 Investigaciones arqueológicas en Cerro Baúl, un enclave Wari en el valle de Moquegua. *Gaceta Arqueologica Andina* 26: 87–120.

Williams, Patrick Ryan, and Donna J. Nash 2002 Imperial Interaction in the Andes: Huari and Tiwanaku at Cerro Baúl. In *Andean Archaeology I: Variations in Sociopolitical Organization*, edited by William H. Isbell and Helaine Silverman. Pp. 243–65. New York: Kluwer Academic/Plenum.

Wilson, Gregory D., Jon Marcoux, and Brad Koldehoff 2006 Square Pegs in Round Holes: Organizational Diversity between Early Moundville and Cahokia. In *Leadership and Polity in Mississippian Society*, edited by Brian M. Butler and Paul D. Welch. Pp. 43–72. Carbondale: Center for Archaeological Investigations.

Winterhalder, Bruce, and Douglas J. Kennett 2006 Behavioral Ecology and the Transition from Hunting and Gathering to Agriculture. *Behavioral Ecology and the Transition to Agriculture*, edited by Douglas J. Kennett and Bruce Winterhalder. Pp. 1–22. Berkeley: University of California Press.

Wirth, Louis 1938 Urbanism as a Way of Life. *American Journal of Sociology* 45(1): 1–24.

Wolf, Eric. R. 1982 *Europe and the People without History*. Los Angeles: University of California Press.

Wright, Henry 1977 Recent Research on the Origin of the State. *Annual Review of Anthropology* 6: 379–97.

1981a *An Early Town on the Deh Luran Plain: Excavations at Tepe Farukhabad*. Ann Arbor: The University of Michigan Museum of Anthropology.

1981b Appendix: The Southern Margins of Sumer: Archaeological Survey of the Area of Eridu and Ur. In *Heartland of Cities*, edited by Robert McC. Adams. Pp. 295–345. Chicago: University of Chicago Press.

1994 Prestate Political Formations. In *Chiefdoms and Early States in the Near East: The Organizational Dynamics of Complexity*, edited by Gil Stein and Mitchell S. Rothman. Pp. 67–84. Monographs in World Archaeology no. 18. Madison: Prehistory Press.

2001 Cultural Action in the Uruk World. In *Uruk Mesopotamia and its Neighbors: Cross-Cultural Interactions in the Era of State Formation*, edited by Mitchell S. Rothman. Pp. 123–47. Santa Fe: School of American Research Press.

2006 Early State Dynamics as Political Experiment. *Journal of Anthropological Research* 62(3): 305–19.

2007 Ancient Agency: Using Models of Intentionality to Understand the Dawn of Despotism. In *Settlement and Society: Essays Dedicated to Robert McCormick Adams*, edited by Elizabeth C. Stone. Pp. 173–84. Los Angeles: Cotsen Institute of Archaeology.

Wright, Henry, and Gregory A. Johnson 1975 Population, Exchange, and Early State Formation in Southwestern Iran. *American Anthropologist* 77: 267–89.

1985 Regional Perspectives on Southwest Iranian State Development. *Paléorient* 11(2): 25–30.

Wright, Katherine 1994 Ground Stone Tools and Hunters and Gatherer Subsistence in Southwest Asia: Implications for the Transition to Farming. *American Antiquity* 59(2): 238–63.

Yaeger, Jason, and Marcello A. Canuto 2000 Introducing an Archaeology of Communities. In *The Archaeology of Communities: A New World Perspective*, edited by Marcello A. Canuto and Jason Yaeger. Pp. 1–15. New York: Routledge.

Yerkes, Richard W. 1989 Mississippian Craft Specialization on the American Bottom. *Southeastern Archaeology* 8: 93–106.

1991 Specialization in Shell Artifact Production at Cahokia. *New Perspectives on Cahokia: Views from the Periphery*, edited by John B. Stoltman. Pp. 49–64. Madison: Prehistory Press.

2005 Bone Chemistry, Body Parts, and Growth Marks: Evaluating Ohio Hopewell and Cahokia Mississippian Seasonality, Subsistence, Ritual, and Feasting. *American Antiquity* 70(2): 241–65.

Yoffee, Norman 1993 Mesopotamian Interaction Spheres. In *Early Stages in the Evolution of Mesopotamian Civilizations: Soviet Excavations in Northern Iraq*, edited by Norman Yoffee and Jeffrey J. Clark. Pp. 257–69. Tucson: University of Arizona Press.

2005 *Myths of the Archaic State: Evolution of the Earliest Cities, States, and Civilizations*. New York: Cambridge University Press.

Young, Bilone W., and Melvin L. Fowler 2000 *Cahokia: The Great Native American Metropolis*. Urbana: University of Illinois Press.

Zeder, Melinda A. 1991 *Feeding Cities: Specialized Animal Economy in the Ancient Near East*. Washington, DC: Smithsonian Institution.

2003 Food Provisioning in Urban Societies: A View from Northern Mesopotamia. In *The Social Construction of Ancient Cities*, edited by Monica L. Smith. Pp. 156–83. Washington, DC: Smithsonian Institution.

Zuidema, R. Tom 2002 Inca Religion: Its Foundations in the Central Andean Context. In *Native Religions and Cultures of Central and South America*, edited by Lawrence E. Sullivan. Pp. 236–53. New York: Continuum.

Index

writing systems: and bureaucratic structure at Uruk-Warka, 69, 75, 129; early urbanism and development of, 50–1

Yaeger, Jason, 43
Yenshi (China), 52
Yerkes, Richard W., 83, 85, 96
Yoffee, Norman, 39, 44, 45, 46, 55
Young, Bilone W., 68, 71, 77

Yup'ik Eskimos (Alaska), 137

Zagros Mountains, and Uruk expansion, 71
Zeder, Melinda A., 45, 46, 54
Zengzou (China), 52
Zhongba (China), 52–3
Zhu Di, 26
Zuidema, R. Tom, 4